FRANCE ON FILM

FRANCE *on* FILM

reflections on popular french cinema

edited by Lucy Mazdon

WALLFLOWER
LONDON

First published in Great Britain in 2001 by
Wallflower Press
16 Chalk Farm Road, Camden Lock, London NW1 8AG
www.wallflowerpress.co.uk

ISBN 1 903364-11-6 hbk
ISBN 1 903364-08-6 pbk

Book Design by Rob Bowden Design

Printed in Great Britain by Creative Print and Design Group, (Wales) Ltd.

Lucille Cairns is Senior Lecturer in French at the University of Stirling. She has published two books and numerous articles both on French women's writing and on male and female homosexuality in French literature, cinema and society. Her third book examines representations of lesbianism in post-1968 French realist works.

Maria Esposito recently completed a PhD on French heritage cinema at the University of North London. Her special research interests include the economics of the French film industry.

Will Higbee is Lecturer in Film and French culture at the University of Exeter and is completing a thesis on marginality and ethnicity in the French cinema of the 1980s and 1990s.

Anne Jäckel is Senior Lecturer and Researcher in European Cinema and Film Policy at the University of the West of England. Her research interests include international co-productions and she is currently writing a book on the European Film Industries for the BFI.

Lucy Mazdon is Senior Research Fellow at the University of Southampton. She is the author of *Encore Hollywood: Remaking French Cinema* (BFI, 2000), as well as numerous articles on film and television.

Phil Powrie is Director of the Centre for Research into Film and Media at the University of Newcastle-upon-Tyne. He has published widely on French cinema, including *French Cinema in the 1980s: Nostalgia and the Crisis of Masculinity* (Clarendon, 1997) and, as editor, *French Cinema in the 1990s: Continuity and Difference* (Oxford, 1999). He has recently completed a monograph on the films of Jean-Jacques Beneix.

Howard Seal is currently researching for a PhD in historical representation and film at the University of North London.

Alison Smith is Lecturer in European Film Studies at the University of Liverpool. She has published a monograph on the work of Agnès Varda (MUP, 1998) and several articles on aspects of French 'social' cinema in the 1970s. Her current research interest is the use of theatrical and performance concepts in cinema, notably in the work of Patrice Chéreau.

Lyn Thomas is Faculty Research Director in the Faculty of Humanities and Education at the University of North London. Her research interests include French and British media, as well as contemporary French women's writing. Her book *Annie Ernaux: An Introduction to the Writer and Her Audience* was published by Berg in 1999.

Darren Waldron is completing a PhD on Gender and Sexuality in contemporary French film comedy at the University of North London. He teaches on undergraduate courses on contemporary French popular culture and cinema.

Emma Wilson is Lecturer in French at Cambridge University and a Fellow of Corpus Christi College. She is author of *Sexuality and the Reading Encounter* (Clarendon, 1996), *French cinema since 1950* (Duckworth, 1999) and *Memory and Survival: The French Cinema of Krzysztof Kieslowski* (Legenda, 2000). She is currently working on a study of childhood and trauma in contemporary cinema.

INTRODUCTION

Lucy Mazdon

The title of this book begs a number of questions. What exactly do we mean by 'French' film and how do we define 'popular' cinema? Clearly the films studied in this book are not representative of French cinema in general. Rather they are a selection of recent works, ranging from Claude Berri's *Jean de Florette* of 1986 to Catherine Breillat's *Romance* of 1999. In other words, the French cinema we will examine here consists of recent or contemporary production, or more specifically films of the 1990s (with Berri's film featuring as an obvious, but important, exception). This is one of this book's particular constructions of French cinema and, as we shall see, it contains a number of others.

What we understand by French cinema depends very much upon the actual act of description or construction. The French cinema articulated in this book might be quite different to that described in other works on the subject. The French cinema experienced by a French film audience is also likely to be significantly different to that experienced by a non-domestic audience. In Britain for example, knowledge of French cinema may be confined to a handful of films shown in a select group of art-house cinemas, late at night on BBC 2 or Channel Four or on specialist subscription channels such as Film Four. Indeed, although French films are among the most widely distributed foreign-language works in Britain, their presence is still slight. Britain is by far the least successful market for French films in Europe. Whereas Eastern European and Francophone countries are highly receptive to the French cinematic product (for example, in 1994 Switzerland bought 74 and Belgium 55 of the 115 films released in France that year), British screens are invariably dominated by Hollywood productions.

The Martell French Film Tour, established in 1999, paradoxically bears witness to this limited presence. The tour shows a selection of French films, some of which have yet to find a British distributor, in association with the Odeon cinema chain. Films selected for the 2000 tour include Diane Kurys' costume drama *Les Enfants du siècle* (1999), Andrzej Zulawski's *La Fidelité* (1999), and Stéphane Giusti's gay comedy *Pourquoi pas moi?* (1998). The organisers (who include the French Embassy in London) present this event as an opportunity to extend the exhibition circuit for foreign-language films in Britain whilst simultaneously enabling the Odeon chain to test its audiences' response to less mainstream production. This is indubitably a commendable initiative, however it also underlines the very limited presence of French film in Britain. The exhibition of these films in the Odeon's venues is, for the most part, unusual and a number of the works shown may only ever be screened in the UK via specialist tours and festivals of this kind.

If we compare this limited knowledge to the numerous films experienced by French audiences in cinemas across France, on all television channels, often at prime time, it becomes clear that we are talking about two quite different forms of cinematic experience. A cultural product which to many British cinema-goers is unfamiliar and perceived as something 'other' plays an absolutely central role in the French audiovisual landscape. Coupled with this unfamiliarity is the fact that those films that do receive a British distributor undergo shifts in identity via the act of cultural transposition. As they move from popular venues to art-house screens, from prime-time television to niche broadcasting, so their status as 'popular' or 'high cultural' product is called into question. Moreover, specificities apparent to a French audience are often undecipherable to a British viewer. Thus the Provence constructed in *Jean de Florette*, described by Maria Esposito in her chapter in this volume, will mean quite different things to a domestic and a non-domestic audience. These shifts in identity, the elision of the cultural specificities of time and place, are often deliberately extended by a film's foreign distributors. Trailers for foreign-language films frequently contain little or no dialogue and connect the advertised work to films already familiar to the target audience. Perhaps the most extreme example of this process of cultural transformation is the remake in which foreign language-films (often French) are reproduced in Hollywood, their cultural and aesthetic specificities effaced to make way for the American version.[1]

Some so-called French films may have their cultural specificities called into question at the moment of production. This is the case for co-productions which have long played, and indeed continue to play, an important role in the French cinematic landscape. Although the Centre National de la Cinématographie (CNC) has a clear set of guidelines for the attribution of a national identity to co-productions, it is clearly far from straightforward to describe many of these films as 'French'. According to the CNC, Nikita Mikhalkov's *Le Barbier de Sibérie* (1999) may be a French film. However, as a Russian/French/Italian/Czech co-production, directed by a Russian film-maker, set in pre-Revolutionary Russia and starring an international cast, audiences may find it rather more difficult to pin down. *Nikita* (Besson, 1990), discussed in this volume by Alison Smith, is also a co-production, this time between France and Italy. Moreover, the national identity of Besson's film is further complicated by its very explicit referencing of American and indeed Hong Kong cinema (an intertextuality which provoked much criticism amongst French commentators).

Let us consider for a moment Mathieu Kassovitz's highly successful film of 1995, *La Haine*. As Myrto Konstantarakos points out, the film has been described as belonging to a group of works termed the '*cinéma de banlieue*' or *banlieue* films (1999: 160). As Will Higbee reveals in his chapter in this collection, this term is not without its problems and it would be misleading to describe it as a clearly defined and definable genre. Nevertheless, a number of films did emerge in France throughout the 1990s set in the *banlieue*. Examples include Malik Chibane's *Hexagone* (1994), Jean-François Richet's *État des lieux* (1995), Paul Vecchiali's *Zone Franche* (1996) and of course *La Haine*. The *banlieue* carries a very specific set of connotations in French that can not be easily rendered in English. Although literally translated as 'suburbs', the French *banlieues* lack the comfort suggested by this term. Instead, as Higbee points out, they are large, generally run-down housing estates located on the periphery of French cities. A significant proportion of their inhabitants are from immigrant backgrounds and unemployment and poverty is rife. A number of violent clashes between young people and police erupted in the *banlieues* in the 1980s and as a result they now tend to bear popular connotations of violence and crime.

Interestingly, *La Haine* was initially entitled *Droit de cité*, emphasising the role of location in the film.[2] Kassovitz himself denied that the film's subject matter is the *banlieue*, claiming instead that his aim was to reveal and criticise police *bavures* (errors) and brutality (see Konstantarakos 1999). However, the movement from periphery to centre, from the *banlieue* to Paris, and thus from one form of alienation to another is a primordial feature of the film's narrative and thematic concerns. Whether or not we accept the director's assertions, it is undeniable that the film creates meanings very specific to its context of production and reception. In other words, the film offers a version of space and experience familiar to a contemporary French audience either via first hand experience, political discourse, or the media. Indeed the film's opening sequence shows scenes of riots transmitted by television and thus seems to offer an explicit (albeit highly stylised) critique of the mediatisation of these locations and events and their construction in the minds of the broader public. The film's specificities, its very forceful portrayal of contemporary social problems, are perhaps best revealed by the response of government ministers who, after its release, organised a special screening of the film in an attempt to gain a clearer understanding of the predicament it revealed.

Nevertheless, *La Haine* is not a realist film. It is highly stylised and draws heavily on other cinematic and cultural forms, notably popular music (French and other) and American cinema (for example Vinz's (Vincent Cassell) attempt to emulate Robert de Niro in *Taxi Driver* (Scorsese, 1976)). These references clearly begin to complicate the film's identity as a 'French' production. Yes, it draws heavily upon the contemporary social context and refers to specifically French social problems (or rather a specifically French version of them). However, its intertextual referencing of non-indigenous cultural forms also suggests a somewhat more fluid identity. Certainly it was this fluidity that was stressed in the film's distribution and marketing in the non-French context. In the sub-titled version of the film released on video in Britain, the subtitles borrow from the language of contemporary Afro-American slang and the text on the video box draws parallels with Spike Lee's *Do the Right Thing* (1989). Thus the film is marketed to an audience already familiar with Lee's films (and the works of other Afro-American directors) and its French specificities are downplayed. As Konstantarakos reveals, this process was picked up by many Anglo-Saxon reviewers of the film, who tended to compare *La Haine* to the so-called 'hood' films, emphasising its depiction of racial tensions (which in fact play a rela-tively minor role in the film) in order to underline this connection.

So the identity of individual films such as *La Haine*, and indeed that of cinema more generally, shifts and alters as works move across cultures. Per-haps the dominant conception of French cinema in Britain is its status as 'art cinema'. Indeed 'French cinema' and 'art cinema' are seemingly synonymous terms in Anglo-Saxon countries. French cinema tends to be defined as intel-lectually stimulating, slow-paced, with an emphasis on narrative rather than action in opposition to the less worthy, action-packed Hollywood product. This perception is partly a legacy of the French New Wave of the late 1950s and early 1960s. The impact of the early films of directors such as Jean-Luc Godard, François Truffaut and Claude Chabrol upon both histories of French cinema and film more generally, has meant that these aesthetically innovative works continue to colour perceptions of French film.

Of course these perceptions have far more to do with distribution and exhi-bition practices than with the films themselves. Many of the so-called New Wave films were positioned outside mainstream cinematic culture in as much as they condemned much contemporary production (Truffaut infamously described it as the '*cinéma de papa*'), setting out to produce a new cinema via aesthetic and technical innovation, and frequently focusing on characters at the margins of society. Nevertheless, a significant number of these films also achieved a cer-tain degree of popular success; although his first full-length feature, Godard's *A bout de souffle* (1960) was his most successful work in terms of box-office, attracting almost 260,000 spectators in the seven weeks of its first run in Paris. In other words, the films of the New Wave cannot be described in any simple sense as 'art' films.

If we turn our attention to more recent films we can see that such definitions remain equally problematic. As discussed above, those films which manage to achieve distribution in Britain and the United States tend to be confined to art-house cinemas, whatever their domestic success. The combination of venue and their subtitled format immediately renders them 'difficult' or 'challeng-ing' to a large proportion of the cinema-going public and thus their status as 'art' cinema is assured. A recent attempt to escape this pigeon-holing in many ways serves to underline its prevalence. Gérard Pirès' *Taxi*, produced by Luc Besson, proved a great hit at the French box-office in 1998 and went on to achieve wide-scale release in Britain in both dubbed and subtitled form, accompanied by the tag-line 'Hollywood doesn't make them like this any more'. This was the first French film to be distributed in Britain in this fashion for over thirty years and it is striking that the only way distributors seemed to believe this action-packed comedy adventure could achieve success in Britain was by down-playing its French origins and comparing it to the products of Hollywood.

So it would seem that what we perceive to be an 'art' film or a 'popular' film depends as much upon the particular context of reception as upon the identity of the film itself. This is not to suggest that such definitions are entirely redundant. Evidently some films are more aesthetically or thematically challenging than others and will demand quite different modes of reception to those invited by the mainstream product. However, such definitions are a highly complex matter, subject to change and influenced, as we have seen, by production, exhibition and reception. Suffice to say that it is highly misleading to describe all French film as 'art' cinema. Indeed, one of the key aims of this book is to problematise this vision, revealing instead the diversity of recent French production and the extremely popular works (in terms of both narrative concerns and box office success) that fill French cinema screens. The prime example, discussed by Anne Jäckel in this volume, is *Les Visiteurs* (Poiré, 1993) which attracted over 13.6 million domestic cinema viewers, making it the second most successful film in France (after Gérard Oury's *La Grande Vadrouille*) released in 1966. *Les Visiteurs* vastly outstrips other films in terms of box-office revenue, nevertheless other films discussed here also proved highly successful with audiences. *Jean de Florette* attracted over 6 million spectators, *Gazon maudit* (Balasko, 1995) nearly 4 million, Luc Besson's *Nikita* over 3.7 million, Robert Guédiguian's *Marius et Jeanette* (1997) over 2.6 million and *La Haine* just over 2 million. Clearly these films can all be described as 'popular' films in terms of their box-office success. Other films discussed in this book may not have matched these impressive careers; nevertheless films such as *Chacun cherche son chat* (Klapisch, 1996) with around 680,000 entries and *Y aura-t-il de la neige à Noël?* (Veysset, 1996) with over 800,000 certainly performed extremely well considering their small budgets and relatively limited distribution and marketing.

In many ways the films discussed in this volume underscore some of the problems associated with definitions of popular cinema. It is a relatively straightforward task to describe *Les Visiteurs* as a popular film. It is a light-hearted comedy, featuring a host of well-known French stars and it proved a huge commercial hit. A film such as *Jean de Florette* is perhaps more problematic. This was a box-office success, it starred a number of prominent French actors and it draws upon the popular novels of Marcel Pagnol and the long-standing traditions of literary adaptations for the screen. However, as Maria Esposito reveals, the film was also part of a concerted effort on the part of the then socialist government and, more particularly, the Culture Minister, Jack Lang, to promote a more 'cultural' cinema. In 1985 Lang appointed the publisher Christian Bourgeois to the head of the *avance sur recettes* committee, briefing him to support 'culture'.[3] This enabled the production of both *Jean de Florette* and its 'sequel', *Manon des sources* (1986), films that typify the simultaneously cultural and popular French cinema espoused by Lang. In an explicit attempt to disseminate French cinema both domestically and abroad (and of course to counteract the dominance of the Hollywood product), Lang set out to support a 'cultural cinema for the masses'. In other words, he promoted those films which drew upon French cultural heritage (and thus carried the trappings of 'high culture') whilst at the same time providing popular entertainment for a broad public. Thus these so-called 'heritage' films, which, as we shall see, played such an important part in the French cinematic landscape of the late 1980s and 1990s, are neither straightforwardly popular nor high cultural. Whilst appealing to the mass audience they distinguish themselves from other popular works (notably Hollywood films) through their heritage pretensions.

Other films discussed here pose even greater problems in terms of their status as 'high' or 'popular' culture. *Bye-bye* (Dridi, 1995), a low-budget work, was not especially popular with audiences, gaining only 120,000 admissions in France. Moreover, its explicitly political subtext, as discussed by Will Higbee, in some ways aligns it more comfortably with experimental or political cinema than with mainstream production. Nevertheless, the film's linear narrative trajectory, familiar themes and – most importantly – focus on the lived realities of protagonists in recognisable communities renders it a thoroughly accessible film. Like *Chacun cherche son chat* and *Marius et Jeannette* which, as Lucy Mazdon and Phil Powrie point out, both hark back to the social cinema of the 1930s, this film engages with social realities via a dramatic and compassionate narrative in a gesture which echoes earlier popular works such as Jean Renoir's *Le Crime de Monsieur Lange* (1936) and Julien Duvivier's *La Belle Équipe* (1936). It is then perhaps fair to say that *Bye-bye, Marius et Jeannette, Chacun cherche son chat* and indeed, *Y aura-t-il de la neige à Noël?* offer another version of the 'popular': a cinema that is rooted in everyday, 'popular' experience.

Of all the films studied in this volume, perhaps the one that most problematically lends itself to definitions of the popular is Catherine Breillat's *Romance* (1999). As Emma Wilson discusses in her chapter, *Romance* offers an extremely challenging and transgressive account of a young woman's sexual encounters. Wilson describes Breillat as an *auteur* who, throughout her career, has set out to explore and reinvent female sexuality. Clearly all this places *Romance* in a firmly high cultural context, a positioning which, as Wilson reveals, was confirmed by the decision of the British Board of Film Classification to pass the film uncut due to its status as a 'serious' and 'philosophical' text. Nevertheless, to describe even this film as 'art cinema' is perhaps to tell only part of the story. As Wilson points out, the film actively blurs boundaries between art cinema and pornography (not perhaps a 'popular' cinematic form but not 'high cultural' either). Moreover, the explicit nature of the film provoked a widespread media debate which in turn perhaps led to relatively healthy audience figures for a film of this kind. So in other words, although the film itself may make high cultural demands upon its spectators, it does this through a negotiation of non-high cultural forms which led to a widespread media response which in turn may have created a new audience for the film.

It is apparent that to describe all French cinema as 'art cinema' or indeed to define any single film in terms of high or popular culture is a far from straightforward enterprise. As the following chapters will reveal, recent French film is, in many ways, characterised by fluidity and diversity as much as by any rigid definitions of national identity or cultural status. In a useful overview of French cinematic production of the 1990s, Phil Powrie (1999) describes the hegemony of the heritage genre in the early years of the decade. The big-budget cultural/popular films described above dominated the domestic box office, displacing the previously ubiquitous comedies and thrillers.[4] This genre was arguably instigated by *Jean de Florette*, and it is for this reason, along with its particular problematisation of the high/popular culture divide, that the film demands a place in this volume. As Powrie goes on to demonstrate, and as the following chapters make clear, the heritage film was far from being the only type of cinema produced in France in the 1990s. Powrie pinpoints as principal strands of production of the period a reinvigoration of *auteur* cinema (mobilised in particular in response to Hollywood production and the increasing place of television in the French audiovisual landscape) and the return of political realism (evidenced in many of the *films de banlieue* described above and in the response of many film-makers to the *loi Debré* of 1997).[5]

Nevertheless, despite this relative diversity, international perceptions of French cinema tend to be dominated by the heritage genre. Films such as *Cyrano de Bergerac* (Rappeneau, 1990), *Germinal* (Berri, 1993) and *Le Hussard sur le toit* (Rappeneau, 1995) have, thanks to state support and extensive promotion, come to represent contemporary French cinema for many non-domestic spectators. As we have seen, these films were very actively mobilised by the state in an attempt to stave off the threat of Hollywood production and increase the international presence of French cinema. Their relative success overseas (*Cyrano de Bergerac* for example was nominated for an Oscar for best foreign-language film and a great many of the so-called heritage films have achieved international distribution) bears witness to the fruition of this project. These films did (albeit in a limited fashion) raise the profile of French cinema, notably in Britain and the United States, achieving new audiences for the French product. Nevertheless, they were also instrumental in *curtailing* French film, squeezing less expensive, non-heritage works out of international distribution and suggesting a homogenous vision of French cinema.

As the following chapters indicate, French production of the 1990s is in fact characterised as much by diversity as by shared attributes. The films studied here range from Poiré's big-budget time-travelling action comedy to Veysset's poetic yet disturbing portrayal of rural family life, from Balasko's brash 'lesbian' comedy, *Gazon maudit*, to Alain Berliner's rather more low-key exploration of gender ambiguities in *Ma Vie en rose*. Indeed, diversity or difference is a key theme of many of the films analysed here: sexuality, race, class and the tensions and uncertainties they provoke all come under scrutiny in a number of these films. Identity can be defined as a key theme and the films discussed (even the most mainstream amongst them) reveal identity in all its forms to be constantly open for negotiation. These concerns can be traced back to the 1980s: preoccupation with national identity, gay and lesbian issues, and ethnicity are key themes in many of the films of that decade. This continuity is perhaps symptomatic of broader changes taking place in French culture and society. The renegotiation of the revolutionary tradition in France from the 1980s, provoked by immigration and increasing globalisation, meant that what it was to be 'French' could no longer be seen to be clear-cut. The promotion of the heritage film, of a specific version of 'French' culture, is one response to these changes. However, the exploration of difference revealed in many of the films discussed in the following pages offers a rather more positive response to social changes.

Many of these films do explore difference and yet they also share a number of attributes. The past surfaces as a frequent concern, notably the negotiation of war-time occupation and collaboration discussed by Howard Seal in his chapter on *Un Héros très discret* (Audiard, 1996). As this essay reveals, the film examines France's failure to come to terms with her war-time past, a failure which moved to the centre of political and cultural debate throughout the 1990s. In rather different ways, *Jean de Florette*, *Marius et Jeannette*, and *Chacun cherche son chat* also negotiate the past – Berri's film through its globally targeted depiction of a lovingly rendered region and the works of Guédiguian and Klapisch through nostalgia and community and a specifically cinematic harking back to the 1930s. This focus on community, or upon the specificities of place, is of course another shared concern. We have already noted the centrality of location in the *cinéma de banlieue* and Dridi's *Bye-bye*. Space and place also play an absolutely vital role in *Chacun cherche son chat*, *Marius et Jeannette*, *Y aura-t-il de la neige à Noël?* and of course *Jean de Florette*. Whereas Paris (or a particular Parisian *quartier*) lies at the heart of Klapisch's film, the latter three works are firmly located in the South of France. This suggests another form of continuity: Paris and the South have long figured as central locations in French cinematic production, notably in films of the 1930s. However, it equally provides another layer of diversity, an emphasis on the regions that has been actively supported by the government via a series of regional funds which have provided subsidies as a means of encouraging film-makers to shoot their films outside central Paris. It may seem somewhat paradoxical that a state which promoted the global aspirations of the heritage film should also support such regional initiatives and indeed this bears witness to the types of identity renegotiation experienced in France described above. However, as Powrie points out here, global and local aspirations can go hand in hand, a combination he pinpoints in *Marius et Jeannette*.

If we return to the questions which began this Introduction – what is French cinema and what is popular cinema – it seems that we are left with no easy answers. Neither can be easily defined and any definition provided in this volume is likely to be rapidly overturned by subsequent books and filmic production. So perhaps we should conclude by stressing once again the diversity of recent and contemporary French film production. This book provides only a snapshot of that diversity and yet the films analysed and the themes they explore make it very apparent that 'French cinema' cannot be reduced to a single entity. The notions of performance explored by Darren Waldron and Lucille Cairns in this volume are perhaps pertinent here. Our understanding of what constitutes French cinema should always remain fluid, open to reinterpretation, its dependence upon exhibition and individual acts of perception fully acknowledged. Identity of all kinds can never be entirely fixed. What I hope the following chapters will provide is a taste of that hybrid, multifarious cultural form which is recent French cinema.

Notes

[1] See Lucy Mazdon (2000) *Encore Hollywood: Remaking French Cinema*. London: BFI.

[2] *Droit de cité* literally means citizenship although *avoir droit de cité* also carries the more figurative meaning 'to be accepted'. *Cité* is a term also used to describe the large blocks of flats that dominate the *banlieues*. This early title thus refers to the film's specific space (the *cités* inhabited by the three main protagonists) and the 'citizenship' and 'acceptance' that, in so many ways, is denied them.

[3] The *avance sur recettes*, first established in 1959, is a loan advanced by the French government to film-makers. They are expected to repay the loan from subsequent box office takings although many fail to repay in full.

[4] Of course, there were obvious exceptions, notably the highly successful *Les Visiteurs*.

[5] See chapters by Powrie, Higbee and Thomas in this volume for discussion of this response to the *loi Debré*.

JEAN DE FLORETTE: *patrimoine*, the rural idyll and the 1980s
Maria Esposito

It is crucial to include Claude Berri's 1986 film in this collection for a number of reasons. Firstly, *Jean de Florette* marked a new departure for the costume drama in France; it can be considered as the first example of what can be termed the '*film de patrimoine*'. This mode of film-making is determined by a strong relationship between protectionist cultural imperatives, industrial strategies of large scale and cost, and an aesthetic of nostalgia which tends to idealise and prettify the past and the nation's geography.

Although costume dramas have been a constant feature of film production in France on varying scales, with larger productions predominating in the 1940s and 1950s and smaller feature films and television productions persisting through to the present day, Berri's first instalment of the Pagnol diptych ushered in a new formulation of this genre. While this film can be said to have reinvigorated a tradition of film-making in France known as *la tradition de la qualité*,[1] the particular combination of elements – the concept of popular cinema, the canonical source-text, the stars, the high budgets, the extremely high-profile release and promotion of the film, the use of natural locations to evoke nostalgia for a lost France – mark the contemporaneity of the film. Part of its specifically modern approach lies in the representation and significance of the past, a characteristic which allows us to liken the *film de patrimoine* to the British heritage film. Both types of film production undoubtedly use the past not only as a spectacle but as a means of shoring up notions of national identity in unstable, increasingly global times. Both modes use the past as a space in which to play out the anxieties of contemporary society, as Andrew Higson (1991) has previously noted. For example, archetypal British heritage films such as *A Room with a View* (Ivory, 1986), *Howard's End* (Ivory, 1992) and *Chariots of Fire* (Hudson, 1991) can be interpreted as a commentary on multiculturalism, the fear of the disintegration of a certain social order, the rise of materialism and meritocracy and, in Phil Powrie's (1997) view, a loss of origins. While I maintain that the *film de patrimoine* has its own distinctive national features which set it apart from the heritage film, the same logic can be applied to *Jean de Florette*. It frames the nation's nostalgic territory, presenting the landscape of Provence as the locus of the nation's idealised rural past. It also highlights such diverse issues as the marginalisation of outsiders in society, questions of inheritance and the ethos of individual material gain. This film is indicative of a certain protectionist attitude to national cinema; it underlines the French film industry's will to affirm itself in the representation of the past.

Jean de Florette and the 1980s

As suggested above, the British heritage film utilises the space of the past in order to reflect on contemporary issues. While it is my contention that the *film de patrimoine* does differ from the heritage film in significant ways, it is worth considering whether *Jean de Florette* engages with concerns particular to the 1980s in France. In a critique of the heritage film published in Britain, greed emerged as one of the issues expressed through the *mise-en-scène* (see Craig 1991). *Jean de Florette* does indeed revolve around the idea of acquisition and loss, not only on a material level, but also in terms of the loss of idealism. The materialist drive associated with the 1980s finds an accurate reflection in the characters of Papet and Ugolin, who strive to possess Jean's land at all costs. Although Ugolin sometimes softens in the face of Jean's increasing pathos, they form a brutal pair, willing to kill the old man for his land at the start of the film and then bring about Jean's downfall, not only by blocking up his spring but also by alienating him from the community from within. The scale of their materialist drive is illustrated by Papet's wish to rebuild the old family orchard, creating a thousand-tree 'cathedral', and Ugolin's dream of growing field upon field of carnations which we see stretching before him in a moment of fantasy projection. Their brutality is made greater by Jean's own modest intentions – to be financially independent through the cultivation of his land and the rearing of rabbits, an aim which it would have been possible to realise if the Soubeyrans had not intervened.

This contrast between materialism and idealism is intensified by Jean's attitude to the land. Jean is clearly driven by a desire to bond with his environment through a close daily connection with the earth. Jean refers to 'the hell of urban life' which contrasts sharply with his rural haven.[2] Berri underlines this contrast rather bluntly with the scene which follows Jean's comment, where we see a typical view of the village square complete with a game of boules on a Sunday afternoon. Jean attempts to live harmoniously with his environment from a modern perspective instead of relying on traditional modes of self-sufficiency. Despite Papet and Ugolin's ridiculing of Jean for his unusual ideas about the sowing and positioning of crops and his reliance on books, Jean's initial harvest attests to the successful marriage of a utopian desire with ecological awareness and scientific knowledge. It is this marriage of approaches which marks out Jean's approach as specifically modern and potentially New Age.

The main themes in *Jean de Florette* find their synthesis in three male protagonists. Jean and the Soubeyrans act out neatly juxtaposed ideas and ideals such as the future versus the past, official knowledge versus accepted wisdom, utopian return to the land versus harsh ruralism. This configuration of characters also outlines the divide between outsider and the community, raising issues of centre and periphery and social alienation. These issues would have had resonance for a French audience at the time of the film's release given the downward turn in fortunes which set in during Mitterrand's first five years of presidency. Whereas the year after the 1981 elections was marked by a sense of euphoria, the period thereafter became increasingly turbulent and 'enthusiasm slowly turned to disappointment'.[3] From 1982 onwards, economic, political and social rifts opened among the French population as a result of many shifts in domestic policy as well as international events which damaged France's reputation internationally.[4] The most relevant factor in this context is immigration, for this issue has serious implications for concepts of national identity and social exclusion and inclusion. In 1985, immigrants in France accounted for approximately eight per cent of the total population and naturalised or first-generation French accounted for three per cent.[5] Although the majority of this community had arrived in France before 1981, much political debate on this subject took place in 1985.[6] While right-wing groups are partly to blame for the heightened visibility of this issue, linking the rise in criminality in France to the presence of immigrant communities, these communities are also marked by their differences from the ethnically French population: by religion, higher birth rates and levels of unemployment. The state's attitude to immigrant communities in terms of citizenship, rights, and benefits has also highlighted this issue and raised the question of French national identity and the demands placed upon individuals adopting it, that is, to assimilate or to retain one's cultural and religious identity. The question of immigration is very much on the contemporary French political and social agenda, as illustrated by *La Loi Debré* (1997), which once again highlights the disparity between French nationals and the immigrant community.[7]

France was faced with similar difficulties to Britain in this period; both were forced to recognise the obsolescence of traditional concepts of national identity in an increasingly multiracial society. A reaction to this situation is the British heritage film which can be regarded as visual, if not narrative, affirmation of tradition and permanence. In *Jean de Florette* we find images which correspond to this longing for the stability and security of the past, in the form of the house and its context. The 1980s witnessed the emergence of the past as a potent signifier in contemporary French society. Given the sense of flux, instability and conflict experienced in this decade, the past offered a firm point of cultural, historical and national reference. This generated a process which can be termed 'patrimonialisation' whereby an increasing number of areas in both public and private life have been and are continuing to be incorporated into the official notion of *patrimoine*. Moreover, the idea of *patrimoine* has been absorbed into contemporary cultural life resulting in a style of visual representation which is visible in cinema and in commercial branding. Where *patrimoine* traditionally referred to pictorial and monumental art, it has now opened up and includes, amongst other things, gastronomy, regional ethnography and urban heritage, all of which have been added to the official definition of patrimoine in the last two decades.[8] In cinema the *film de patrimoine* is an example of the way in which patrimonialisation can idealise and genericise the past; Berri's *Jean de Florette* constructs Provence as an idyllic place through his long sweeping pans of the panorama and practically static 'tableau' shots of the house which are in a pictorial fashion. This mode of portraying Provence leads to a stylisation of representation where the idea of the past and the nation is reduced to the visual signifier of a nostalgically projected Provence. Already imbued with nostalgia by intertextual references (Pagnol and his position in national culture, advertising, experience of rural exodus and tourism), these sites are patrimonialised by Berri. There is a tension, however, created by the storyline; Jean's marginalisation by the villagers based on his hometown, his education and his physical deformity, undercuts the heritage elements of continuity, resulting in a conflict between aesthetics and narrative. Jean's story can be seen to function as an allegory which uses the distance provided by the past to comment on features of contemporary society.

Another feature which marks the contemporaneity of the film is the significance attached to land. There has been a tendency in France to 'patrimonialise' land, particularly urban space, in the last two decades (Gravari-Barbas 1996: 55). To illustrate this point one could give the example of gastronomy, which is closely linked to both culture and the land in France, the image of France as home of high quality cuisine being a nationally coded value. *Les produits du terroir* provide an example of consumer goods which are symbolic of regional identity. Due to high levels of mobility among the population it is difficult to develop a rooted sense of social identity, a situation which has resulted in a drive to extract an idea of continuity from the immediate physical space utilised by a community in the past. Therefore space is attributed the role of *'ciment identitaire'* for a group and local institutions or key features such as schools or forges are considered as sites of minor heritage (Gravari-Barbas 1996: 65). Taken on a broader level, the imagery of Provence can be said to function in a similar manner, providing visual sites for national identification. Through Berri's choice of locations and the camera work used to showcase them, the sites of typical Provençal living invite nostalgic contemplation. These regional sites are elevated to the level of the symbolic, representing an attachment to the nation and to a version of its rural past through a set of very specific physical markers. This tendency to root ideas of authentic French identity in the country also surfaces in contemporary films, for example, *Le Bonheur est dans le pré* (Chatiliez, 1995), which juxtaposes urban living and emotional corruption with rural living and happiness. The rural setting of Condom, while not as impressive as Provence, still contains the typical features; the stone country house set in lush gardens with views to the hills beyond. This image of the rural home has been reiterated in contemporary cinema and is very resonant for many French people who engage with narratives of return to the land as exemplified by *Jean de Florette* on the level of fantasy and nostalgia, perceiving the symbolic value of the rural family house as the site of a better past, or perhaps, in Powrie's view, of 'the certainty of an hierarchical rural social order' (1997: 61). It may also resonate for those who see the reflection of their own '*retour à la terre*', an alternative lifestyle popular in the wake of 1968.

Opening sequence: hooks for a contemporary audience

The first few minutes of *Jean de Florette* impart considerable information about the positioning of the audience vis-à-vis the film's relationship with national culture and the nostalgia aroused by the physical and temporal setting. It is the journey depicted at the start of the film which is particularly significant for the audience. The journey is essentially Ugolin Soubeyran's return from military service to his home. However, we only realise this when he steps out of the car and walks towards Papet's house towards the end of the sequence. Up until this point the journey has been an anonymous one; we have not been aware of Ugolin's existence nor of his relevance to the narrative.

The opening shot is the misty Provençal landscape seen through a car windscreen. The camera adopts the position of a passenger in the car looking out. Given that the camera seems to be showing our perspective as audience, literally looking over our shoulders to the view of the mountains in front of us, it can be suggested that the audience is implicated directly in this journey, travelling in parallel with Ugolin. While he returns to his real home within the diegesis, the audience is involved in a more mythical excursion; the movement shown here is essentially nostalgic, transporting the spectator back to the past. The movement shown here is symbolic; we are moving from darkness to light, that is from the negativity of the present to the safety and security of the past, from the urban to the rural, from the mundane to the visually and geographically exotic.

The past on display for our consumption and identification is strongly shaped by romanticism and nostalgia, composed of many almost stereotypical elements: the crowing of the cock as daylight approaches, the winding country roads, the cobbled streets of the village and the typically southern solidity of its buildings, the grandeur of the valley and the mountains. This scene is evocative on a number of levels. It is a representation of the past as lived by recent generations; France made the transition from rural to urban nation relatively late and thus the experience of rural existence may be separated from many spectators by only one or two generations. The spectator may also have childhood recollections of this journey to the Midi to visit grandparents, or to the family's second residence in the country, a common occurrence in France.[9] Moreover, the journey south has contemporary resonance, given the huge exodus by the urban French population each summer to the Midi.[10] In the light of these levels of identification the opening sequence can be accused of cinematic tourism and, despite the cruelty of nature and the rural community depicted in the film, the overriding image of Provence as rural idyll established at the start ultimately persists.[11]

There is great emphasis on the geographical setting in the opening sequence. This is particularly clear in the long pan which follows the shot of Ugolin emerging from the car. In the course of one long take the camera pans slowly from left to right, sweeping across the top of the valley and gradually lowering its focus onto the trees and roads until it reaches Papet's house set against the mountains. At this point we have caught up with Ugolin, who is simultaneously approaching this location on foot. The long pan has not, however, been Ugolin's perspective on the landscape; on one level it can be construed as a classical establishing shot, taking the focus of the film from the universal (the general landscape of Provence) to the specific (the home of Ugolin where the drama will unfold). On another level it can be suggested that this shot is reinforcing the spectator's position as nostalgic traveller, given that the camera is involved in a heritage moment whereby it seems to echo the typical eye movement of an anonymous, disembodied spectator as s/he scans the panorama from a typical tourist vantage point. This perspective has the effect of drawing the audience into direct nostalgic contemplation of the view. From this point onwards it appears that we are located outside the narrative, looking in on events from this initial distanced perspective of longing and visual appreciation. This is particularly evident when considering the heritage nature of many long shots which, as discussed below, frame archetypal Provençal markers and vistas for their evocative quality or sheer beauty rather than their narrative importance.

Heritage encoding

The opening sequence introduces many of the key elements which, when taken as a whole, codify *Jean de Florette* as an example of a *film de patrimoine*. Berri's preferences in terms of locations and shooting style lead one to make a direct comparison with the aesthetic of the British heritage film. While the country house and the gentle pastoral settings of Southern England and Tuscany have come to typify the heritage aesthetic, the aesthetic focus of *Jean de Florette* is both formal and less moneyed; Berri's camera tends to train languidly on the wilderness and expansiveness of the Provençal landscape, creating an aesthetic specific to French cinema. This can be seen in other recent Pagnol adaptations, such as Yves Robert's *Le Château de ma mère* (1990) and *La Gloire de mon père* (1990), Jean-Paul Rappeneau's *Le Hussard sur le toit* (1995), Philippe de Broca's *Le Bossu* (1997), and Bernard Tavernier's *La Fille de D'Artagnan*. In these films, as in *Jean de Florette*, certain sites particular to French culture and to the southern French landscape are privileged through the camera work and their positioning within the overall form of the film. These sites are the village, the bar, the mountains and, particularly in the Pagnol films, the house at the centre of the narrative. These sites allow other typical features of representation to come into play, forming a conceptual cluster which visually enunciates the idea of a lost and exotic Provence. Following Maria Gravari-Barbas' (1996) theory about the patrimonialisation of space, these local sites have been invested with accrued significance in recent times as a result of the disintegration of the rural community and the high mobility of the urban population. The loci of communal life and tradition, here expressed through the village setting and Jean's house, can be read as geographical and historical points of reference, providing visual interaction with the past and the sense of community and historical cohesion it imparts.

The stereotypical images of Provence: character and spheres of action

The Midi is a region which has inspired greater numbers of films than any other in France. It has been reduced in filmic terms to the representation of Provence thereby excluding the Southwest and Corsica.[12] In his article 'Images of Provence', François de la Bretèque (1990) outlines the many stereotypical characters, spheres of actions and events which mark out films set in the South of France. Thus films such as *Le Boulanger de Valorgues* (Verneuil, 1952) or *Manon des sources* (Pagnol, 1951) contain the typical range of Provençal characters: the loud Southerner, the taciturn peasant, the patriarch, the farmhand, the young virgin, the outsider, the bad guy, the witch and the *enfant sauvage*. These characters are seen engaged in traditional rural activities (farming in all its forms, particularly harvesting and planting) or in other artisanal occupations such as baking or milling flour. They inhabit a world which consists primarily of the emblematic sites of the Provençal village: the café, the fountain, the square, the market.

The emphasis on Papet, Ugolin, and Jean has resulted in the reduced narrative importance of secondary characters, particularly of the women in the text who, as Powrie points out, have been silenced to heighten the sense of melodrama amongst the three male leads (1997: 55). This leads to the superficial representation of the inhabitants of Jean's village whereby they function on a metonymical level in an equally metonymical space; they have been diminished to the role of visual markers of Provence who no longer exercise a narrative function. This runs against Pagnol's own stated preferences as a writer and a director.

The 'gallery' of characters was one of the essential elements in Pagnol's films. Everyone had an equal place in the picture, creating, through each individual stroke, a picture of a community both united and divided by its contradictions, caught up in its dramas.[13] They are only relevant in relation to Jean and the unfolding of his story, and not seen independently of this. In Berri's film they have become a heritage feature, furnishing the tableau-like long shots of the countryside with authentic human activity. Thus they are indicative of a heritage aesthetic in more ways than one, providing authenticity and excess of signification. Firstly, they can be likened to a living display of lost agricultural life-styles in a heritage museum/park. We see the background characters involved in various processes which strongly connote the past and man's lost connection with the land, such as harvesting grapes, sowing seeds, pruning olive trees and carrying water. We also see other figures who are emblematic of their rural environment, such as the peasant riding by on a donkey, a woman cooking and serving her male relatives in the farmhouse, the farmer going to market, the baker in his shop. The shots featuring these symbolic, nostalgia-inducing activities lend the film a certain regional credibility. Secondly, they provide *Jean de Florette* with a visual texture and local colour through their appearance, usually grouped together in crowd scenes in the village or in the fields. Berri's tendency to condense the secondary characters to emblematic, undifferentiated figures, seen collectively, indicates a deployment of extras as heritage detail as well as the articulation of a rudimentary notion of group identity. Thus, the inhabitants of Les Bastides Blanches are portrayed in public spaces, for example in the village square, in the bar or in their space of work (the fields, in the bar or the bakery), rather than in their personal spaces, thereby providing a human heritage backdrop against which the personal narrative of Jean, Ugolin and Papet finds sharp definition.

Images of patrimoine: the house and garden

On analysing *Jean de Florette* it becomes apparent that only four main spaces are utilised by Berri, namely Jean's house and gardens, the Soubeyrans' property, the village and the vistas of the region. This utilisation of space builds up a sense of place and identity, with each locus forming a layer of identification which cumulatively express the idea of Provence. Jean's house articulates a stereotypical image of Provence from the angle of an individual space. The solid, shuttered, stone farmhouse is an image commonly associated with this area. The bastide is a typical element in the established iconography that circulates in French and also, to a certain extent, in British culture. Pagnol's work, especially his autobiographical novels, placed the bastide at the centre of the highly nostalgic narrative and of Southern living. The first instalment of the autobiography is aptly named *Le Château de ma mère*, in reference to the house. Adapted from the first two novels in the Pagnol series, Yves Robert's films are centred on the holidays spent at the summer house and showcase this particular location in a nostalgic, reverential manner. In Britain this image surfaces in a number of areas: in Peter Mayle's hugely successful books – his accounts of living in Provence – *A Year in Provence* (1989), *Toujours Provence* (1991), and *Encore Provence* (1999) and the subsequent television adaptation of the first book by the BBC in 1993 as well as the fictional *Hotel Pastis* (1993), in advertising such as the Stella Artois television advertisements, where Verdi's *La Forza del Destino* is used to heighten the Berri connection. It is also a more generic signifier for Mediterranean countries, featuring in advertisements for cars and food.

The house in *Jean de Florette* is a key image. It contains within it the ideas of inheritance and tradition, idealism and loss, which are articulated through Jean's relationship with it. Jean's vision of his existence in the house combines the past and the future, his desire to cultivate a traditional rural lifestyle informed by modern science and official knowledge, in a manner reminiscent of the heritage couplet outlined by John Corner and Sylvia Harvey. Corner and Harvey comment that 'if the spirit of enterprise offers itself as the motor of change, innovation, and development, the spirit of heritage offers the reassurance of continuity with a shared past' (1991: 72).

Jean's vision of utopia is predicated on a very idealistic view of rural self-sufficiency which combines the past and present: he claims that 'the only way to be happy is to get back to nature. I came here to cultivate the real. I want to eat vegetables from my garden, make oil from olives on my trees, eat fresh eggs from my hens, get drunk on wine made from my own vines'.[14] He foresees the realisation of his own version of utopia through the application of modern farming methods to a very traditional context. Not only does the house embody discourses related to heritage culture, but it is also very much represented in a heritage style: it is often seen in medium to long shot, positioned in the centre of the frame, surrounded by the gardens and the mountains, thus very securely anchoring the house in its geographical context. Jean is also strongly connected to the house and its environment. For example, in one long take which seemingly spans one whole day we see Jean engaged in clearing the garden. The camera pans to the right through the trees and plants and finds Jean working in the distance. As the camera continues to move to the right the light and shadows change, suggesting the progression of time, and it finally rests on a shot of the house at twilight with smoke rising out of this chimney. This scene appears to present Jean as an organic part of this particular landscape, interacting with his environment and imbuing this space with his identity.

Papet and Ugolin's homes and land are accorded less attention in the film. Papet's house, however, is an important location, for it is here that we see the cold plotting of the Soubeyrans. Indeed, the two locations function in opposition to each other: while Jean's associative location in the first half of the film is his garden where he is happily involved in the spring-time process of planting and tending crops, the Soubeyrans, by contrast, are presented in the dark interior of Papet's house, hatching their scheme. Thus, Jean's optimism and delight find their visual echo in the beauty of his external surroundings. When Jean's project starts to fail his associative location changes; from this point onwards Jean is mainly seen either carrying water or brooding in his house. The garden is no longer the terrestrial paradise he discovered on his arrival but rather a very material display of his impending failure. Jean's unravelling is visually heightened by the use of the weather, which casts the garden as a scene of disaster of operatic dimensions. Where the garden was once lush and green in the spring-time, the extreme summer temperatures result in devastation and Jean's increasing bewilderment and sense of betrayal. The blindingly bright sand storm and night of lightning transform the garden into a visually alien space. For the former a filter is used, creating a hallucinatory vision of the garden; upon opening the door to the garden Jean is disorientated by the vicious light, which changes the rural space outside into a forbidding desert. For the latter, the garden is shot from above in the dark, which has the effect of dwarfing Jean and underlining his small tragedy in relation to the wider concept of nature. In both cases the perspectives adopted to shoot the garden disrupt the gentle idyll created by Berri's eye-level slow pans and lingering long shots.

The village and markers of the regional space

It was suggested above that only four main spaces are utilised in Berri's film. Along with the prominent locations of Jean's house and garden and then, in descending order of importance, the personal spaces of the Soubeyrans, the other two geographical spaces shown in *Jean de Florette* are the village and the general panoramas of the Provençal mountains where we see the villagers at work. Unlike the main protagonists, who are also depicted in their personal space, the inhabitants of Les Bastides Blanches are mainly depicted in two areas – in the village and on the land. These two areas impart a sense of the generic. Where Jean's space is the embodiment of his, and by implication the spectator's, nostalgia for an individual connection with a lost way of life, the village and the mountain vistas generate meaning at a far more general level, creating a distinctive sense of place (here, the region) through the use of established markers. Although one could accuse Berri of producing a picture of Provence by including stereotypical images and characters, it could equally be argued that this recourse to the general for the narrative backdrop intensifies the unfolding of Jean's personal tragedy. In portraying the grandeur of the landscape, the unchanging cycle of seasons, and exposing the fundamental flaws in human nature, Berri locates and delimits the fate of a man, underlined by the choice of Verdi's *La Forza del Destino* as Jean's theme, against Destiny and the wider fate of the human race as opposed to the individual. The generic aspects of the film allow Berri to relate his story in bold and simple terms such as nature, community and timeless human emotions (greed, grief, longing and envy), lending the film a certain universality and timelessness.

The representation of the village of Les Bastides Blanches provides the greatest illustration of Berri's tendency to create a generic image of Provence. The village is the main point of interaction between the primary and secondary male characters where they either discuss Jean in the bar or, more rarely, see him walking with his family through the village. Given that the breadth of the source text has been condensed in *Jean de Florette* to highlight Jean's particular setting and story, the village and its inhabitants are also reduced to their emblematic qualities. Thus the elements of the village depicted on screen are those which symbolise the French rural community and way of life. The village is not depicted in its entirety; we mainly see it from the central perspective afforded by the square which, as de la Bretèque comments, is 'a synthesis of a number of places ' (De la Bretèque 1990: 67). This is the place where we find the game of *boules*, the fountain, the plane trees and even the old straw seated chair reminiscent of a Van Gogh painting. We also see two internal spaces: the bakery briefly and the bar on several occasions. Although the bakery is clearly a marker of the Provençal world with films such as *La Femme du boulanger* (Marcel Pagnol, 1938) and *Le Boulanger de Valorgues* (Henri Vallorgues, 1952), *Jean de Florette* does not exploit this particular avenue and instead concentrates on the bar as the main area of action and village intrigue. It is a pivotal location where we find the men of the village, uniformly dressed in their black Sunday best, drinking and discussing local business. Here the camera focuses on the small details which impart a sense of the way of life in Provence; for example, we see Papet in close-up, slowly pouring Pastis over a sugar cube in his glass. The simple rhythm of life is also underlined by this location where the locals convene for a drink on a Sunday after working all week on the land. The snatches of dialogue reinforce the film's regional specificity; the Midi accent is apparent here and, given Jean's standard spoken French, highlights his difference from the local community. Again, there is little differentiation or individualisation of the assorted men in these bar scenes; they merely serve the purpose of adding heritage texture to the film and conveying the idea of community. Moreover, one can draw out cultural associations suggested by the scenes in the bar which resemble paintings by Cézanne (see 'The Cardplayer' series of paintings (1890–96) and 'The Smoker' (1891–92)).

The shots of the mountains also function in a number of ways. Firstly, they have painterly connections; the panoramic views of the countryside around Les Bastides Blanches recall paintings of Mont Saint Victoire by Cézanne. Secondly, they establish the geographical parameters of the film and, through the preferred camera movements, angles and length of take, indicate the value attributed to the physical setting. From the opening sequence alone, it is clear that Berri imbues the mountains around Aubagne with a sense of nostalgic longing. In one long take the camera slowly pans from left to right from a high vantage point, sweeping across the valley at dawn and eventually finding Ugolin on his ascent to his house. The screen time preceding Ugolin's appearance would seem to be a heritage moment where the lingering long shots and tracking shots of the landscapes are not directly motivated by the narrative. Instead, the landscape is offered for our lengthy contemplation, much in the same manner as the opening sequence of *Howard's End*, where the camera lovingly trails Vanessa Redgrave walking through the long grass around the house at twilight before shifting its focus to events taking place inside. While the treatment of the settings is similar in terms of the slow moving, steady and even reverential camera work, the object of this attention is very different in *Jean de Florette*. The country house, set in its own grounds of the British heritage film, finds its equivalent in the old stone farmhouse set against the rugged backdrop of the Provençal mountains. Both British and French audiences can relate to these contexts, not only through the retrospective movement of nostalgia but also through present-day leisure activities such as days out at National Trust properties or holidays in Provence. This type of leisure-time pursuit highlights the contemporary pleasures to be gained from revisiting the past as presented by the heritage industry and indeed the heritage film. There are clearly nationally specific facets to the heritage consumer's relationship with the national past displayed in museums or at the cinema. In terms of cinema, a French audience's relationship with the concept of the past generated by the idea of Provence is coloured by the post-war rural exodus. Thus *Jean de Florette* and other Pagnol adaptations reveal a world distanced from the present, not only by its sheer exoticism and grand physical scale, but also by it very pastness – that is, in its depiction of a pre-lapsarian world which has not yet experienced the dislocating effects brought about by the mutation of the society from agricultural to urban. While the lifestyles and settings in *Jean de Florette* patently belong to the past they are nonetheless close by virtue of the temporal proximity of the exodus for contemporary spectators and of their interaction with the heritage/leisure industry. Berri facilitates a nostalgic excursion into this lost world through his use of a classical iconography of Provence complete with a soundtrack capturing the cicadas, the birds, the sounds of carts travelling on stony ground and the movement of grass. Cumulatively these features lend the film a picturesque quality, each lingering shot of the mountains or Jean's house creating a living tableau of Provence. It is perhaps telling that Berri, on reading *L'Eau des Collines*, considered the novel to be a grand fresco of the region.[15]

Jean de Florette, stars and the media

Part of *Jean de Florette*'s appeal for cinema-goers lay in the actors chosen to play the main roles. According to a survey by SOFRES, the actors provided the second main incentive for going to see the film (Frodon and Loiseau 1987: 217). Yves Montand and Gérard Depardieu are clearly the stars of the film; Daniel Auteuil had not yet become a prominent screen actor by this stage. The three principal actors were widely used to promote the film prior to its release with interviews on television, on radio (a whole day of interviews on *France Inter*) and in the press. Montand was the most prolific in this sense, appearing in a profile on TF1 entitled '*Yves Montand à la rencontre de Pagnol*' (Frodon and Loiseau 1987: 215). The film was screened at pre-release premieres throughout France, most notably in Aubagne at the Pagnol cinema and in Paris where it was attended by Jack Lang and his successor, Philippe de Villiers, which is indicative of the support received from the Ministry of Culture for Berri's concept of high budget, state-funded popular cinema (Frodon and Loiseau 1987: 216). This promotional strategy clearly succeeded: *Jean de Florette* was seen by one million French cinema-goers in its first week of exhibition, outperforming *Rambo* and *Raiders of the Lost Ark* at the box office (Zimmer 1988: 67).

Depardieu is perhaps the more important star in this film for a number of reasons. In terms of stature and international recognition he has been described as the contemporary equivalent of Maurice Chevalier and Jean Gabin (Vincendeau 1993: 343). Where Montand is indicative of the old school of French male stars who largely appeared in dramas, comedies or mixtures of the two,[16] Depardieu functions across genre and across gender (Vincendeau 1993: 344). In the construction of a new cultural identity in the post-1968 era in theatre and later in cinema, Depardieu has been a prominent figure, embodying ambiguous sexuality, unstable masculinity and social marginality often from the position of a '*loubard*' – a small-time criminal from the suburbs.[17] There is a resonance of real life in Depardieu's roles given his emergence from a working-class background into petty crime before finding his vocation as an actor. This is clearly not the role that Depardieu assumes in *Jean de Florette* which is more in line with his secondary career of *vigneron*; in this film his populist origins are on display but he is a character closely aligned with high culture (opera, classical music, literature) as well as with modern science. He desires a return to his roots from an informed rather than traditional position, again recalling Harvey and Corner's heritage couplet, which unites tradition and modernity as a strategy to face an uncertain future. This couplet can be seen to express Jean's Frenchness given that cultivated urbanism and ruralism articulated in the Paris versus province (or indeed in this case Provence) form a binary upon which French national identity is often based. Where a French audience can appreciate the nuances of urban and local identities on display in *Jean de Florette* carried in the accents, locations and narrative themes, a foreign spectator is more likely to perceive Jean as typically French, 'an icon of Frenchness erasing class and/or regional difference' (Vincendeau 1993: 361). He is thus a useful promotional tool for films distributed outside France which cannot escape their national provenance given their linguistic specificity and usual exhibition on the art-house circuit. This function of Frenchness is illustrated by his appearance in subsequent *films de patrimoine* (*Tous les Matins du monde* (Corneau, 1991), *Cyrano de Bergerac* (Rappeneau, 1990), *Le Colonel Chabert* (Angelo, 1994), *Germinal* (Berri, 1993), *Camille Claudel* (Nuytten, 1988), *Uranus* (Berri, 1990), and briefly in *Le Hussard sur le toit*). He therefore holds value for audiences and film-makers: for the former he is an attraction by virtue of his star status, and for the latter he is an assurance of quality necessary for investors in such high-budget films.

It is this assurance of quality that is crucial to high-budget French film-making in the climate of the 1980s and 1990s. In satisfying the demands of the two major forces in the film market – American products and, more recently, television – the single or multiple use of stars is an essential element; as Vincendeau points out, it is common to see two stars in contemporary cultural super-productions.[18] To secure funding and then small- and big-screen audiences and the sale of video rights, increasingly high-budget *films de patrimoine*, which are the most conspicuous example of the drive to protect national cinema through a cinema of expensive, cultural attractions, require guarantees. This is achieved in part by the presence of the star or stars.

Jean de Florette can thus be regarded as a film which is unusually expressive of the present. It points to the way in which contemporary society and dominant cultural production retrospectively cast the past as an anchor for identity by harking back to a time prior to the rural exodus in France. *Jean de Florette* depicts a time when family, community, and the rigours of agricultural life gave a definite structure to life in sharp contrast to the insecurities and mutability of modern urban living. Jean plays on this negative/positive, city/country, present/past dichotomy, referring to his escape from '*l'enfer des villes*' and his rural existence as natural and harmonious. The past is, therefore, a haven, a form of reassurance despite the catastrophes Jean is subjected to in the film. The past, in the shape of Provence, is the main character in the film, a constant nostalgic spectacle which Berri's reverent camera paints as beautiful, solid and permanent. This past is, of course, a modern-day fiction based on the way that we see Provence from our distanced, tourist's perspective. The *maison de campagne* is a good example of this perspective; it is reinscribed as a symbol of a lost community and the associated discourses of tradition and continuity which place a very firm contemporary stamp upon the film. The way in which the *maison* and indeed the key sites of the region are re-valorised and appropriated by collective nostalgia is indicative of the process of patrimonialisation. *Jean de Florette* is also expressive of the nation's film industry and state strategies to boost its presence at the domestic box office. It tells of the industry's constant battle with American film and the French response: the *film de patrimoine*, a cultural blockbuster which packages French culture in a high-budget format. Berri's film was arguably the first to deploy this strategy, which has since become the defining formula for dominant contemporary French cinema.

Notes

[1] *La tradition de qualité* was a style of mainstream film-making which predominated in the 1940s and 1950s in France. It displayed a preference for high production values, studio-based filming, stars, literary adaptations and high budgets supported by significant levels of government funding. This form was favoured by directors Claude Autant-Lara, Yves Allegret and Jean Delannoy and scriptwriters including Jean Aurenche and Pierre Bost. Films made in this vein are *La Reine Margot* (Dreville, 1954), *Le Rouge et le noir* (Autant-Lara, 1954), *Nana* (Christian-Jacque 1954) and *La Fête à Henriette* (Duvivier, 1952). Stars appearing in these films include Gérard Philippe, Jean Gabin, Daniele Delorme, Danielle Darriuex and Martine Carol.

[2] '*l'enfer des villes*'

[3] '*l'allégresse fait place peu à peu au désenchantement*' (Ambrosi, A. and C. Ambrosi (1991) *La France: 1870-1990*. Barcelona, Bonn, Milan, Paris: Masson, 372).

[4] The major events which took place in France in this period are the devaluation of the franc twice in nine months, decentralisation, strikes caused by unfavourable changes in unemployment laws and the suspension of inflation-linked pay increases, the rise in unemployment, the drop in the standard of living, terrorism in Corsica and mainland France, insurrection in New Caledonia, and the Greenpeace affair. These events are discussed in depth by Ambrosi 1991.

[5] Ibid, 395.

[6] Ibid.

[7] The reforms on immigration drafted by Jean-Louis Debré in effect impede the entry of immigrants into France while also clamping down on immigrants already on French territory. This law, which increased the power of the police (for example, authorising greater searches on vehicles and in companies thought to be harbouring immigrant labour) while reducing the power of judges to free imprisoned immigrants, draws a crucial distinction between the French and those simply born in France, indicating that the latter status does not license the entry of relatives into the country.

[8] Historical tourism also attests to the public's interest in visiting sites of historical importance: in 1981 30 per cent of the public visited a heritage site, a figure which rose to 57 per cent

in 1993 (P. Faucher 1994 'Mise en valeur du patrimoine du territoire', in *Cahiers des Espaces* 37). Patrimonialisation is also evident in consumer tastes and commercial trends. There has been a growth of shops with a heritage theme such as *L'Occitane* and *La Méditerranéene*, the magazine *Côte Sud*, brands such as *Côté bastide*, *Comptoir du Sud*, *Les Olivades* and *Souleiado*, which have taken the theme of Provence as their *'image de marque'*.

[9] In 1990 there were 2,822,295 *résidences secondaires* in France of which 84.9 per cent were owned rather than rented. Ownership can be broken down by occupation as follows: executives and liberal professions 24.1 per cent, craftsmen and businessmen 16.1 per cent, middle management 10.7 percent, employees 7.1 percent, manual workers 4.7 percent and farmers 4.2 per cent. *Résidences secondaires* accounted for over 70 per cent of the total number of beds used by tourists in France (12,071,000 of 17,238,000). Figures taken from *Quid 1998*, 1323 and 1742.

[10] Of the 157,800,000 holidays enjoyed by the French in France in 1995, 106,300,000 were spent in Provence-Alpes-Côte-d'Azur. Compare to 18,800,000 in Rhône-Alpes, 12,500,000 in the Ile-de-France, 11,400,000 in the Loire, 10,400,000 in Brittany, 9,900,000 in Languedoc-Rousillon, 9,600,000 in Aquitaine and 8,400,000 in the Mediterranean Pyrenees. Moreover, compare to the number of French going on holiday outside France: 11,900,000 went to another European country, 1,400,000 to Africa, 900,000 to the Far East and 1,400,000 to the American continent in contrast to the 157,800,000 holidays spent in France. Figures from *Quid 1998*, 1743.

[11] Guy Austin has commented on the picture-postcard version of France presented in *Jean de Florette*. Berri, he observes, creates a 'touristic, facile picture of Provence' (1996: 161).

[12] The representation of the Midi has been further arrested in recent times by the tendency to focus on one of the two contradictory traditions of writing and film-making associated with this region. De la Bretèque contends that the comic-maritime vein predominates over the tragic-rural vein (1990: 59). The Pagnol adaptations of the 1980s and 1990s, however, illustrate the popularity of the latter; films set around the ports of Marseille, for example, may well have prevailed in the 1930s and 1940s under the impetus of Pagnol's own adaptations of his literary works. Today, *Jean de Florette* and the films which followed in its wake attest to a dominant, nostalgic rural image of Provence with smaller films such as *Marius et Jeannette* (Guediguian, 1997) or *A la place du coeur* (Guediguian, 1999) and *Un, deux, trois soleil* (Blier, 1993) portraying the contemporary urban side of the equation.

[13] 'La 'galerie' de personnages constituait un des éléments essentiels des films de Pagnol. Tous avaient droit à la représentation, dessinant ainsi, trait par trait, les contours d'une collectivité à la fois soudée, et prise dans ses contradictions, son drame interne' (Toubiana 1986: 51).

[14] '... le seul bonheur possible c'est d'être un homme de la nature. Je suis venu ici pour cultiver l'authentique. Je veux manger des légumes de mon jardin, recueillir l'huile de mes oliviers, gober les oeufs frais de mes poules, m'enivrer du vin de ma vigne'

[15] Press Release from Cannon films for *Jean de Florette*.

[16] In this context Vincendeau lists Louis de Funès, Bourvil, Fernandel, Raimu, Bach and George Milton (1993: 344).

[17] In reference to Depardieu's sexuality one can cite *Les Valseuses* (Blier, 1973), *Inspecteur La Bavure* (Zidi, 1980) and *Tenue de soirée* (Blier, 1986).

[18] It is common to see two stars in *films de patrimoine*. Vincendeau points to Montand and Depardieu in *Jean de Florette*, Depardieu and Deneuve in *Fort Saganne*, Depardieu and Adjani in Camille Claudel, Depardieu and Marielle in *Tous les matins du monde* (1995: 360). In the later *films de patrimoine* multiple stars are in evidence, indicating the continuing pressure to provide attractions and guarantees. Hence we see Depardieu and Ardant in *Le Colonel Chabert* (Angelo, 1994), Adjani, Perez and Anglade in *La Reine Margot* (Chereau, 1994), Ardant, Rochefort and Berling in *Ridicule* (Leconte, 1996), Binoche, Cluzet, Depardieu, Yanne in *Le Hussard sur le toit* and Auteuil, Perez, Noiret, in *Le Bossu* (de Broca, 1997).

NIKITA as social fantasy
Alison Smith

Luc Besson's *Nikita* (1990) has retained a reputation as one of the most stylish exponents of what has come to be known as '*le cinéma du look*' of the 1980s and 1990s.[1] In fact, insofar as that title corresponds to a definite genre, *Nikita* could be said to be the peak which, perhaps, preceded its dissolution. Jean-Jacques Beineix, who inaugurated the genre with *Diva* in 1981, had already passed the peak of his popularity, and his last film to date, *IP5* (1992), drifted from brief notoriety to semi-obscurity. Even the explosive *Les Amants du Pont-Neuf* (Carax, 1991), which Guy Austin (1996) considers the apogee of the genre, has not exerted such a lasting hold on the imagination as *Nikita*. The film, however, was coolly received by the French critics, who by and large accused Besson of a kind of populism, and of playing to a notional 'youth-market' in his choice of theme and style. Audience figures soon bore out Besson's belief that he was indeed able to engage the imaginations of a cinema-going public in France, and the film's subsequent career has shown that the effect is durable. Besson's critical reputation has, however, always been higher in Anglo-Saxon countries than in France, and it was partly in response to this that, after *Nikita*, he moved his centre of operations more clearly across the Atlantic to make *Léon* (1994) and *The Fifth Element* (1997).

The French cinema of the 1990s has tended – in broad terms – to divide its attention between relatively traditional blockbuster fare, such as costume dramas and comedies, and a renewed interest in social realism.[2] The urban fantasy which characterised the *cinéma du look* has in the 1990s found expression mainly in the BD-inspired creations of Jeunet and Caro (*Délicatessen* (1991), *La Cité des Enfants Perdus* (1995)), in whose hands the labyrinthine worlds which Beineix, Besson or Carax delineated in a still identifiable Paris have become wholly imaginary.

By 1997, with the appearance of *The Fifth Element*, Besson seemed to have moved definitively into the elaboration of baroque futuristic fantasy. In *Nikita*, however (as in *Léon*), his imagination is still restrained, visually and contextually. The film's world is recognisable, almost credible, and it is this which gives the fantasy its force. For *Nikita* is undeniably a fantasy, and the spectator certainly receives it as such, and it is with *Nikita* as fantasy that this chapter will be primarily concerned.

Any fantasy involves a representation of the world which corresponds to the desires, or the fears, or most likely both, of its author. This is of course true – to some extent – of any film, and one could perhaps claim that all films are more or less fantasies; where the genre is openly espoused, however, this definition and the questions that it imposes becomes central to understanding the functioning of the film.

These questions are threefold: firstly, they concern the content of the representation; secondly, the identity of the author, for a fantasy must imply a fantasising mind; thirdly, the way in which the fantasy acts upon its audience. This chapter will thus seek to explore the world of *Nikita* from the following angles: What is being represented? Whose representation is it? Or, in other words, is there an approximation to an authorial position contained within the film? What is the function of the representation, both for its author and for its audience?

These questions have to some extent been evoked by Susan Hayward (1997) in her extremely erudite study of Besson's work, to which this chapter is much indebted. Hayward has shown how the film's delineation of a society based on surveillance-systems, where the young protagonist is representative of youth in general as an alien and distrusted class, can convincingly be related to perceived developments in French society in the 1980s. She has also discussed in detail the complex gender issues which the film expresses. *Nikita*, in fact, tells the story of the development of the protagonist from genderlessness to a gendered identity, through the mediation of a 'father-figure', Bob. Hayward has shown how the film can be related to the Oedipal scenario, and the difficulties which arise from the lack, in Nikita's development, of a credible mother-figure. In fact, femininity in *Nikita* seems to be presented as a form of masquerade, with the protagonist being encouraged to put on the costume, make-up and names associated with it in order to fit into society and also to attain a form of manipulative power. Apart from Nikita herself there is only one female character, Armande, who is the spokesperson for just this attitude to gender. Nikita is kitted out with a selection of costumes for her various assignments which correspond to different imagined constructions of femininity until, in the final assignment, she 'cross-dresses/transgresses', a move for which, in Hayward's analysis, her final failure and disappearance is a punishment.

In this chapter I have elected to concentrate on the elaboration of Nikita's story as an expression of the functioning of order in society, and the issue of gender will be considered only insofar as it is directly relevant to this. The reader is referred to Hayward's work for a detailed analysis of some of these issues.

What fantasy?

Given, then, that *Nikita* is a fantasy, what is the content and how is it represented? From the start it is defined as an urban fantasy, and as we shall see, its concerns will increasingly prove to be with the organisation of society, a distinctly urban preoccupation.

The first images, in a rainy, unidentifiable city, present a group of teenagers marching purposefully along the street. They are fairly distant and therefore unidentifiable, but visually coded, by clothing and manner, as aggressive, and when we do at last see them closely, they are shown at a low-angle, which again creates a sense of menace. Throughout the first, exaggeratedly violent, sequence, the group remains menacing and incomprehensible – a series of stereotypes of 'delinquent youth' incarnated in the four characters. They are junkies: they turn to violence as the first solution to even the most simple obstacle (Zap); they indulge in it for – or at least with – pleasure (Rico); they are totally divorced from any sense of family (Coyotte) while able to use other people's sense of it to their own advantage when menacing the innocent small businessman (Rico, briefly); they are exhibitionist (Zap again), and inconsequent (everybody). The climax of the anarchic violence which they unleash – even if the police then take over – is the shooting of a policeman by the only member of the gang left alive, the woman, who is hiding in a corner.

If the gang members are never more than names and stereotypical behaviour, the 'forces of order' are even less individualised, being nothing more than a faceless front of firepower until one of their number uncovers Nikita. In the seconds before he is, literally, blown away, we see him in close-up in a shot-countershot sequence with Nikita. He is thus humanised; we are also allowed to retain an indistinct but definite image of him, and we may assume that this is also true for Nikita. It will be of significance later that both we and she should have retained the image of this anonymous face.

Nikita, however, becomes individualised as for the rest of the film she alone represents the 'danger' which she and her gang at first embodied. The rest of the film depicts the way in which society extracts from her – what? Justice? Or vengeance? Or advantage? Or, finally, proof that complete socialisation of such anarchic elements is either impossible, or at least, very dangerous.

My argument will be that *Nikita* presents itself as a fantasy about 'justice', seen as the neutralisation of a danger to all the values of an ordered society, a danger constructed by the film in the first sequence. This fantasy, however, is not unequivocally endorsed by the film at any time, and indeed is more and more clearly shown to contain within itself elements which negate it.

The narrative explicitly presents Nikita's fate as a process of justice, or rather as a sequence of alternative processes, all of which have strong connotative power. The sequence begins with the conventional judicial scenario (trial and sentence), but this is almost incidental. The next scene – apparently – substitutes a hidden, primitive, justice of a life for a life in which, due service having been paid to the forms, she is to be killed by lethal injection. Not, as we know, always a fantasy, but in societies where capital punishment is not part of the system its possibility remains a powerful collective fantasm which is always resurfacing. The scene proves to be a red herring, however. Nikita awakens in a cell and for the rest of the film will 'serve her sentence' as a state killer.

However, the scene of her 'death' is not so easily forgotten. Firstly, she is indeed officially dead, and the way in which this is covered up indicates that there is no safeguard in the system which ensures that she is not so for real. Secondly, there is the manner of her awakening.

If we allow ourselves to imagine, for a moment, that the execution has been for real, and that the scene which follows takes place in 'the afterlife', we find that many of the visual clues are appropriate; there is a blinding light, a white room, a figure sitting in judgement, and when Nikita asks the figure 'Am I in heaven, sir?'[3] the question seems not unreasonable. Neither, in fact, do Bob's answers provide any real denial, although I presume most spectators instantly reject this possibility which, if acceptable, would irremediably weaken the film.

Nonetheless, such strongly coded images can hardly be innocent. I would argue that they increase the tendency to read Nikita's subsequent fate not only as a fantasy, but as a fantasy which bears a direct relation to her previous existence. They add, by connotation, another layer to the sequence of systematic judicial recriminations with which Nikita has been faced – the concept of heaven and hell, after all, is only another fantasised process of justice.

Such a reading is further reinforced by the appearance of the Judge. Certainly his dark clothes, his position, his stern face and discreet stubble make of him a phallic father-figure and a representation of authority, but that face and that stubble bear more than a passing resemblance to another face already seen, that of the doomed policeman of the first sequence. A comparison of the two stills bears this out, although detailed study and the credit list seem to confirm that the policeman is not Tchéky Karyo. Thus the controller of Nikita's rebirth, and process of socialisation, is, at least, very similar to the victim of her previous violence, a similarity which, if we perceive, we may assume that Nikita, too, is aware of.

Thus the answer to our first question – what is being represented – may be said to be a fantasised process both of retribution and of neutralisation of the kind of anarchic violence which constitutes a disturbance to 'normal' society and kills its agents. The neutralisation, however, will take place not by denying the violence but by disciplining it and turning it against the 'enemies of society'. That sentence should not be read, however, as implying that the disciplined violence is to be turned against itself (or its own earlier form). The 'enemies' against whom Nikita is used are coded, inasmuch as we can give any character to the targets at all, not as the anarchic, frightening, but finally vulnerable youth of the first scenes, but as highly organised, socialised, yet strangely 'foreign' beings. This is certainly true of the ambassador at the end, and apparently of the somewhat Oriental-looking VIP at the beginning, while one might perhaps argue that the woman in Venice is 'foreign' to the corridors of power that she presumably moves in simply by her sex. The violent elements in society, tamed, are to be used not to repress violence, then, but difference.

However, the film does not allow a full engagement with this representation. The issue of the name is enough to make us wary. Briefly – the protagonist when she first appears, outside all socialisation, a danger and a desire (*'j'en veux'*), nothing else, has no name; but when one is demanded of her, she provides it. The name Nikita has many connotations. There is its source in (a very established form of) popular culture, its genderlessness, its three sharp syllables which make it sound like a martial arts war cry when Nikita first uses it. Most importantly, it is quite probably a name she has chosen herself and which has not been given to her, and it comes to represent the part of her which is not controlled by Bob (who uses it when speaking to her at the moment of separation when she is most clearly an unpredictable love-object and when he therefore cannot feel control).

It is also the title of the film, and thus applies to the whole of it – the protagonist never ceases to be Nikita, even when everyone calls her either 'Marie' or 'Joséphine', she is thus never quite neutralised or incorporated into others' images.

Whose fantasy?

We now turn to the issue of the authorship of the fantasy. That is, who is the author of the representation of justice above described, and to what extent is it shared, subverted or even rejected by other intervening voices – and, finally, by the audience?

Issues of authorship in *Nikita* are complex, but the first central question, is whether there is a place for an 'author' within the narrative of *Nikita*? The very fact that, as mentioned above, the film provides strategies to prevent us engaging fully with the fantasy, indicates the presence of what might be called a 'meta-author', who is outside the author of the fantasy and can cast doubt on it, and that usually implies that one way or another the author on whom doubt is cast has to be wrapped up in the text somewhere. The question is – where?

There are several layers to this question. Firstly, one has to ask whether Bob, or indeed Nikita herself, can be positioned as the author of the fantasy. Superficially, one is tempted to reject Nikita's candidacy out of hand, and to see strong arguments for that of Bob. Nikita is so clearly in the object-position throughout – gazed at, disguised, constructed according to the images created by various controllers – that the whole film seems to do nothing but manipulate her. However, her position is not perhaps so powerless as it seems with regard to her own image. Neither, of course, is the suggestion that the fantasy involves her own punishment an argument against her authorship of it, and her position contains considerable ambiguities, recognised by Hayward in her discussion of the difficulties involved for a female spectator in identifying with Nikita.

Bob, on the other hand, has a strong claim to be the 'author' of the re-vamped Marie/Joséphine character that Nikita becomes. He is apparently a father/authority figure – he is certainly the authority which Nikita quite quickly recognises. He initiates her training and provides (and is seen to provide) the ideals on which she is to model herself – be they a judo tutor, Armande, or a poster of a ballerina. In the famous sequence where, after her 'release', he comes to dinner with Marco and Marie, he becomes, literally, her author, and as he recounts her reconstructed childhood, the film gives us long frontal views of Nikita's face listening enthralled to her own story being written, and then being obliged to hide her fascinated interest when Marco looks at her. His place in her life is infinitely more central than that of Armande, the only credible 'mother', who is no more than an appearance (and says as much; she is there to teach Nikita not to *be* a woman but to *act* as a woman), and, of course, his link with her is justified by his apparent pre-destination as the victim who therefore has the right to exact retribution.

However, there is no sense in which Bob occupies the authorial position in the film. Technically, he does not enjoy the 'point of view' particularly often – rather less, in fact, than Nikita herself – neither are his emotions revealed (through close-ups) more often than Nikita's. Narratively, his control stops with Marie/Joséphine (not even, really, Nikita) over whom he has been able to gain some ascendancy because of his fulfilment of some of her personal desire for direction. Bob is under the control of an immediate superior, faced with whom the film reduces him to a state of infancy comparable to the infantile state to which Nikita is reduced in front of Bob (in these sequences as in earlier ones with Nikita, this is effected mostly through angle shots and an impressive use of shadows – menacing silhouettes are a recurring symbol in this film of Power-Which-Cannot-Be-Argued-With). In a sense this superior acts as Bob's conscience in the same way that Bob gradually appears to gain a status as Niki-ta's 'conscience', reproaching him for indulging in the pleasure of a presence that he cannot discipline. Bob's response is to increase the discipline. In the sequence before his interview with his superior, the film shows him watching Nikita's defeat of her judo teacher – which is totally against the rules – with obvious enjoyment; in the sequence after we see him rejecting Nikita's progress to date. It is worth noting that in the sequences prior to this episode, she is dressed in the punky clothes which she came to the Centre in, and her walls are covered with rebellious scrawls. The first reading of this tends to be that she is not quite 'tamed' yet – but it needs to be taken a little further; we have had quite enough information to know that she is in a totally controlled environment, and therefore her possession of the clothes and the paint represents a choice on the part of someone. Until Bob's interview with his boss we have had no reason to suppose that he is not in total charge of this building, and, even after it, it still appears that Nikita is his responsibility, that he regulates her life. Her residual rebelliousness is certainly with his indulgence then, and apparently gives him pleasure – but, when the boss says so, it has to stop!

However, there is no suggestion in the two sequences where the superior appears that he, personally, controls the point-of-view – and he does not have ultimate control of the centre either. 'If it had been up to me,' he says to Nikita when she is about to graduate, 'I'd have let you croak'.[4]

The fact that these two apparent authority figures (and there are no others of anything like comparable status) do not wield the point-of-view, however, does not mean that a central point-of-view cannot exist. In fact, the implication throughout is that Nikita is living in a controlled environment, and that this control and surveillance (which is of course the prerogative of the camera, from whose eye she is scarcely ever absent, and when she is it is always to show someone waiting for her, looking for her or talking about her: we will return to this) is exercised within the narrative space (the self-contained world in which any story takes place. An author puts her/himself within the narrative space whenever s/he appears as a character able to interact with other characters. Clearly, in this case, Besson does not exist within the narrative space, but the Centre does).

The evidence of this seems to be even more widespread than has usually been recognised. Not only does Marie's mission consist in a complex web of watching and being watched, and not only is this watching taking place in real time and all the time, as we understand through the commentary on her mission in Venice, when the voice in her headphones scolds her for dallying when she does not immediately get a perfect aim on her target, but the final scene after she returns from the botched mission to the embassy throws doubt even on the most private part of her private life.

This is not simply in the sense that Hayward suggests 'in her private life with Marco the camera may not be there (but who is to know?)' (1998: 93) – if she is watched as she aims out of the bathroom window, then the camera is almost certainly there at other times, but even more menacingly, by implicating Marco himself. His revelation that he knows all about her secret life ('the stake-outs, the tailings' ('*les planques, les filatures*')) – is, on reflection, inexplicable, unless he has either been informed or has been following her consistently himself. Although our first reaction tends to be relief that Nikita is spared the need for explanation, it is an ambivalent relief. Also, just before this revelation, Marco makes a comment on the career which is too hard for her, which holds considerable significance. He focuses on her hands – 'these little hands ... they mustn't age'.[5] This immediately recalls Armande's comment long ago in the Centre – 'Is it my hands you're looking at? ... they were beautiful you know – now they give me away'.[6]

There is no narrative reason to make this connection, but the recollection helps to create the (paranoid) conclusion that everybody around Nikita is part of the central plan. If, then, no one person is given the point-of-view, this is because all the characters are contained within the purview of a single all-embracing surveillance system, contained within the narrative space. '*Le centre*' is presented as all-seeing and all-controlling, and can therefore realistically be placed in the position behind the camera. When Nikita disappears from the control of the centre, she goes out of frame and becomes invisible. 'The Centre', then, takes up the authorial space, and allows for the incorporation into the narrative of a very nearly omniscient narrator – which is an interesting feat.

We began by saying that *Nikita* presents itself as a fantasy of social justice. By placing 'the Centre' in the position of the author within the narrative, the film-maker also attributes to it the elaboration of this fantasy of justice, and insofar as the Centre is identified with (organised/civil) society, to make it a social or communal creation. This allows any individual, film-maker or spectator, to attain a degree of detachment from the fantasy, although at the cost of rejecting that society which, it is suggested, formulates it.

Such detachment allows us not only to find it potentially terrifying – identification with the author would not preclude that – but to make sense of the destructive elements contained in the film and formulate some kind of critique. It is through this degree of detachment that the position of the spectator, and more especially the female spectator, with regard to the film is made viable – we are, certainly, 'positioned as male, the State even' (Hayward 1998: 111) by the camera, but that position has at once a clear identity within the story and no thoroughly human face – we can therefore recognise the existence of a subjective element in the telling of the tale without having much encouragement to identify with that element. This may well be even more true of the female spectator recognising her implication in the destiny of the woman Nikita, although it seems that the tendency to identify or not with Nikita is not governed purely by the gender of the spectator concerned.

The means of disposing of Nikita

The actions of the Central Control seem aimed at the destruction of Nikita, the 'dangerous' element (the danger does not stem from her violence, as we shall see, but perhaps from her ability to exist outside the social structures presided over by 'the Organisation', an ability which remains latent in the character and is often expressed through gender). Her destruction will be achieved, however, not by annihilation (ruled out by the boss of the Centre as impossible) but by absolute incorporation, the destruction of her capacity for independent action.

It is in this way that the final mission should be read. Although Nikita is *told* that she is acting independently, the sequence of action is designed to prove that, in fact, she is unable independently to arrive at the appropriate result; the Organisation will always know more than she does. The voice which in her previous missions has controlled her at a distance, through radio or telephone, (and which, like the point-of-view, is fairly clearly *not* Bob, despite his role as the 'face' of the Centre for most of the film) informs her that 'surveillance' has informed 'it' (or 'him', as it is always male, or 'them' as it frequently adopts the 'we' which indicates that it speaks for the Centre) that her information is inadequate. Her abilities cannot match those of the anonymous Organisation; and, in the following scenes, she is more and more directly culpabilised for this inevitable failure. It is implied not only that an independent individual cannot survive fighting *against* the Organisation (of social authority), but that s/he cannot even effectively fight *with* it. The individual is inadequate and must be subordinated to the whole. The fascistic overtones of this are underlined by the 'solution' presented to Nikita: the chilling figure of Victor – absolute violence, nothing else.

Here it becomes very clear that the threat which must be eliminated by the social fantasy has nothing to do with violence. Until this point it might, just, have been supposed that the ideal was to assimilate the anarchic violence represented by Nikita and her gang and train it to restrict itself to the minimum necessary – one quiet shot, if all goes well – but Victor kills quite as unnecessarily as Rico. What has disappeared is the autonomy, and the pleasure. Victor is more or less a programmed robot, unable to think independently, unable to react to what he is doing either in revolt or in enjoyment, and his violence is entirely subordinate to the narrow immediate needs of the Organisation. He seems absolutely closed to any discussion – and yet Nikita does in desperation succeed, through a brief use of the technique of 'femininity' taught her by Armande, in persuading him to compromise very slightly and give subtlety a chance. Perhaps even in Victor all spark of autonomous reaction is not lost (and this brief flicker no doubt suggests Besson's desire in his next film, *Léon*, to explore this absolutely dehumanised character and to give him a vulnerable side).

However, at the end of this mission it seems fairly clear that Nikita's future with the organisation can only pass through a total renunciation of all pretence at independent action as a punishment for her initial attempt at complete, if desperately inadequate, independence. In this sense Victor represents her possible (probable, inevitable) fate, and it is clear that it is not a fate that she is capable of accepting. Faced with Victor she experiences a physical revulsion which indicates the extent to which her personal reactions are still an integral part of her. She also shows a degree of independence of thought which enables her, even in panic and without a clear plan, to manipulate Victor and inflect his programme slightly.

The flaws in the fantasy

As Hayward points out, the logic of *Nikita* is that the independent, anarchic element cannot be integrated into society and must disappear. This is the fantasy of justice represented by the film – which seems really to be closer to a fantasy of revenge, since the rogue element is to be annihilated slowly; but perhaps the two things are indissociable.

However, rather than complete annihilation, the film opts for, precisely, disappearance. That is to say, Nikita – and the impulses and desires which she represents – simply leaves the screen, or the viewpoint of the camera. She still exists, but out of view. Hayward's interpretation of this ending seems to evolve in the course of her work, from an initial entirely negative reading to a more empowering one: 'there is considerable power in Nikita's disembodied powerlessness because she no longer functions as an assertion of male power – she marks through her absence' (1988: 157).

I would like to emphasise this latter view. When Nikita disappears from the field of vision, it is as if the camera has, with her concurrence, pushed her out of view. Effectively, then, she has been repressed, pushed into the social unconscious (in Freudian psychoanalysis, this refers to functions of the personality which we cannot be aware of but which influence our action without our knowing it. The concept tends to be presented as being 'situated' in a 'place' in the personality – hence, *in* the unconscious); and, of course, to be pushed into the unconscious is not in any sense the same as being definitively annihilated. The content of the unconscious has all sorts of effects and it seems that to take the logic of the fantasy to its fullest extent is to accept that the film's conclusion is that, much as society (constructed as the organised, ever-threatening, Centre) might like to annihilate the menace which threatens its security, it is able only to push it out of sight, and therefore once again out of control.

Further, the film proposes that this is not only the inevitable, but the desired result, even if this is far from fully admissible. Throughout the film, the visible – and therefore the human – face of the Organisation, Bob, who is also equated with the individual directly wronged by Nikita, has a scarcely-veiled attraction to her. Certainly, he takes pleasure in his ability to control her and to infantilise her, but he also takes pleasure in her rebelliousness. In the scene where she returns furious from her first test mission, a scene which is central to the portrayal of their relationship, her attack on him is highly sexualised (by the film, not the characters) and ends in a kiss; she is the initiator both of the violence and of the sexuality, but his response is decidedly positive. Faced with Nikita, Bob's whole attitude seems to be tinged with regret – she is in some way forbidden. Such a prohibition clearly springs from the demands of the Organisation, and it is perhaps this willing – even pleasurable – submission to its restraints which lies behind Nikita's words when, after her Venice trip, she accuses Bob of 'sickness'.

In the last words of the film Bob expresses regret at her going: 'we'll miss her' ('*elle va nous manquer*'). Given that her disappearance, one way or the other, was logically the aim both of Bob's Organisation and of the film, it is remarkable that the anarchic 'threat' which Nikita represents should be so clearly desired even by the elements of society most at risk from it. Bob, in fact, states his willingness to 'protect' Nikita, provided, presumably, she does not resurface into the organisation's consciousness.

Marco's role in this last scene is also interesting given that the previous sequence has apparently implicated even his private role in the functioning of the Organisation. Here he attacks the logic represented by Bob, apparently from an independent position: 'Do you only count them [killings] when it suits you?'.[7] Bob's response is a wry smile, which suggests that the accusation neither surprises nor confuses him: he is prepared to take the charge on board, as if he was expecting it.

Bob and Marco, it appears, are on the same wavelength in many ways. They understand each other's point-of-view, and their negotiation takes account of the other's aims. They agree also in their ambiguous attraction to Nikita (and here I do mean Nikita, and not Marie or Joséphine), and their wish that she should go on existing within their consciousness. In this, Bob diverges from the central line of the author-of-the-fantasy, although he has throughout the film been the agent of 'the Centre' which is that author. Marco, more openly independent than Bob although still socialised, acts as an encouragement to Bob's tendency to protect Nikita.

To put this together, Bob and Marco represent, within the ambit of the Centre and therefore within the social fantasy, ambivalent elements, and intermediate positions, between that of absolute social authority – the position which monopolises the point-of-view, thereby watching both Marco and Bob, and which cannot accept the visibility of Nikita – and that of complete rebellion or escape from the control of authority, represented by Nikita herself – but *not*, of course, Marie or Joséphine. The fact that the point-of-view in *Nikita* is identi-fied with a universal social agency allows room for the individual (extradiegetic author or spectator) to appropriate the instincts and opinions of any of the characters, and to position him or herself anywhere along the line between the Centre and Nikita.

As far as Besson's own position is concerned, at the conclusion of the film it seems to be that the social fantasy of neutralisation of the threat, and/or of justice/vengeance for the affront to order, is not effective, because even within the socialised and ordered sphere which it is presumably intended to protect (and even within itself) the Organisation encounters ambivalent attitudes to the attractive danger of asocial freedom, and also because the kind of total organisational control – with no independent elements – which seems to be the central aim, implies the use of an unthinking, undiluted violence, represented by Victor. This is presented as radically undesirable, unattractive, and to be rejected physically – we share Nikita's reaction of physical revulsion at the methods employed – and, additionally, it is actually inefficient because Victor is unable to compete against greater force.

As regards the composition of the social psyche, the same elements remain at the end of the film as at the beginning, but further layers of complication have been added. The anarchic element, Nikita, has been brought into contact in the course of her training with various disguises which will, we may realise, enable her to pass unchallenged within society without necessarily accepting the real-ity which the disguise implies, and which notionally allow her to be simulta-neously visible and invisible, once a (temporary?) invisibility has allowed the Centre to lose track of her. In one of Besson's proposed endings to the film, Nikita returns to her punk dress before her disappearance, but with the knowl-edge that this is only one of many possible disguises. In fact, the attempt at neutralisation has resulted in a multiplication of the possibilities available to Nikita in her interactions with 'Society', and the repressed threat may indeed, in the logic of the education which it has received, re-appear as something quite unrecognisable.

I would read this ending as an affirmation of the indestructibility of Nikita, but at the same time of her inassimilability. She cannot be eliminated by Soci-ety, but at the same time she cannot be accepted into it without losing the radi-cal *un*conventionality which is, effectively, her identity. Whether we read this as positive or negative will no doubt depend firstly on the extent to which we have identified with Nikita and therefore wish her to remain herself; secondly on the importance which we place on *social* existence. Nikita pays for her anar-chism by the loss of everything that constitutes happiness as it is usually per-ceived – a lover, a home, a domestic life – but on the other hand she ends the film in a position in which she *cannot* be controlled, in which she exists, unpredictably, within the social unconscious, which as we have seen is a place of considerable, perhaps fundamental, influence.

Notes

¹ The name '*cinéma du look*' has been given to a number of films made in the 1980s and very early 1990s, characterised by their preoccupation with striking stylistic effects, and their improbable plots usually based on permutations of the urban thriller genre. The main exponents of the *cinéma du look*, which openly derived inspiration from advertising films and video-clips, were Jean-Jacques Beineix, Luc Besson and Léos Carax.

² Not that all such films need be 'traditional blockbuster fare': there is always room for the exception, as Patrice Chéreau has triumphantly shown.

³ '*Suis-je au paradis, Monsieur?*'

⁴ '*S'il n'avait tenu qu'à moi, je t'aurais laissée crever*'

⁵ '*ces petites mains ... il ne faut pas qu'elles vieillissent*'

⁶ '*C'est mes mains que vous regardez? ... elles étaient belles tu sais – maintenant elles me trahissent*'

⁷ '*est-ce que vous ne les comptez que quand ça vous arrange?*'

LES VISITEURS: *a feelgood movie for uncertain times*
Anne Jäckel

The most popular film of the decade

At the beginning of 1993, in a France already anxious about the outcome of the GATT negotiations, nobody imagined that *Les Visiteurs*, the new comedy by Jean-Marie Poiré and Christian Clavier, would become the biggest French box-office hit of the decade and the second most successful French film of the post-war era. One has to go back to the mid-1960s to find a film which achieved more than the 13.6 million admissions of *Les Visiteurs*. The record is held by *La Grande Vadrouille* (1966), the most popular French film of all time.[1] In contrast with Gérard Oury's much awaited wartime comedy of the 1960s, the time-travel farce of Poiré and Clavier received little attention from French film critics when it was first released on 27 January 1993. Its 220-copy launch in France (45 of which were in the Paris region) was modest compared to the heavily promoted releases of Claude Berri's *Germinal* and Steven Spielberg's *Jurassic Park* (370 and 450 copies respectively) later that year. However, after winning over 1 million fans in its first two weeks, *Les Visiteurs* not only went on to beat Spielberg's dinosaurs (*Jurassic Park* was number one in most countries in 1993) but, in France, the film became the most talked – and written – about of the year, attracting the attention of politicians, historians, psychologists, and educationalists alike.

Deeply rooted in national mythology and cultural traditions (language and humour), comedy is the genre most prone to stereotypes, and *Les Visiteurs* is no exception. This chapter explores the complex network of determinants, both textual and contextual, that have contributed to make this French comedy the most popular French film of the last quarter of the twentieth century.

The plot

On the face of it, the adventures of a twelfth-century knight, Godefroy de Montmirail, and his loyal serf Jacquouille la Fripouille, transported to contemporary France, follow a somewhat facile and familiar tale of culture clashes and mistaken identities. The film opens with the return of the two protagonists to their native Languedoc after years of fighting abroad. The chivalrous knight is to marry his betrothed, Frénégonde, but, under a witch's curse, he mistakes his intended father-in-law for a bear and kills him with an arrow. He drinks a magic potion hoping to travel back in time and undo his deed but instead he and his servant find themselves in 1990s France where they meet their respective descendants, the effete Béatrice de Montmirail, married to a dentist, and the insufferable *nouveau-riche* Jacquart, who runs the former Montmirail estate, now an up-market château-hôtel-restaurant. Finding an ancient spellbook in the dungeon of the castle, Godefroy drinks a second potion which allows him to successfully return whence he came, while Jacquouille manages to stay in the 1990s with Ginette, a colourful homeless woman he met in a car park. Jacquouille-the-serf drugs Jacquart-the-hôtelier and, via a last-minute switch, sends him to the Middle Ages in his place. *Les Visiteurs* ends with Godefroy de Montmirail and his beloved Frénégonde reunited and their lineage assured.

An unexpected success?

With hindsight, French producers Patrice Ledoux and Alain Terzian believe the film's success is not difficult to explain. According to Ledoux, the male duo was able to synthethise, in the two protagonists, the noble hero and the resourceful commoner ('*le prolo débrouillard*'), what is essentially 'the French character'. As for Terzian, he believes that *Les Visiteurs* has turned into a social and cultural phenomenon in France because it thrives on something which belongs to the French psyche, something both simple and fantastic, like a cartoon character. 'To children,' he explains, 'Jacquouille has become a character as basic as Mickey Mouse!' (Ferenczi 1998: 24).

A year after the release of *Les Visiteurs*, the Communist newspaper *L'Humanité* gave other reasons for the film's enormous success at the box office: people's need to escape the current recession, their search for identity and, above all, the socio-political function of humour. They quoted a certain Robert Ebguy, Director of Research at the Centre for Advanced Communication (CCA), explaining that laughter has always been used to expose society's failings in order to make them more acceptable:

> Comedy has a function. It is one of social reintegration. Watching this film, the French are laughing at themselves and at the society in which they live. What is the first symbol of modern France in *Les Visiteurs*? A Guadalupian, in a Post Office van: the idea of a France sold over to foreigners. It is not innocent, and the fact that so many French people have been laughing is rather a good sign. In this respect, one of the reasons for the film's popularity is that the film sends us back our own image, one which is ridiculed, almost as in a huge mass psychotherapy. (Quoted in Capvert 1994: 18)

In April 1993, the French magazine *L'Evênement du Jeudi* had already consulted a psychoanalyst, Gérard Lassalle, for his expert opinion on the matter. Lassalle, too, believed that the search for identity was one of the key elements of the film and the main reason for its success: 'In the film, identity is affirmed in the strength of the family clan and its perenniality throughout the ages, and reinforced by phantasms of immortality.' According to Lassalle, such archetypes and phantasms of France's brave ancestors, 'defenders of the land and of their noble heritage', inform on the deeper feelings of the French nation towards Europe: 'However obsolete those values may be, however much they make us smile,' he said, 'they also enable us to dream of a former glory. In all this, Europe is the target' (Berthemy 1998: 99).

While one may disagree with Lassalle and argue that the mass-appeal of ancestral heritage (as shown in the film) is not peculiar to the French but common to most Europeans, it is nevertheless true that *Les Visiteurs* belongs to a long tradition of popular culture anchored in national mythology, the presence of which still pervades the French imagination, from the portrayal of Vercingétorix, the Gallic hero of schoolchildren's history books, to the Astérix theme park outside Paris.

A film genre: French comedy

Humour relies on familiarity. Innovation has rarely been a strong point of (French) comedies, and *Les Visiteurs* presented domestic audiences with many traditional features common to the genre. The use of the male duo, for instance, has proved a recipe for success almost since the beginning of cinema (e.g. Laurel and Hardy). In France, it was particularly popular in the 1940s, when the Franco-Italian *Don Camillo* series – starring the French comic Fernandel, who plays the eponymous priest opposite Gino Cervi in the role of Peppone, the village Communist mayor – dominated the box office both at home and in Italy. It continued in the 1950s with Bourvil and Jean Gabin (*La Traversée de Paris*, 1956), in the 1960s with the Bourvil-de Funès team, in the 1970s with the Jean Poiret and Michel Serrault duo (*La Cage aux folles*, 1978), and even in the 1980s – a time when comedies and thrillers tended to be relegated to television – some of the most popular films were the action comedies of French director-scriptwriter Francis Veber starring Gérard Depardieu and Pierre Richard (*La Chèvre* (1981), *Les Compères* (1983) and *Les Fugitifs* (1986) later to be turned into American remakes). Today, Depardieu may be one of the few French stars known outside France but, in the wake of 1968, France developed a substantial pool of comedians whose reputation was an almost guaranteed source of success at the domestic box office in the 1970s and early 1980s.

A well-established tradition of comic actors

Among these comedians, Christian Clavier – who plays the hilarious Jacquouille and Jacquard in *Les Visiteurs* – had already enjoyed a long career in comedy. Clavier and Jean-Marie Poiré, the director of *Les Visiteurs*, share a close relationship to the *café-théâtre* movement which developed in the 1970s. This style of alternative comedy, based at the *Café de la Gare* and *Le Splendid* theatres in Paris, was brought to film-goers in 1973 by Bertrand Blier with his notorious *Les Valseuses* (starring Gérard Depardieu, Patrick Dewaere and Miou Miou). In addition to the trio of *Les Valseuses*, the *café-théâtre* movement produced some of the most popular actors of the post-1968 era. They include Coluche, Josiane Balasko, Gérard Jugnot, Michel Blanc and Thierry Lhermitte. In the early 1980s, three performances from *Le Splendid* theatre were directed for the cinema by Jean-Marie Poiré: *Les Hommes préfèrent les grosses* (1981), *Le Père Noël est une ordure* (1982) and *Papy fait de la résistance* (1983). All three films were extremely popular with French cinema audiences. In *Le Père Noël est une ordure*, Christian Clavier is the Father Christmas of the title, a drunkard and a tramp who pairs with a bag-lady, Josette, played by Marie-Anne Chazel (the friendly vagrant lady who befriends Jacquouille in *Les Visiteurs*). Valérie Lemercier, the kind-hearted snob Béatrice of *Les Visiteurs*, was also a member of *Le Splendid*. The name of the theatre points in a mocking way to its marginal relationship to conventional French theatre. Members of the group showed a predilection for social satire, popular language and clichés.

Social satire and class differences

Contrasting the medieval heritage with present-day values, *Les Visiteurs* makes it clear that social differences have dramatically changed. Godefroy de Montmirail is scandalised to learn that his lands have been shared out democratically and that the owner of his castle is now the descendant of a serf. As far as the master-servant relationship is concerned, there has almost been a reversal of roles. Once Jacquouille realises that the French Revolution has abolished feudal servitude, there is no way that he would willingly return to the Middle Ages. Even though the film clearly plays on stereotypes, and its characters are treated with little nuance or finesse, as a social satire *Les Visiteurs* does allow for social commentary on the foibles of the provincial bourgeoisie of the 1990s.[2] In a four-page article examining the film's steadily growing performance at the box office in August 1993 ('10 million spectators in just under seven months!'), *Le Parisien* pointed out that *Les Visiteurs* was a film in which the rich were ridiculed, a film made by the common people for the common people: 'It's Molière in the year 2000,' wrote *Le Parisien*'s film critic, 'Valérie Lemercier as a *Précieuse ridicule* against Jacquouille la Fripouille as a merry Scapin' (Vavasseur 1998: 11). Yet, while there are times when the film shows a sense of irony verging on irreverence, on the whole and as far as politics is concerned, *Les Visiteurs* sends conflicting messages, in turn pleasing right-wing and left-wing movements (with both its anti- and pro-Revolutionary statements) and ecological groups (by showing the pollution and the ugliness of the twentieth-century landscape).

In the film, the conflict between medieval customs and modernity is also linguistic. The serf, transported to modern-day France, rapidly discovers that using the language of a certain class brings membership of that class. On the one hand, he learns Ginette's coarse language in order to stay with her, on the other, he is literally fascinated by the 'super', 'hyper' and 'cousin Hub' of Béatrice. He senses that the use of such expressions will enable him to enter the circle of people he wishes to join. To acquire this new system is to move up the social ladder.

Language

Unconventional in its use of social satire, the *Splendid* team purposely used popular language to comic effect. All the stock-in-trade of the *café-théâtre* tradition – clichés, slogans, catch-phrases, aphorisms – are present in *Les Visiteurs*.

Valérie Lemercier gives a particularly memorable performance as Béatrice, combining to perfection a *bon chic bon genre* appearance with a haughty form of speech which incorporates 'franglais' and an upper-class accent reminiscent of the language spoken by some of '*Les Bronzés*', the *Club Med* members in Patrice Leconte's 1980s popular comedies of the same title. Marie-Anne Chazel (Ginette) excels in her cameo role of Josette (the bag-lady of *Le Père Noël est une ordure*). She uses back slang (*verlan*), slang (*argot*) and bad grammar, with a coarse Parisian accent reminiscent of the popular films of the 1930s and 1940s. The courtly speech of the valiant knight (played by Jean Reno – the favourite actor of Luc Besson), is a peculiar mix of formal speech and anachronistic vocabulary which contrasts with the mixture of slang and rejuvenated old French spoken by Jacquouille (whose vulgar-sounding name, containing the French word for 'balls', has been fittingly translated into English as Jacqu-ass-e). The serf's speech has also much in common with the stylistics and the scatological witticisms of medieval literature.

Many of the expressions used by the characters of *Les Visiteurs* have become catchwords in France. Whether in schools, universities or offices, '*ça puire*' (it stinks), was soon to replace '*ça pue*'; '*les fillotes*' (girls), '*les filles*'; '*charriotes*' (cars), '*voitures*'; and the word '*sarrasins*' is now often used to refer to people with any shade of skin colour darker than white. Christian Clavier's aping of Lemercier's clipped and snooty pronunciation of 'OK' (Okkaayy!) or *'c'est dinnngue!'* and weird expressions such as *'mais qu'est-ce que c'est que ce Bin's'* have become national catchphrases.

The fascination of the French for such a way of speaking may seem odd in a country which has always been prone to defend its own language. After all, the year of *Les Visiteurs* was a time when the Minister heading cultural affairs bore the title 'Minister of Culture and Francophony' and Bernard Pivot's *dictée* (a particularly difficult dictation broadcast nationally) was one of the favourite programmes on television. Yet the 1980s and 1990s have also been, for France, a period when deviations from the norm (*verlan*, Americanisms, the use of slang words and local colloquialisms) have proliferated.

On the one hand, deviations from the French standard, so blatant in *Les Visiteurs*, may appear subversive to such guarantors of the purity of the French language as *L'Académie Française* or *Le Haut Comité de la Défense de la Langue Française* but, on the other hand, the re-appropriation of old forms and the interest in – if not the obsession with – the French language may further reinforce the argument made by Robert Ebguy that *Les Visiteurs* is a film which uses national mythology to foster social reintegration.

On the Middle Ages and 'Gallic humour'

Some of the language spoken in the film may be coarse and several of the jokes crude, but they belong to a medieval tradition of short stories claimed to have been written to entertain the common people. Under the title *Les Visiteurs* appears the caption 'they were not born'.[3] The so-called 'Gallic humour' of *Les Visiteurs* draws on a tradition of coarse realistic comedy which is found in medieval literature in general and in the 'fabliaux' of Rabelais (1494–1553) in particular. Such a form of humour has been described as 'characteristic of the lower orders of society and thus inevitably concerned with the baser instincts' as well as 'the inferior relative of the comic genius of French people'! (Trotter 1993: 71). David A. Trotter gives a fascinating account of 'Gallic Humour' in an article entitled 'L'Esprit Gaulois: Humour and National Mythology', in which he argues that it is only in the middle of the nineteenth century – a period when considerable efforts were made to create a national consensus in France and when 'medieval literature, decent or indecent, was drawn on as a source of national and nationalistic inspiration' – that this inferior form of Gallic humour became a national signifier. Today, a parallel can easily be drawn between the appropriation of '*l'esprit Gaulois*' as a national signifier in nineteenth-century France and the 1993 public acclaim and subsequent critical reappraisal of *Les Visiteurs* at a time when France was, on the domestic front, compelled by economic forces to redefine its identity in popular terms and, on the international scene, determined to fight to the bitter end to obtain the exclusion of cultural productions from the General Agreement on Tariffs and Trade (Jäckel 1996).

Les Visiteurs and popular film genres

Since 1983, Jean-Marie Poiré has written exclusively with Christian Clavier, and the subversion of standard genres has been a thread running through their work. *Les Visiteurs* also borrows from various popular film genres: the French burlesque comedies of the 1960s starring Bourvil, Fernandel and Louis de Funès are one, slapstick comedy is another. The misunderstandings arising from the knight and his servant's arrival in the twentieth century generate numerous slapstick gags and a great deal of the film's humour is grounded in Godefroy and Jacquouille running up against modernity (their discovery of electricity, telephone, motorways, cars, meat wrapped in clingfilm, and so on). The film successfully mixes silent cinema gags, Pythonesque one-liners and a reputedly German scatological sense of humour. Montmirail and Jacquart washing their hands and face in the toilet bowl, or the bowl of soup landing on the businessman's head, are hardly new gags, but the film's frantic pacing and extreme camera angles, along with the actors' frenzied performances, make them work.

Guy Austin (1996: 139) argues that the film is also 'related to three other genres beside popular comedy: fantasy cinema, poetic realism and the heritage film'. He finds the former connection 'manifest above all in the time-travel plot, the Gothic scenes concerning the Witch of Malcombe, and the action sequence in the dungeon, which,' he writes, 'recalls Steven Spielberg's *Raiders of the Lost Ark* (1981)'. Other critics have mentioned the obvious references to *Back to the Future* (Zemeckis, 1985; 1989; 1990). Jean-Marie Poiré would certainly agree with Austin since he has often stated that, as somebody who 'likes films which tell stories', he is a great admirer of Hollywood popular genres such as American adventure films, comedies and westerns. The French director even admitted that he found his inspiration for Jacquouille in the character of 'the Bad' in *The Good, the Bad and the Ugly* (Leone, 1967) (see Baudin 1993).

Austin, however, is less convincing when he argues that the medieval scenes of *Les Visiteurs* 'tend to pastiche the historical settings of such poetic realist films as Jacques Feyder's *La Kermesse héroïque* (1935)', even though *Les Visiteurs*, comparing as it does, the responses of one social group to those of another, has a structure reminiscent of that of many 'poetic realist' films of the 1930s.

As far as heritage film is concerned, the medieval heritage had already made a successful comeback in France in the 1980s with Daniel Vigne's *Le Retour Martin Guerre* (1984) and Jean-Jacques Annaud's 1986 adaptation of Umberto Eco's novel *The Name of the Rose*. The two films received public and critical acclaim both at home and abroad (unlike *Les Visiteurs*, whose performance outside France was, with a few exceptions, generally poor).[4] According to Camille Nevers, the film critic of *Cahiers du Cinéma*, Annaud's influence on *Les Visiteurs* even extended to *L'Ours*, the film Annaud made in 1989: basing her argument on the scene at the beginning of the film when Godefroy de Montmirail inadvertently kills Frénégonde's father as the knight's vision becomes blurred and a bear takes the place of the old man, Nevers suggested that the knight's killing of his future father-in-law represented an overturning of Annaud's 1989 film. Guy Austin offers a more persuasive reading of *Les Visiteurs*' connection to the heritage film – and one somewhat different from that of *Cahiers*. Building on Nevers' contrasting of 'the film's vigorous but culturally low humour with the high culture of the expensive décors and the historical setting', Austin contends that Poiré uses the film's reliance on the heritage genre to take on the French cultural policy of the time:

> The film in fact begins by conforming precisely to the conventions of the historical drama, with period costume, spectacular landscapes shot from high and wide angles, lush music and an authoritative voice-over which situates the action in 1123. First undermined by the loutish violence of the English soldiers in the credit sequence, the heritage code is placed under increasing strain by the burlesque energy of the subsequent scenes. *Les Visiteurs* thus engages in combat with the values of Claude Berri's *Germinal* (1993), its major French box-office competitor, and with all the 'cultural' projects which Poiré and Clavier protest are better supported by the State, easier to finance and easier to cast than popular comedies. (Austin 1996: 140)

Austin certainly has a point. One only needs to recall the two extraordinary French premières of *Germinal*, one attended by François Mitterrand in northern France, where VIPs from the political and artistic (overwhelmingly) Parisian élite had been brought by a specially hired TGV, and the other, in the new Pathé twelve-screen multiplex in Thiais on the outskirts of Paris, in the presence of the Minister of Culture and Francophony, Jacques Toubon, not to mention the thousands of tickets the French Educational Authorities had bought for schoolchildren to receive Berri's cinematic lesson in French history.

In the wake of Jack Lang's stance on popular culture and France's rigorous defence of its film industry, the cinematic climate of the time favoured large-scale films. Even though *Les Visiteurs* did not qualify for France's selective aid – *l'avance sur recettes*, an interest-free loan reserved for first films or Auteur-films – Poiré's and his producer Gaumont's previous successes at the box office guaranteed *Les Visiteurs* a substantial sum from the automatic aid. A '100 per cent French film', *Les Visiteurs* was co-produced by Gaumont and France 3 cinéma, the cinema arm of the French public television channel. According to trade industry figures, it was the sixth most expensive French production of the year (*Germinal* came first with a reported budget of FF172m). The FF60m-budget of *Les Visiteurs* allowed for high production values (special effects, spectacular landscape).

Today, *Les Visiteurs* is often cited as a case-study and a pedagogical tool in the study of 1990s France. In Britain, Martin Bright (1993: 62) has suggested that: '*Les Visiteurs* could easily be shown to British school students as a guide to the French class system. It demonstrates better than most audiovisual aids that it is the lumpen-bourgeoisie who are the dominant class in France today and that the aristocracy is just a subculture among many.' All cross-cultural exchanges involve a minimum of mental effort on the part of people coming from different cultures. Noting the extent to which each side remained convinced of their own righteousness in Poiré and Clavier's film, Françoise Ploquin (1993: 11) ended her review of *Les Visiteurs* in *Le Français dans le Monde* by recommending it to all those teaching civilisation and languages.

It is not coincidental that a film confronting class differences appealed to the whole political spectrum of the French population in the year when the French economy was particularly hit by the recession and the Socialist government of François Mitterrand lost the elections. It is also ironic that the year which ended with the exclusion of film and other audiovisual programmes from GATT saw *Les Visiteurs*, a comedy made with American (production) values by a fervent admirer of Hollywood popular cinema, become 'a national icon' and the most popular film of recent times in France. Decades of low esteem for a genre considered at best as a lower form of entertainment prevented the French establishment from making more than a token gesture towards a film conceived by its creators as a crowd-pleasing fantasy: in December 1993, the French authorities granted Poiré and Clavier's comedy a special derogation allowing an early video release. Still, the pre-Christmas exemption was well-timed, families rushed to buy the film and, with over 2 million cassettes sold, *Les Visiteurs* became the best-selling French film on video.[5]

The French historian and film critic Jean-Pierre Jeancolas likes to remind his readers that Renoir's masterpiece *La Règle du jeu* was a flop when it was first released in 1939. Jeancolas wrote extensively on the popular cinema of the 1950s, and particularly on a special type of comedy, an 'inexportable cinema' which he calls 'Franchouillard', comedies 'based on pre-existing forms of entertainment, well-known comics and a parodic view of national history, poor films without "auteurs", aimed solely at national consumption and that involve a connivance with an undemanding audience' (1992: 62–3). Over the years and in a climate increasingly referring to film as part of the 'culture industries', the great works of cinema released in various outlets under different forms have also become commodities.

It would certainly be a sign of the times if, in France's increasingly mercantile cinematic climate, the most popular French film of the 1990s – however 'Franchouillard' it may be – were to enter the pantheon of the great French films of the century.

Notes

[1] *La Grande Vadrouille* sold more than 17.2 million tickets in 1966. It starred the two greatest comics of the period, Bourvil and Louis de Funès, and built on as well as pastiched the wartime settings of such contemporary successes as *Paris brûle-t-il?* (Réné Clément, 1965) and *La Nuit des généraux* (Anatole Litvak, 1966).

[2] This applies to all types, 'aristo' (Béatrice), *nouveau-riche* (Jacquart) and 'prolo' (Ginette).

[3] '*ils ne sont pas nés hier*'

[4] For a survey of *Les Visiteurs*' performance abroad, see Jäckel (1996: 42): the film made 400,000 admissions in Germany. The version dubbed by Mel Brooks was not found satisfactory in America and *Les Visiteurs* was subsequently released with subtitles – and with little success – on the art circuit.

[5] In 1993 in France, a film which claimed over 400,000 admissions in its first theatrical release in the Paris region normally had to wait for a whole year before it could be released on video. Cyril Collard's cult film, *Les Nuits Fauves* (1992), was denied the privilege granted to *Les Visiteurs*, but in 1992, Ridley Scott's *Thelma and Louise* and Régis Wargnier's *Indochine* had also been allowed an early video release.

Hybridity, space and the right to belong: Maghrebi-French identity at the crossroads in Karim Dridi's BYE-BYE
Will Higbee

Bye-Bye focuses on the experiences of two brothers of North African origin, Ismaël (Sami Bouajila) and Mouloud (Ouassini Embarek) who, in the face of opposition from both white French racism and pressure from their North African parents, attempt to establish their own sense of identity and rightful place within the *Hexagone* (France).[1] The film begins with the brothers' arrival from Paris in Marseilles, where they are to stay with their uncle and extended family. It soon transpires that the brothers will depart Marseilles for the Maghreb: Ismaël has been instructed by his father to accompany Mouloud to the *bled* (family home) where he will remain with his parents indefinitely. Mouloud is, unsurprisingly, strongly opposed to his enforced 'return' to a country and culture he hardly knows. His refusal to obey the father's instructions precipitates a slide into delinquency which leads to his involvement with a local North African drug dealer, Renard (Moussa Maaskri). Meanwhile, Ismaël, unable to enforce the law of the father, and haunted by the earlier death of his handicapped brother for which he feels partly responsible, drifts into a job at the local shipyard. Here he befriends a white work-mate, Jacky (Frédéric Andrau), and his girlfriend, Yasmine (Nozha Khouadra) – to whom Ismaël becomes attracted. The culmination of a series of events: Ismaël's sexual encounter with Yasmine; Mouloud's delinquent activities; the father's demands that they return to the *bled*; and threats from a local gang of racist thugs, force the brothers to flee Marseilles at the end of the film, in search of a new future in an undetermined location.

Released in September 1995, *Bye-Bye*, Franco-Tunisian director Karim Dridi's second feature, appeared at a moment of both cinematic and socio-political significance in France. In cinematic terms, the year was marked by the emergence of what critics labelled the *cinéma de banlieue*: a number of independently released commercial features (of which Mathieu Kassovitz's *La Haine* (1995) was by far the most prominent) that tended to focus on social exclusion found within the disadvantaged periphery of larger French cities.[2] Although French politics would be dominated by the same issues addressed in the majority of these *banlieue* film – unemployment, delinquency, *fracture sociale* – politically the mid-1990s was also a period in which the return of the Right to power was to be marked by an increasingly hostile and suspicious attitude towards the presence of non-European immigrants and their descendants in France.

Soon after the Right's election victory in March 1993, the new Minister of the Interior, Charles Pasqua, introduced a series of reforms which toughened legislation concerning immigration, revoked the automatic right of citizenship for the descendants of immigrants born in France, and increased police powers to stop and detain any individual suspected of residing illegally within the *Hexagone*. The right-wing government's position was further consolidated in 1995 with the election of Jacques Chirac as President – a politician who in 1986 had unsuccessfully attempted to introduce more restrictive French nationality laws similar to those implemented by the *loi Pasqua*, and who remained unpopular among France's ethnic minorities for remarks from a (now infamous) speech made in 1991, in which he expressed sympathy with French people who disliked the 'noise and smell' associated with immigrant families (*Le Monde*, 1999: 6).

Finally, the summer of 1995 saw massive police operations in Paris, Lille and Marseilles, aimed at eradicating groups of Islamic terrorists presumed to be active within the *Hexagone*. In reality, the series of bomb attacks which instigated this crackdown was perpetrated by a small, isolated group of alienated youths of Algerian immigrant origin from the disadvantaged *cités* (housing estates) of the urban periphery, directed by Islamic extremists fighting against the Algerian government. Nevertheless, the combination of uncompromising political rhetoric and intense media attention which accompanied the police action fuelled an image of the *banlieue* as a common recruitment area for Islamic terrorist groups, whilst equating the Muslim community in France (and by extension North African immigrants and their descendants) exclusively with Islamic fundamentalism.[3]

In light of the political climate outlined above, the open and sympathetic portrayal of the Maghrebi community and their descendants beyond the confines of the disadvantaged *cité* offered in *Bye-Bye* is highly significant. Dridi was praised for challenging the negative stereotypes commonly associated with the North African immigrant population, without eliding either the realities of discrimination and delinquency, or the complex issues of identity and difference, faced by Maghrebi-French youth during the 1990s.[4] It is, therefore, rather ironic that a film which is at such pains to reject the essentialist cultural and socio-spatial identities imposed upon the French-born descendants of Maghrebi-immigrants, should, on occasion, find itself defined in these self same reductive terms.

Firstly, even though the majority of the narrative is located in the working-class districts of Marseilles, the inclusion of a limited number of scenes in the disadvantaged *cités* of the urban periphery seem to be sufficient to include *Bye-Bye* as part of the *cinéma de banlieue* phenomenon which emerged at the time of the film's release (*Bye-Bye* appeared on French screens barely three months after the intense media attention and box-office success of *La Haine* had brought the notion of the *banlieue* film to the attention of a wider public). Secondly, the fact that *Bye-Bye* is made by a Franco-Tunisian director and focuses on characters of predominantly North African origin has caused the film to be identified with the problematic (and increasingly redundant) notion of *cinéma beur* – a label which threatens to marginalise the Maghrebi-French film-maker as 'other' in relation to the dominant cultural norm. Through an analysis of the representation of space, cultural difference and hybridity in *Bye-Bye*, this chapter will consider the extent to which Dridi is able to offer a portrayal of the North African immigrant community which transcends the potentially reductive paradigms of the *banlieue* film and *beur* cinema, thus leaving the film better equipped to explore the complex hybridity of the Maghrebi-French subject.

Let us first consider the representation of cinematic space in *Bye-Bye*. During the 1990s, largely as a result of the representations offered by main-stream media, the *banlieue* emerged as a new and highly stigmatised social space. The term is now used almost exclusively in reference to the most disadvantaged housing estates (*cités*) of the urban periphery, and qualifies the *banlieue* as a site of delinquency, violence and alterity, identified predominantly with male youth of North African origin (Hargreaves 1996). This notion of the *banlieue* as marginalised site of socio-economic exclusion is to be found in nearly all the so-called *banlieue* films of the 1990s: dehumanising and degraded *cité*scapes dominate the *mise-en-scène* of *La Haine, Raï* (Gilou, 1995) and *Ma 6-T Va Crack-er* (Richet, 1997). Although the majority of these films focus on an underclass of multi-ethnic youth, Maghrebi-French characters tend to occupy a central position within this social group. It is precisely this association with the stigmatised space of the *banlieue* from which Dridi is attempting to distance his protagonists of North African origin from in *Bye-Bye*.

Originally, the director had hoped to locate the film in Belleville, where he had lived as a child. Although a largely working class *quartier* with a significant non-European immigrant population, Belleville is nonetheless situated within the *arrondissements* that form the central hegemonic space of Paris. As such, the district's inhabitants are not stigmatised or excluded to the same extent as those minority social groups living in the disadvantaged *cités* on the extreme margins of the capital. However, the redevelopment of Belleville during the 1980s and 1990s resulted in the fragmentation of the local community around which Dridi had hoped to base his film (Rémy 1995: 52). Forced to search elsewhere for his location, Dridi went to Marseilles, where he again eschewed the run-down HLMs (*habitations à loyer modéré* – subsidised housing) of the urban periphery, in favour of Le Panier, a district near to the city's old port with a large and diverse immigrant population (Dridi 1995a).

Unlike the uniform concrete towers of the alienating post-war *cités* which dominate the outskirts of larger French cities such as Marseilles, Paris and Lyon, the architecture of Le Panier – its courtyards and maze of narrow streets – forms an instantly recognisable part of the city itself. The fact that the district was constructed by the first wave of Italian immigrants to arrive in the port during the nineteenth century further highlights the long-established presence of an immigrant community in Marseilles. Le Panier is thus a space which identifies the immigrant population as part of the collective historical development of the city. Since the arrival of the first Italian immigrants, the district has housed waves of Armenian, Spanish, and Portuguese immigration, and is now home to a significant population of North African origin.

Dridi emphasises the plurality of cultural and ethnic origins to be found in Le Panier through the use of both image and sound in *Bye-Bye*. The camera contemplates multi-ethnic groups of children playing in the streets of the *quartier*, as well as the mixture of white, black and Maghrebi youths who flock to the *raï* concert on the beach. Similarly, the film's soundtrack associates an eclectic mix of music – including rap, *raï* and ragga – with Le Panier. Amidst the confusion caused by the eviction of a neighbouring black family which greets Ismaël and Mouloud upon their arrival at the family apartment in Le Panier, strains of Italian *bel canto* emanate from another part of the building, reminding the spectator of the cultural heritage of the district's original inhabitants.

Le Panier is characterised not only by its multicultural population but also the presence of an established working class community. Dridi is careful to identify the North African immigrants and their descendants as an integral part of this popular heritage. The brothers' uncle, played by Benhaïssa Ahouari, has a permanent job in one of the local shipyards, where Ismaël is also offered temporary work. The North African community of Le Panier is thus represented as economically integrated within the wider French working-class population. Moreover, by placing the Maghrebi-French subject in this environment Dridi distances him/her from the stigmatised space of the disadvantaged *cité*. Ismaël is not identified with the economic exclusion caused by unemployment which effects nearly all protagonists of North African origin in the banlieue films of the 1990s: *Hexagone* (Chibane, 1994), *La Haine* and *Raï*.

However, the representation of the *banlieue* as site of violence, delinquency and exclusion is not entirely absent from *Bye-Bye*. The disadvantaged *cité* is portrayed in a limited number of scenes involving Renard, a dealer of North African origin from a deprived estate situated on the outskirts of Marseilles with whom Mouloud becomes involved. On the one hand, the inclusion of these scenes is understandable. They serve to highlight the dangers of the precarious socio-economic position (poor housing, unemployment, exclusion) occupied by many young people of North African origin in the *banlieue*. Frequently, these individuals find themselves further marginalised by racism experienced at both an institutional and personal level – the most obvious example being discrimination in the job market.[5] These experiences compel a small number to reject the conventional path of education and a traditional work ethic in favour of illegal activity within the *cité*; mostly drug dealing and petty crime (Jazouli 1991; Malouk and Lederman 1999). Renard appears to be an example of one such individual who, excluded by society, has opted for involvement within this clandestine economy.

In spite of his well-intentioned efforts to highlight the potential dangers faced by Maghrebi-French youth within the *cité*, the methods used by Dridi to introduce the spectator to these marginalised minorities within the disadvantaged urban periphery are somewhat disingenuous. The opening to the first sequence in the *cité* runs as follows: from an establishing shot of a run-down HLM estate, the camera cuts to a group of black and Maghrebi-French youths playing basketball, panning across to an individual tower block and finally cutting to the interior of an apartment where Renard, knife in hand, prepares to divide up a large block of hashish. The fairly clichéd images of the dehumanising HLMs indicate our arrival in the 'ghetto' of the disadvantaged *cité*. Furthermore, the initial sequence establishes a discursive chain which associates the *banlieue* to Maghrebi-French youth and drug dealing. Renard's persona as the paranoid, gun-toting, cocaine-snorting dealer, is exaggerated to similar effect. Given the fact that in the rest of the film Dridi is careful to avoid any stereotypical representations of the Maghrebi immigrant population and their descendants, the manner in which both the disadvantaged *cité* and the dealer of North African origin are portrayed in *Bye-Bye* is somewhat surprising.

It is clear, however, that Dridi did not intend for Renard (who only plays a secondary role) to provide the dominant representation of Maghrebi-French youth in the film. Significantly, the dealer is portrayed as a solitary figure – he never appears in Le Panier – and is thus isolated from both the North African community and wider French society. The larger than life performance offered by Moussa Maaskri as Renard and the rather clichéd representation of the *banlieue* further distances his character from the intimate realism employed by Dridi to portray the everyday lives of the extended immigrant family. Whether Dridi intended this division between Le Panier and the *cité* to be as pronounced as is suggested here is unclear. Nevertheless, away from the stigmatised and heavily stereotyped space of the *cité* in *Bye-Bye*, a more nuanced and complex portrayal of the extended North African family is allowed to develop.

Carrie Tarr suggests that this 'new emphasis' offered by Dridi on the extended immigrant family allows for 'more fully individualised characters capable of challenging stereotypical expectations' to emerge (1997: 77). This is particularly true of the female characters. The aunt (Jamila Darwhich-Farah) is portrayed as a strong, compassionate and intelligent woman. In one scene she is shown giving English lessons to her daughters: a far cry from the stereotype of the North African immigrant mother as little more than a poorly educated housewife. In contrast to the rigid authoritarian approach adopted by Mouloud's father (endorsed by the uncle, with little success) the aunt is able to empathise with and accept her children's position, defying the patriarchal authority of the *bled* to suggest that both Mouloud and her own children should remain in France. Cultural differences are present within the family home – the aunt converses with the grandmother in Arabic; the family watch an Arabic show on television – although not foregrounded. Significantly Islam, generally perceived by the French as the greatest barrier to the successful 'integration' of the North African immigrant population is barely represented in the film. By challenging the stereotypes commonly applied to the North African immigrant population and their descendants, Dridi attempts to break down the perceived 'difference' which marks the North African community in France as 'other'. In this respect, the representation of the Maghrebi immigrants and their children found in *Bye-Bye* is similar to the diverse range of protagonists of North African origin present in both *Hexagone* and *Douce France* (1995) by Maghrebi-French film-maker Malik Chibane.

Commenting on the wider significance of Marseilles as the location for *Bye-Bye* beyond the microcosm of Le Panier, the immigrant family home and the disadvantaged *cité* inhabited by Renard, Dridi (1995: 39)has stated: 'Setting my film over there [in Marseilles] allowed me ... to look at Africa from the other side. Just as I am half Arab and half French, so Marseilles is a city at an intersection, a very hybrid city'.[6]

The multi-ethnic community of Le Panier quite obviously illustrates this notion of Marseilles, as miscegenated, multicultural space. However, the film-maker refuses to reduce the *espace métisé* of Marseilles to an over-simplified vision of pluri-ethnic utopia. Interethnic relationships, founded on the tolerance of cultural difference, are formed within the diegesis, the most obvious example being that of Ismaël and Jacky. Yet these friendships are contrasted with the hostility displayed by Jacky's brother, Ludo (Philippe Ambrosini), and the gang of racist thugs with whom he associates, towards the non-European immigrant inhabitants of Le Panier.

The scene towards the end of the film where local residents are shown celebrating a mixed-race marriage well illustrates this underlying tension within the hybrid space of Marseilles caused by such xenophobia. The camera contemplates the black groom and his white bride, in western wedding dress, dancing to North African music, surrounded by black, Maghrebi and white French guests (including Ismaël, his aunt and uncle, Jacky and Jasmine). The fact that neither the bride nor bridegroom appear anywhere else in the film emphasises the symbolic function of their union in relation to the narrative. Rather than foregrounding the individual subjectivities of these two characters, Dridi wishes us to focus on the mixed race marriage in *Bye-Bye* on two levels: as a symbol of Marseilles as miscegenated space, and, by extension, a reflection of Ismaël and Mouloud's hybridity.

Yet the wedding reception's function as a site of multi-ethnic tolerance rapidly degenerates into one of racial conflict with the arrival of Ludo. Having insulted the newlyweds – insinuating that the white bride has chosen to marry her black husband because she has already 'had' every other man in the *quartier* ('you're not the first or the last'),[7] Ludo delights in generating further tension by revealing to Jacky that Ismaël has slept with Yasmine. His presence in this scene not only embodies the xenophobic tendencies of the far right in France – Ludo's fear of *métissage* is manifested through his aggressive opposition to mixed race unions – but also emphasises the way in which the success of such discourse comes as a result of exploiting the fears and insecurities of the white French population. Ismaël's 'betrayal' of Jacky thus plays on the stereotype of ethnic 'other' as a sexual threat to the white male. The scene ends with Jacky, who has been portrayed throughout the film as a tolerant figure, entirely comfortable within the miscegenated space of a multicultural Marseilles, spitting in Ismaël's face. Jacky's justifiable anger at both Ismaël and Jasmine is thus exacerbated by Ludo's xenophobic discourse. The dispute is transformed (or even hijacked) by Ludo from the question of infidelity between friends to that of an apparently racially motivated act, which forms part of an ongoing conflict between the white majority and those of non-European origin who live in the *Hexagone*.

In addition to this notion of Marseilles as a site of *métissage*, the city's status as a port emphasises the transitory nature of this space for Mouloud and Ismaël, as they 'return' to the *bled*. Perhaps more important, though, is the geographical and historical significance of Marseilles in relation to North Africa. The visual motif of Ismaël staring out to sea as boats leave the port bound for Africa, reflects the geographical proximity of France to the Maghreb. However, it is also representative of the migratory flows and cross-cultural exchanges which have taken place between North Africa and the *Hexagone* during the past 150 years – of which Ismaël and Mouloud are the living embodiment. In this respect, the port offers a symbolic link with the cultural heritage of the Maghreb and also with France's colonial past. Marseilles would have served as a gateway for the post-war migration of North Africans to

France; a point of return for French soldiers and colonial administrators following de-colonisation; and the entrance to a land of exile for the *harkis* and *pied noirs* who arrived from Algeria in 1962.[8] Therefore, sealed within Marseilles' history are reminders of the events that have led to the permanent settlement of North African immigrants within the *Hexagone* and thus shaped the dual cultural identity of their children. Given this symbolic importance of Marseilles, it is hardly surprising that Mouloud and Ismaël are forced to question the consequences of their own hybridity, when placed in this space 'at the intersection' between France and the Maghreb.

The child of a French mother and Tunisian father, by his own admission 'the creation of two cultures' (Rémy 1995: 52), Dridi is careful to articulate the complex questions of identity facing the descendants of North African immigrants in France today. Indeed, the cultural identification of each individual represents a unique response to their own hybrid subjectivity: one which is articulated in different ways, and expressed to varying degrees, as a result of personal experiences. These identifications can range from an almost total rejection of North African culture, to a sense of self defined solely in terms of Maghrebi/Muslim consciousness, motivated by a feeling of exclusion in both socio-economic and cultural terms from the dominant societal norm. Most, however, occupy an intermediary position: feeling an intuitive sense of belonging in France, yet still maintaining a strong attachment to their parents' North African culture (Dubet and Lapeyronnie 1992).

The dilemma faced by Ismaël in *Bye-Bye* – whether to uphold the patriarchal law of the *bled* and return Mouloud to Tunisia, or allow him to remain in France and determine his own future – is therefore representative of these issues surrounding identity and belonging which continue to confront French people of North African origin. Mouloud, is vehemently opposed to returning to the *bled*, feeling a much stronger affinity with the French/western culture in which he has been raised and educated. The extent to which many French youths of Maghrebi immigrant origin share this sense of almost complete alienation from their parent's religion and culture is well illustrated by the scene in which Mouloud and his cousin take shelter from racist thugs in an Arab household of Le Panier. The youths inadvertently enter in on the proceedings of a Muslim funeral. Mouloud looks on at events as a total outsider. As he attempts to make sense of the scene before him, the camera follows his gaze: panning across the women in traditional Arab dress into another room in which the men are seated and finally resting in an antechamber where the *immams* (holy men) who surround the shrouded corpse are reciting passages from the Koran.

In contrast, the stronger attachment felt by Ismaël to his North African origins is reiterated on a number of occasions – the repeated image of Ismaël staring out across the sea toward the Maghreb being the most obvious example.

Elsewhere in the film he actively participates in the traditional dancing taking place at a local North African bar. Ismaël's more open identification with the *bled* and the culture of his parents can, perhaps, be explained by the age difference between the two brothers. Given the fact that he is in his twenties, it is possible that Ismaël was not born in France and thus arrived in the *Hexagone* having spent at least some of the formative years of childhood in Tunisia. Mouloud, on the other hand, is far more likely to have been born and raised in France.

However, the younger brother's apparent 'rejection' of his parents cultural heritage is not only motivated by the fact of his socialisation within the *Hexagone*, but also a desire to reject the patriarchal discourse of the *bled*. The father's demand that Mouloud 'return' to Tunisia indefinitely, fails to acknowledge the powerful attachment to French society and culture which informs his son's hybrid subjectivity. The Maghrebi-French subject's desire to determine his/her own identity within the *Hexagone* is, therefore, shown to be opposed by forces within both French and North African society. Mouloud's refusal that his own identity be determined by a third party – be they the racist stereotypes of the French far-right or the patriarchal authority of the *bled* – is most emphatically articulated through the rap he has written entitled '*Beur pourri*' (rotten *beur*) with the refrain '*ne m'appelle pas beur, car ce mot m'écœure*' (don't call me *beur*, that word makes me sick). The fact that Mouloud focuses on the word *beur* is, of course, highly significant. Initially seen as an empowering self affirmation of their hybrid identity, the term *beur* has since been rejected by the majority of the Maghrebi-French population, who feel it has been appropriated by mainstream French culture – especially elements within the media – to signal their difference from the dominant social norm (Durmelat 1998).

The portrayal of the dealer of North African origin in *Bye-Bye* further highlights the extent to which these externally imposed (mis)representations offered by the dominant social norm marginalise Maghrebi-French youth. Renard sees a world of violence and drug dealing as the only means for him to acquire the material wealth and respect of his peers denied him by white French society. However, acquiescing to this stereotype of the North African male from the *cité* as the delinquent, marginalised other, means he must *perform* an identity, not be one. In the attempt to cultivate this image as the tough dealer, he appears to imitate the dress, lifestyle and mannerisms of a Hollywood gangster: the violence and drug-fuelled paranoia that surrounds Renard in *Bye-Bye* is reminiscent of Al Pacino in *Scarface* (De Palma, 1983), whilst the white vest he wears conjures up images of Harvey Keitel in *Mean Streets* (Scorsese, 1973).

Clearly, it is Renard's disadvantaged socio-economic status and the association with the stigmatised space of the *cité* which effect his marginalisation, not any perceived cultural difference. However, when Mouloud visits his apartment for the first time, Renard brings out his gun and, placing the young boy's finger on the trigger, tells him: 'you're a man with that [gun] ... look at how people's reactions change ... you're no longer a dirty Arab ...'[9] As his comments to Mouloud make clear, Renard sees his exclusion primarily in ethnicised, not economic, terms – 't'es plus un bougnoule'. To adopt a Fanonian expression, his identity has thus been 'over-determined from without' (Fanon 1986: 116). Renard's own sense of self is shaped by the stereotypes projected onto his identity by the dominant societal norm: white, republican France. A double (mis)recognition of his own identity is thus effected: firstly as the grotesque caricature of the American gangster films he watches on TV and secondly, the stereotype of Maghrebi-French youth from the cité as delinquent ethnic 'other'.

This sense of the Maghrebi-French subject being 'over-determined from without' has a particular resonance in relation to Dridi's own position as a Franco-Tunisian film-maker and the concept of beur cinema. During the 1980s beur cinema emerged in relation to a handful of commercial films made by directors of North African origin whose narrative themes focused on the experiences of young Maghrebi-French characters (Bosséno 1992). In spite of the fact that the term continues to be used by both scholars and critics, the idea of a separate cinematic genre which can putatively be described as beur cinema has consistently been rejected by those film-makers with whom the term has been associated. Directors such as Charef, Chibane and Dridi object, above all, to what they see as an essentialised (mis)representation of their work which categorises films via criteria based primarily on the grounds of ethnic and cultural difference rather than narrative content of the film, or the aesthetic vision offered by the individual film-maker. Yet far from representing a disavowal of their North African cultural origins, the rejection of this idea of a culture beur by artists, authors and film-makers of Maghrebi immigrant origin seems to be motivated more by the fact that this identity is imposed by, and perceived in relation to, the dominant cultural norm (Rosello 1996).

Rosello's summary of the reluctance shared by many French artists of North African origin to associate themselves with this notion of a beur culture appears to accurately describe Dridi's own position. In an article emphatically entitled 'beur ... je refuse ce mot!' the director disassociated himself from both the generic term beur, and also the associative cinéma beur (Rémy 1995: 51). Dridi went further in a number of other interviews, stating his intention that the film allow for a more universal spectator identification with the characters of North African origin. To emphasise this point, he drew attention to the fact that the central narrative theme in Bye-Bye was concerned with the question of guilt and responsibility. Dridi argued that associating these universal concepts with Ismaël – his guilt over the earlier death of his handicapped brother and responsibility towards Mouloud – would enable audiences, regardless of their own ethnic origins, to identify more directly with the main Maghrebi-French protagonist (Edmond 1995; Dridi 1995a).

Despite this desire to highlight the universal qualities of the Maghrebi-French subject, Dridi was clearly also keen to endorse and embrace the North African cultural heritage that informs his own hybridity. In a television interview two months after the film's release, the director claimed that he had made *Bye-Bye* both to inform a mainstream white audience who had little contact with Maghrebi culture, and also to offer positive images of North African characters with whom spectators of Maghrebi immigrant origin could identify (Dridi: 1995b). In this respect, through the sympathetic portrayal of the extended immigrant family in the film, Dridi positively acknowledges his own North African origins, whilst simultaneously challenging the negative stereotypes which have previously dominated representations of the North African community in French cinema. For example, the director has suggested that *Bye-Bye* offers a counter-point to the *polars* of the 1980s such as *La Balance* (Swaim, 1981) in which nearly all the protagonists of North African origin are associated with criminal activity (Royer 1995). As his comments make clear, Dridi in no way intended *Bye-Bye* to be viewed or received as a product of a *beur* cinema, because of the way in which this externally imposed concept perpetuates the margnalisation of film-makers (and even spectators) of North African origin. Instead, he wanted to offer a positive representation of the North African community in France, determined by subjects of Maghrebi-immigrant origin – in this case, the actors and director himself – with which a wider French audience could also empathise.

Perhaps unsurprisingly, Dridi's highly sympathetic representation of the North African community and their descendants shares similarities with the work of other French film-makers of North African origin during the 1980s and 1990s: *Le Thé au harem d'archimède* (Charef, 1984), *Hexagone* (Chibane, 1994), *La Nuit du destin* (Bahloul, 1997). Nevertheless, the intimate, realist portrayal of the working class inhabitants of Le Panier in *Bye-Bye* is equally reminiscent of the work of British film-maker Ken Loach, of whom Dridi is a great admirer. Significantly, Phil Powrie identifies Loach as one of the British film-makers who has been seen to influence the new wave of young French directors whose work appears more engaged with contemporary social realities affecting France today (Powrie 1999). It could therefore be argued that, rather than existing in isolation as part of the *beur* cinema canon, *Bye-Bye*, in fact, belongs to this wider cinematic discourse surrounding the renewed emphasis on social realism and the political in French cinema in the 1990s (Bouquet 1995).[10] This suggestion is further endorsed by the fact that Dridi was one of the 59 film-makers who, in 1997, signed a public call to civil disobedience against the repressive new immigration laws proposed by the right-wing government.

In the same vein, *Bye-Bye* is quite clearly engaged with the political realities of the period. The manner in which the film positively endorses the rightful place of Mouloud and Ismaël within French society, presents a clear challenge to the right-wing government of the mid-1990s, whose political discourse questioned the 'Frenchness' of those descendants of first generation immigrants born in France (the *loi Pasqua* of 1993 decreed that children born in France of foreign parents were no longer French by birth and would have to offer a manifestation of their 'loyalty' – through a formal request for citizenship between the ages of 16–18 – in order to acquire French nationality). The aesthetic sensibilities and political sympathies revealed in *Bye-Bye* appear, therefore, to be more readily identifiable with the return of the social realism in French cinema of the 1990s than any reductive definition of the film as an example of *cinéma beur*.

In the final scene of *Bye-Bye*, however, the specificities of Maghrebi-French identity are once again called into question. Having rescued Mouloud from Renard's apartment in the *cité*, Ismäel finally decides not to send him back to Tunisia. The brothers flee Marseilles, and in so doing defy the external discourses that would oblige them either to return 'home' to the Maghreb, or else occupy a position of exclusion in marginalised spaces of the urban periphery. One reading of the ending proposed by Dridi, would be to suggest that Maghrebi-French youth should reject the identities imposed upon them by third parties – embodied in the film by the patriarchal law of the *bled*, on one hand, and Ludo's xenophobia, on the other – in order to determine their own subjectivity. This need for Mouloud and Ismaël to forge their own space and rightful place within society (one which demands their hybridity be accepted and valued, rather than feared and repressed) echoes Homi K. Bhabha's notion of 'third-space' as the site of enunciation which allows for the positive recognition of hybridity within which cultural difference may operate (Bhabha 1994: 37).

Yet by the end of the film, far from occupying this empowering 'third-space', the brothers appear to have reached an impasse. Ismaël informs his father that he will not be returning his brother to the *bled*; the camera then contemplates Ismaël and Mouloud, standing opposite the phone box beside their broken-down car, on a deserted roadside overlooking the sea, discussing what their next move should be. By distancing the final scene from Marseilles and focusing solely on the two brothers, attention is diverted from the problems they have left behind. The consequences of Ismaël's betrayal of his friendship with Jacky, for example, are conveniently side-stepped. In Le Panier, the xenophobic discourse propagated by Ludo, which aimed to divide the community along ethnic lines, has not been silenced. If anything, we might argue it is now even stronger, since Ludo has been able to break up the interethnic alliance between Jacky and Ismaël (a factor which contributes to the brothers' decision to leave Marseilles).

The ending does not therefore explain how the brothers can overcome the legacy of the colonial past which informs their hybrid subjectivity and find a (third-)space within French society where they can be accepted on their own terms. Mouloud's final suggestion that the brothers forge a new life together in Spain could be seen as further evidence of the fact there is no future for them in the *Hexagone*. However, the animated dialogue between Ismaël and Mouloud, which fades to credits accompanied by an upbeat *hybrid* mix of *raï* style vocals and flamenco guitar, largely dispels this sense of underlying pessimism. Moreover, Ismaël's refusal to send his brother back to the *bled* effectively represents an empowering defiance of Maghrebi patriarchal law which had threatened to dictate Mouloud's own sense of self. It is therefore possible to interpret a degree of optimism and a determination on the part of the brothers in the final scene of *Bye-Bye*. Mouloud and Ismaël may encounter continued resistance from certain sections of both the French and Maghrebi population, but they will not be deterred in their attempts to establish their rightful place in a post-colonial, multi-ethnic society.

Bye-Bye is a film which, through the plurality of spaces offered to the Maghrebi-French protagonist and a nuanced portrayal of the North African community, refuses to be categorised as (or marginalised by) a simplistic association with either *cinéma beur* or the *banlieue* film. Far from being an extension of films such as *La Haine* beyond the bounds of the Parisian urban periphery, *Bye-Bye*, in many ways, offers a counter-point to the representation of the Maghrebi-French subject found in the *cinéma de banlieue*. Similarly, the film's aesthetic and socio-political sensibilities are more productively analysed through their association with the return of social realism to 1990s French cinema rather than in relation to a putative notion of *beur* cinema.

Through his film, Dridi reiterates that these questions of discrimination, exclusion, cultural difference and national identity, although widely perceived as 'problems' concerning solely the Maghrebi-French population, do in fact need to be addressed by all members of France's post-colonial society. Ludo's inability, for example, to acknowledge Marseilles as a hybrid space, merely leads to xenophobic hostility and confrontation. However, this is not to deny the central position given to Maghrebi-French youth in *Bye-Bye*. Against the background of the multi-ethnic, *quartier populaire* of Le Panier; the transitory space of the port of Marseilles and the marginalised, clandestine economy of the *cité*, Dridi reveals the complex matrix of social, historical and cultural relations within which Maghrebi-French youth must negotiate their own sense of identity. Yet as *Bye-Bye* makes clear, whether Mouloud and Ismaël will indeed find their own place within the *Hexagone* depends largely on the willingness of both French and North African parents to positively embrace the hybridity of Maghrebi-French youth.

Notes

[1] I would like to thank Susan Hayward for her careful reading of the first draft and helpful comments on this chapter.

[2] The supposed emergence of the *cinéma de banlieue* as a new and distinct cinematic genre in the 1990s is, however, problematic. Whilst they may share the same geographical location, films such as *La Haine, Douce France, État des Lieux* (Richet, 1995) and *Raï* offer markedly different perspectives of the *banlieue*, in terms of their aesthetic vision, narrative structure, representation of space and ideology. Moreover, the *banlieue* films of the mid-1990s must be seen in relation to earlier cinematic visions of the post-war *cité*. The urban periphery had formed the focus of French films as early as the 1960s – e.g. *Terrain vague* (Carné, 1960) and *Deux ou trois choses que je sais d'elle* (Godard, 1967) – whilst the themes of exclusion and delinquency amongst multi-ethnic youth that are central to the so-called *banlieue-film* of the 1990s can be found a decade earlier in *Laisse béton* (Le Péron, 1983), *Le Thé au harem d'archimède* and *De bruit et de fureur* (Brisseau, 1988).

[3] See Hargreaves (1997: 88–90) and also Lorcerie and Geisser (1997: 935–8), for further references and more details surrounding these events.

[4] I use the descriptive term 'Maghrebi-French' in relation to both the French born descendants of North African immigrants and also those children of North African origin who arrived in France at a very young age and have thus been raised and socialised within the *Hexagone*.

[5] According to the annual report of the *Commission nationale consultative des droits de l'homme* (as quoted in *Le Monde*, 3 April 1998, 32) although largely hidden, discrimination against ethnic minorities in France remains a deep-seated and widespread problem in both the workplace and the job market.

[6] 'Situer mon film là-bas me permettait de … regarder l'Afrique de l'autre côté. Marseilles c'est une ville à l'intersection, comme moi qui suis à moitié arabe et à moitié français. C'est une ville très métissée'

[7] 't'es ni le premier, ni le dernier'

[8] *Harkis* are Algerians who fought for france during the Algerian War of Independence. *Pieds noirs* are French colonial Algerians.

[9] 't'es un homme avec ça … regarde les gens comme ils changent … t'es plus un bougnoule'

[10] For further information on the return of realism and the political in French cinema of the 1990s and the emergence of a so-called *jeune cinéma français* see Powrie (1999); Garbaz (1997); Herpe (1998).

Fluidity of gender and sexuality in GAZON MAUDIT
Darren Waldron

With 3,981,952 tickets sold, *Gazon maudit* was the second most popular French film of 1995 and enjoyed considerable international success, particularly in Italy and South America.[1] Critical acclaim soon followed; in 1996, the film received the *César* for the Best Original Writing or Adaptation and, perhaps more surprisingly for a mainstream comedy, it became the official French entry for the Best Foreign Language Film category at the Golden Globe Awards and received a nomination.[2]

On the surface, the film's popularity could have been expected; as yet another example of the somewhat tired, but nonetheless highly marketable comic form of the *vaudeville* and based on the sexual and sentimental relationships between three protagonists, *Gazon maudit* seems to comply perfectly with the hallmark of French comedy – the *ménage à trois*. That such success was achieved despite the film's placing of a lesbian couple as one of its central axes provides its greatest surprise. *Gazon maudit* confronted mainstream audiences with an explicit portrayal of a lesbian relationship, previous depictions of which had largely been veiled behind the more acceptable narrative of platonic female bonding.[3] The film's title itself alludes to the frankness of this portrayal as it is a familiar nineteenth-century expression which signifies lesbian.[4] However, the film's transgression of both generic and social convention is not only limited to its representation of an 'alternative' couple; in rejecting established notions of gender as fixed and dependent on biological differences between males and females, the director, Josiane Balasko, presents an original vision of sexual identity and sexuality as fluid.

In her interesting but irreverent criticism of the portrayal of the lesbian couple, Lucille Cairns concedes that 'a more charitable interpretation might argue for the sexual politics of the film as kaleidoscopic: assembling diverse forms of desire, mingling and collapsing them to the point where a unitary analysis becomes impossible and irrelevant' (1999: 234). Without indulging the film or its director, this article will argue that Balasko's deconstruction of established binaries of gender identity, through her favouring of fluidity and transience, constitutes the film's most potentially radical subversion. Moreover, it will posit the contentious figure of the 'butch' lesbian (Marijo) as a catalyst in that her arrival in the lives of the heterosexual couple (Laurent and Loli) pre-empts the shifting of identity which dominates the diegesis. Marijo's effectiveness as a rival for the heterosexual male is rooted in her appropriation of the physique and mannerisms traditionally associated with 'masculinity'.[5]

Although, as Cairns has correctly indicated, Judith Butler's work on imitative and performative gender affords by no means an exact theoretical justification of the construction of gender and sexuality in *Gazon maudit*, its challenge to the perceived status of heterosexuality as a 'gender original' does bear some relevance to this discussion.

The portrayal of gender fluidity will form the principal focus of this article, which will analyse how each character can be said to embark on an individual trajectory towards an ambivalent identity. This will reveal how Balasko deconstructs stereotype through her gradual erosion of the initially caricatural personae of the 'butch' lesbian, the 'philandering' husband and the 'subservient' wife. The central discussion will be preceded by an exploration of how gender is evinced through the structural elements of the film, that is the narrative, iconography, space and location. However, as the theme which has incited the greatest criticism is the portrayal of lesbianism, it is necessary to reveal the principal points of contention, the factors which informed its construction and to explore the perceived influences on the experience of the minority group it portrays.

'Butch-femme': heterosexual stereotype or urban reality?

Lucille Cairns' principal criticism stems from the construction of what she appears to perceive as the early stereotypical 'butch-femme' pairing of Marijo and Loli. She proposes that a more radical portrayal would have been 'for Loli to team up with another equally feminine-looking woman, for in such a union the male element would have been elided' (1999: 229). This appears to coincide with some reviewers who manifest their disapproval by framing discussions of Marijo within conventional, patriarchal discourses of 'masculinity'. In the words of Cécile Mury, Marijo personifies a 'real guy'[6] (1996: 115) whereas Claude-Marie Trémois opines that 'Balasko's choice to make the female lover a lesbian on the verges of transvestism limits the scope of her film ... it is difficult to believe in the seductive powers of such a character' (1995: 28).[7]

This preference for a more 'feminine' character appears to contradict the mood of a film which challenges the very existence of such an identity. Moreover, it can be interpreted as a compliance with the patriarchal construct of 'femininity' and, as such, amounts to a view not too distant from that espoused by the 'macho' heterosexual male character in the film, Laurent. The casting of the 'butch' is central to the film's radical force. As the majority of the female characters are perceived as sexual objects or conquests by Laurent, Marijo's rejection of the traditional, visual attributes of 'femininity' secures her position as his rival (the potency of which would have been severely undermined if she could have been construed as sexual object). Furthermore, as Balasko herself indicates, this renders the deriving of any erotic gratification from her love scenes with Loli improbable: 'I did not want the husband to be sexually attracted to Marijo, to avoid falling within the heterosexual porn genre where there is always a lesbian love scene [to titillate men]' (quoted in Vincendeau 1996: 25).

It would appear, however, that the above commentators' positions are inspired by a desire for the adoption of what they understand as 'positive images' of minority groups. However, although it may be true that the previously restricted and detrimental depictions of lesbians (see note 3) impose a need for more diverse, balanced representations, the very concept of a 'positive image' is embedded in personal, political and cultural points of view. For some, Marijo can be read as caricatural, for others she is radical. That her identity complies with heterosexual stereotype is not reason enough to deny her filmic presence. The 'butch' lesbian is an exisiting identity within a minority; any censorship of her screen representation amounts to a similar level of prejudice to that which motivated the medium's aforementioned narrow view. Finally, were a universally acceptable 'positive image' of lesbians possible, its depiction would be typified by superficial characters and underpinned by a moralistic narrative, thus, simultaneously undermining any reflection of cultural diversity and intensifying the risk of marginalisation.[8]

Balasko, comedy and the unconventional woman

For Josiane Balasko, caricatures of real life characters, such as Marijo, but also Laurent and Loli, are crucial to the potential and value of humour in film comedies: 'If there was no basis in reality, people would not laugh' (quoted in Vincendeau 1996: 25). Exploitation of stereotypes is typical of Balasko's work and stems from her work in *Le Splendid,* one of the *café-théâtres* which flourished in the aftermath of May 1968. Aimed at providing accessible, non-elitist entertainment, the productions were based on a coarse, crude humour within which a serious challenge to social convention was embedded. As Jill Forbes describes, the *café-théâtres* have 'contributed to the establishment of a domain of social comedy which mocks the habits and mores of the petty bourgeoisie' (1992: 175). The comedy exploited by *Gazon maudit* stems from this tradition, as is evidenced by the film's title (see note 4).

A challenge to the beauty culture of the late twentieth century can be said to underpin Balasko's approach to her work. Examples include her incarnation of the 'overweight' secretary in *Les Hommes préfèrent les grosses* (Poiré, 1981), the scenario of which she co-wrote, and her role as the mistress who reignites the passions of Gérard Depardieu, bored with his wife's (Carole Bouquet) cold, classic and distant beauty in *Trop belle pour toi* (Blier, 1989). Her portrayal of the prostitute in *Nuit d'ivresse* (Nauer, 1986) reinforces the emerging rebellious pattern of which Marijo seems to constitute one of the latest examples. Interestingly, such roles appear to strengthen her popularity (following the release of *Gazon maudit*, she was voted the second best director by French spectators (Vincendeau 1996)) and contribute to a star image which, as Steve Warren underlines, appeals to a wide cross-section of French society (she was voted an ideal mother by French children in 1992 and was Grand Marshall of the Gay Pride Parade in 1993 (Warren 1996)).

Taking lesbians out of their closets: media, minorities and Marijo

One of the principal markers of the film's influence is the intense media attention which it attracted and which led to the somewhat optimistic, but premature conclusion that it had facilitated general tolerance of lesbians. Steve Warren's review is typical of this. He describes how the film 'made butch lesbians leave their flannel and leather laden closets and start flaunting it on talk shows in Parisian prime time' (Warren 1996: 1). This view is echoed and broadened in Frédéric Martel's discussion of the French gay movement since 1968; he suggests that the success of *Gazon maudit* illustrates changing attitudes to sexuality 'since it shows that homosexuality has become rather banal' (1999: 316).

One of the 'talk shows' alluded to in Warren's quote above, entitled *Ça se discute* and broadcast on France 2 in the autumn of 1995, discussed the question 'Does lesbian culture exist?'[9] The influence of *Gazon maudit* on the programme was undeniable; key scenes were screened in order to generate debate. Ginette Vincendeau concludes that 'an overwhelming majority of the lesbian audience approved of the film, for putting lesbianism on the agenda' (1996: 24). Elula Perrin, guest, women-only nightclub owner, writer and perhaps one of France's most high-profile 'out' lesbians, asserts that '*Gazon maudit* certainly did a lot for us because it was the first time a lesbian had been the heroine of a film without being ridiculed' (Quoted in Vincendeau 1995: 22).[10]

While such mediatisation of a hitherto largely unpublicised minority may be welcomed, conclusions that this revolutionised lesbian existence may be over-optimistic.[11] The very need to ask the question as to whether lesbian culture exists demonstrates its perceived inexistence. After providing very little evidence of the emergence of this culture, the aforementioned television debate was soon dominated by questions of morality. As one guest tried in vain to demonstrate how homosexuality was 'curable', the familiar references to psychological 'abnormality' returned. For Elula Perrin, such media coverage confirms the marginalisation of lesbians in society: 'At the moment, there is a lot of talk about us because it is fashionable, but we are still considered abnormal. However, we are not freaks' (1995: 22).[12]

Feminine narrative structure, gendered iconography and a female hero

Gazon maudit charts the relationship of Marijo and Loli and its effects on Laurent, the latter's husband. The narrative structure twists and turns from equilibrium to disequilibrium, hence its American title, *French Twist*. With its metaphoric references to notions of the 'female form', this meandering narrative contributes to the 'feminine' iconography of the film.

The spectator is immediately confronted with the dichotomy of 'masculinity' versus 'femininity' through the symbolism of the opening credit sequence. The first shots focus on the back of a van adorned with the reclaimed hippie symbol of a Hindu God. Notions of 'masculinity' and class are evoked by the van's cultural association with *man*ual professions, enhanced by the *man*-made Parisian cityscape, with its angular buildings, multi-laned motorways crammed with lines of speeding vehicles and loud, upbeat rhythms of the background music. The driver, dressed in sunglasses and a cap, smoking a cigar, appears to confirm the image of 'maleness' expected. Moments later, a milder, more harmonious atmosphere, accompanied by the slower, melodic tones of *A Whiter Shade of Pale*, marks the hero's entry into the 'feminine' domain of the countryside. The gentle contours of the rolling hills covered in soft, wild vegetation and flanking the long, meandering road intensify the 'feminine' ambience through their connotations of mother nature and metaphoric references to female corporeality.

As the van crosses a small, Southern town, the hippie symbolism, through its cultural associations with sexual liberation and gender transgression, clashes with the familiar, picture-postcard image of a region where traditional family values and Mediterranean machismo are the order of the day. When the driver's identity as a lesbian is revealed, the importance of location is clarified; Balasko has uprooted her unconventional hero from the relative safety of the big city and placed her within the semi-hostile surroundings of the Midi.

'Feminine' space is not only delineated through geographical location; the boundaries of the home provide the setting for the ever-changing identities of the three protagonists and the gradual erosion of heterosexual complacency. The scene in the lesbian nightclub provides the culmination of the marginalisation of male 'masculinity' through its denial of the man's conventional privilege to gaze. The camera's appropriation of Laurent's eyes as he finally secures his entrance into the establishment and descends the staircase intensifies the hostile atmosphere. As one female reveller growls 'Look, an error',[13] her attack is inadvertantly rerouted and directed at the spectator.

The use of the conventionally 'feminine' symbol of water serves to enhance the poignancy of the rapport between the two women and differentiate this from the more carnal portrayal of heterosexual intimacy. The image of the two women in the bath is underpinned by the tension between sentimentality and potentially gratifying eroticism. Loli's head rests on her lover's upper chest, her left leg and arm exposed, the latter resting on Marijo's bosom, blurred by the soapy water. Water also 'feminises' Diego's 'masculinity'; droplets trickle slowly down his face, framed with long, dark hair, as he returns Laurent's objectifying gaze in the final scene.

Heterosexual symbolism and gender imitation

The poster which accompanied the film's release alludes to the ambiguity to be found in the diegesis. Whereas the universally recognisable heterosexual symbolism of the wedding appears to posit both Loli and Laurent in their traditional ceremonial roles as bride and groom, Marijo, dressed as another 'groom', provokes the initial comic surprise.

However, Marijo's ease at assuming one of the pivotal, symbolic roles of 'masculinity' within Christian society poses a genuine threat to the permanence of Laurent and Loli's 'heterosexual' identities. Marijo's uncomplicated appropriation of the physical appearance of her anatomical opposite appears to endorse Judith Butler's theory of the potential performativity of gender, illustrating her view that there is 'no [gender] original'. Although based on the transgressive spectacle of the drag queen, Butler's theory can be developed and projected onto a more generalised negotiation of gender and sexuality within society. If 'masculinity' and 'femininity' can be imitated by any subject, biological notions of gender identity are greatly undermined and the potential performativity of heterosexuality is intensified (Butler 1998).[14]

The tension caused by Marijo's presence is revealed through closer inspection of the poster; her cool demeanour contrasts greatly with Laurent's unease; his face is stern, his hand grips Loli tightly as he stares angrily at the cause of his indignation, Marijo. Loli's apparent disavowal of the patriarchically defined role of the blushing bride provides a visual manifestation of the consequences of this tension; her gaze engages directly with the viewer, her hands placed on her hips reinforcing the strong defiance she symbolises.

Diesels, devils and damsels: reconstructing stereotype

The film's initial construction of Marijo complies with the notions of the 'masculine' woman described above. She has short hair, wears trousers, drives a van, smokes cigars, mends pipes and plays with a Gameboy and table football. She exploits traditionally 'masculine' tools in agencing desire, but rather than the male becoming the focus of this objectification, it is the female who inspires the erotic and amourous energy. The opening shots of the kitchen scene provides an example of this; the camera is placed at sub-waist level as it focuses on Marijo in 'masculine' plumber mode. Loli's legs come into view to the right of the screen before crossing to the left, a movement simultaneously followed by Marijo's gaze. The camera appropriates the gaze as it settles on Loli who has inadvertently offered her posterior to the appreciation of her admirer. Through this reworking of cinematic convention, Balasko is placing the spectator in the unusual position of enjoying a spectacle of the female form through the eyes of a woman.

Marijo's 'masculinity' is reinforced by her subsequent seduction of Loli in which she masquerades as the romantic, attentive, almost 'gentleman-like' admirer. Her technique bears visible fruits as Loli loses her inhibitions, allowing Marijo free reign to gaze at her naked legs. Loli appears to revel in the intense sexual energy of Marijo's inflamed desires. As Loli tries to remove a hair from Marijo's cheek (hence further references to her 'masculinity'), the air becomes tense; Marijo takes hold of Loli's hands, placing them on her (Loli's) breasts with the warning, 'Stop, because the more you joke the more you excite me', inducing an audible sigh of desire to escape from Loli's mouth.[15]

This technique is reminiscent of both romantic fiction and Hollywood film in which the gentleman hero would create favourable conditions before embarking on the final seal of seduction, the kiss. The fact that the object, the heroine, was forced to wait and her desire for the hero allowed to deepen, heightened her frustration, increasing the potential for conquest. Marijo has installed desire within Loli, who attempts to satisfy this by unsuccessfully initiating intercourse with her husband. The cultural references are potently illustrated by the kiss. The atmosphere is once again filled with sensual tension, reinforced by the dramatic introduction to the song *Une Histoire d'amour*, as Marijo literally sweeps Loli off her feet before pressing her against the tree and kissing her. The camera cuts to an after-the-event shot of Loli, her face comically registering her interior *jouissance*.

In Laurent, Balasko initially exposes the misogynist conventions of both rural Mediterranean society and mainstream cinema. He complies perfectly with the stereotype of the philandering, womanising southern European male who seduces women with his cocky confidence and middle-class affluence. His 'masculinity' depends on his sexual virility, his mistresses representing conquests which strengthen his male subjectivity. He subscribes to traditional patriarchal perceptions of women as either sexual objects or mothers, a convention upheld in film, as Susan Hayward (1998: 160) suggests:

> Mainstream cinema ... functions ideologically to separate the discourses of female sexuality and motherhood, precisely because patriarchy has difficulty combining the two (it cannot represent

to itself the mother as a sexual being). Thus the female is represented as nothing but her sexuality: as whore, vamp etc.; or as everything but her sexuality: virgin, mother. She is either in excess or lack of sexuality.

In her influential discussion of Hollywood representations of women, Laura Mulvey (1975) attributes this perception of the female to a preoccupation with retelling the classic Oedipal narrative within mainstream cinema. To avoid potential castration by the female, the male has a choice of two escape processes: voyeurism and fetishism. Portrayals of 'vamps' and 'whores' are examples of the former, which are based on the male's need to contain the female through subjugation; 'virgins' or 'mothers', with their celestial references, fall within the boundaries of the latter and elevate the female to a higher status within society. Laurent's perception of his mistresses is typified by this voyeurism, as exemplified by the café scene in which he refuses to buy roses for one of them, joking: 'No thanks, we've already had sex'.[16] His seduction technique compounds his voyeurism. His style is direct, devoid of any flattery as he uses professional jargon as a metaphor for seduction: 'So Ingrid, why don't we close this deal straight away. It's not a deal to let go.'[17] The contrast with Marijo is heightened by the *mise-en-scène* as the scene cuts back to her own seduction of Loli.

Laurent's fetishistic admiration for his wife is revealed by the misunderstanding with the barman in which he describes Loli as 'much prettier' than his mistress. The French word '*mignon*' signifies beauty, but not sexuality. Loli's status as wife and mother is established as the camera cuts to an image of her polishing her wedding photograph while engaging in maternal chat with her son. The sequence constructs her as almost angelic; her simple and unflattering clothes symbolising lack of vanity, her domestic and maternal activities evoking notions of selfless charity. This 'lack' of sexuality is underlined by Laurent's response to Ingrid's allusions to Loli's infidelity: 'Listen Ingrid, we have a good laugh, we have good sex and we have a good time together, but leave my wife out of this. She is not the type to get picked up at the school gates when taking the kids home.'[18]

Thus far in the diegesis, Loli's occupation of the traditionally female position of object is embodied by her identity being projected onto her by the subject of desire, atypically in this case, a male and a female. As the focal point onto which the two patriarchically contradictory discourses of motherhood and sexuality converge, Loli's character is both ambiguous and transgressive, and this is potently confirmed in the restaurant scene. For Laurent, the image of Loli and Marijo caressing each other's legs represents an extremely tangible threat to his male subjectivity, for, not only is his status as provider of sexual pleasure to Loli usurped by Marijo, but Loli is transgressing the boundaries of maternity by actively expressing sexual desire. Loli's status as object of desire is endorsed as Marijo lifts her hand to her nose, inhaling the lingering, erotic odours of Loli's sexual being. Laurent's subsequent humiliation of his wife illustrates what Hayward (1998: 161) appears to view as a conventional reaction to the female's active manifestation of her own desires:

> If you attempt to agence desire, be a mother and be publicly empowered then you will be punished ... The only time woman can combine female sexuality and public power is when it is sanctioned by the 'true' parent (the male).

Voyeurism and fetishism also underscore Laurent's attempt to contain the threat represented by Marijo. Initially, he denigrates her as a 'contraption', 'top model' or 'van driver', emphasising her non-compliance with his image of 'feminine' beauty to detract from the lack of desire she bears him.[19] Later, he changes tactics by granting her the metaphorical phallus in order to engage her in physical confrontation. Initially goading her by yelling: 'You play at being a man, but you're scared of getting hit. Don't you have the balls?', Laurent also replies angrily to Loli's concerns, asking: 'Where can you see a woman?'[20] In responding to this by stepping down from her van armed with a cricket bat, Marijo is accepting the conventionally 'masculine' position of enemy in combat. Laurent later confirms Marijo's status as an equal during the card game: 'We're talking between men'.[21]

Gender metamorphosis: Loli gets the power

Loli's subsequent discovery of the extent of Laurent's previous infidelity sees Marijo move into the conjugal bed, an event which precedes a shift in the gender identities of the protagonists. Laurent's 'masculinity' begins to crack; he becomes visibly emotional, performs 'maternal' tasks with increased regularity and waits passively for his wife to return to him. Similar shifts also occur in Marijo's gender identity; in a turnaround of previous events, she prepares the evening meal in Loli's absence. Loli telephones Marijo to say that she will be late, an act culturally perceived as 'masculine' and a version of what Laurent did to Loli earlier. As the two women dine, with Laurent's head hidden behind the newspaper, Marijo happily accepts Loli's patronising ruffling of her hair.[22]

After spending the night with Laurent, Loli occupies the position of sexual subject, agencing desire and forcing both Marijo and Laurent into self-abnegation by granting them equal status as her 'mistresses'. As her 'feminine' sexuality has afforded her this freshly omnipotent status, she intensifies her masquerade, moulding the fetishistic gaze of her mesmerised onlooker in order to secure her privileged position. The overtones of raw, carnal passion are reinforced by an emphasis on her Spanishness; prior to the abovementioned dinner, she parades in front of Marijo, her dance evoking notions of Andalucian women through its sharp, flamenco-like twists and turns accompanied by the flowing, twirling shawl.

The image, however, is characteristic of the ambivalence which underpins the diegesis; on the one hand, it can be said to illustrate what Teresea de Lauretis has termed as 'mutual narcissistic empowerment'. De Lauretis describes how the 'femininity' performed in front of the butch is 'aggressively reclaimed from patriarchy by radical separatism, with its exclusive reference and address to women, [and] asserts the erotic power of the unconstricted, 'natural' female body in relations between women' (1994: 264). This 'aggressive reclamation' of 'femininity' can be said to manifest itself through Laurent's exclusion; the distant outline of his semi-silhouette, with one child in his arms and flanked by the other, his melancholic gaze directed towards the beatific display of the two women's embrace underline his encroaching impotence. Moreover, Loli's act could be described as a punishment of her husband, her display an intended exacerbation of his increasing frustration.

On the other hand, however, Laurent's presence can also be said to dilute the potency of Loli's display, illustrating the limitations and precariousness of her control; despite her newfound power, she is unable to dictate the identity of her audience. In narrative terms, the principal meaning to be derived from the embrace is Laurent's (thus the male's) isolation, as the two women have already been seen in close physical contact in previous scenes. Such complexity endorses the multi-faceted nature of the film's portrayal of gender and sexuality and demonstrates the limitations of unitary approaches to its analysis.

Notions of the precariousness of Loli's power base are strengthened by her later reaction to the presence of Marijo's ex-girlfriend, Dani. Her response is typified by similar forms of fear, jealousy and anger to those which underpinned Laurent's reaction to Marijo; she describes Dani as 'ugly' ('*moche*') and her friend as a 'paratrooper' ('*parachutiste*'). Stereotypical images of the Spanish woman are intensified as she is seen to prepare a deliberately inedible meal, slam drawers, throw tea-towels and make obscene gestures. The consequences of this threat to her command are momentarily manifested as she tearfully asks Laurent to tell her lover to leave and promises to return to her pre-Marijo existence. Her subsequent appearance on the train illustrates that, instead of reverting to her original, subservient role of dutiful wife and mother, she has donned the androgynous look of the contemporary woman. Her initiation of physical confrontation with Marijo's new partner, Fabienne, in the night club provides another example of how her shifting identity appropriates elements which are conventionally associated with 'masculinity'.

Marijo's movement towards conformity and Laurent's passage into passivity take a giant leap in the previous scene. Initiated by Marijo's determination to become pregnant, her decision to engage in heterosexual intercourse with Laurent appears to validate direct contact with the penis as desirable within the procreation process and contradicts her earlier repulsion. Her self-definition as a 'virgin', despite her sexual experiences with women, reinforces the symbolic importance of the heterosexual act. For Laurent, the event constitutes his first intimate connection with homosexuality, not only because his sexual partner is a lesbian, but also because he has constructed her as male. As Balasko (1995: 62) suggests, the scene is crucial:

> What interests me in this scene is her [Marijo's] masculine side, particularly when she turns him [Laurent] over: It is difficult to distinguish between the two bodies. I wanted the scene to be disturbing. I also wanted it to contain a loss of reference points. It starts with a comic tone and finishes with a question. It's one of the most erotic sequences in the film. Voyeurism is never satisfied. How are they going to make love in order to satisfy the conditions of the deal while they hate each other so much? We will never know if they experienced any pleasure or not. Ambiguity persists.[23]

Although both partners attempt a mental evocation of Loli in order to stimulate sexual arousal, as they both open their eyes, they visually acknowledge the true identity of their partner and their new roles. Marijo's success in becoming pregnant could infer that pleasure was sustained, at least by Laurent. However, it can also be deduced that Marijo's subsequent return to her previous existence as an urban lesbian and her description of the event as 'painful' undermines the potentially revolutionary effects of the act on her own identity.

Marijo's penultimate scene symbolises her entrance into relative social conformity. As the camera shifts from Laurent and Loli's bedroom to that of Marijo, her presence in the family home implies an acquiescence to Loli's earlier moralistic remark, 'a child needs a mother and a father'.[24] It seems as if a revalidation of heterosexuality is underway through the reconstruction of the couple Loli/Laurent and Marijo's banishment from the conjugal bed. Motherhood and sexuality are once again separated as the focus on Marijo and her baby is devoid of any visual signs of her previous gender identity and sexuality. The scene also re-establishes the conventional distribution of gender through its delineation between Marijo and Laurent along traditional parental lines; as the former awakens from her deep slumber, incidentally 'feminised' by her silk pyjamas, the latter places the baby into her arms, thus emphasising the maternal bond and loosely reconstructing the biblical image of 'virgin mother and child'. The conventional symbolism of the scene is finalised as Marijo insists that Laurent buys the correct nappies before waving her baby's hand and whispering '*Au revoir, papa.*'

However, the final close-up of Marijo, Loli and the baby undermines this conventional conclusion. Although the short embrace between the two women does not imply the continuation of a sexual relationship, its distinct intimacy suggests the existence of some sentimental attachment. As the two women coo over the latest offspring, a new, alternative vision of community consisting of a baby, two children and three parental figures – two mothers and a father – is constructed.

Laurent's entry into passivity is explicitly finalised in the last scene as he succumbs to the charms of his male client, Diego. For Cairns, Laurent's inferred homosexual infidelity represents nothing more than a '*dalliance*' which does not threaten his reinstated role as '*père de famille*' (1999: 236). However, through the camera's repeated focus on Laurent's mesmerised, enamoured face, a sentimental as well as sexual energy can be said to be activated, reminiscent of the initial seduction scenes between Marijo and Loli. Over breakfast, the sexual dynamics predominate as Diego toasts his guest with the Catalan expression 'Salut i força al canut'; the metaphoric use of 'canut', meaning vagina, coupled with the sharp raising of his fist transmit his carnal intentions. That Laurent repeats this, much like a language student would repeat unfamiliar words in an attempt to learn them, signifies his acceptance of the 'lesson' Diego is offering him.

To suggest that a 'macho', 'heterosexual' male may indulge in homosexual intercourse is subversive enough; to imply that he will become its passive object constitutes the film's most serious challenge to male subjectivity. However, Josiane Balasko's film goes further than merely developing representations of the 'crisis of masculinity' by portraying the male's ultimate passivity; *Gazon maudit* provides a highly original and subversive contribution to representation by challenging the fixity of gender and sexuality. Differences between 'masculinity' and 'femininity', 'maleness' and 'femaleness' and 'heterosexuality' and 'homosexuality' are obscured and a new vision of community, in which permutations of sexuality are permitted without engendering punishment or ostracism, is constructed. *Gazon maudit* allows the spectator to enter into this 'permissive' society in which both men and women can agence desire and become its object, appropriate the objectifying gaze and provide its spectacle, give sexual pleasure and rejoice in its reception.

For Cairns, Josiane Balasko's attempts at subversion fall short of the 'truly radical end-scenario ... of a lesbian family' (1999: 236). Cairns appears to attribute what she perceives as a lack of radical will to regional cultural differences between the north and the south. The south, with its Latin roots, may well be 'tolerant, relaxed enough to have fun' but it is 'ultimately committed to preserving the two foundation-stones of its identity – the family, and the Law of the Father, which is what, in the end, it is all about' (1999: 236). However, as the above alternative reading suggests, Balasko could be said to confront the heterosexual complacency of the southern provinces by bringing her urban lesbian hero out of her ghetto and placing her within more hostile surroundings. In this sense, the film contributes to a national social and political challenge to traditional notions of union, the family and patriarchal law. The lengthy debating and recent voting of a piece of legislation effectively recognising homosexual union, the PACS (Civil Pact of Joint Responsibility – *Pacte Civil de Solidarité*), may have brought attention to differences in regional attitudes to homosexuality, but it also succeeded in imposing and establishing an extremely progressive law throughout the French republic.

It is within the changing social and political climate in France that, since the release of *Gazon maudit*, a string of comedies have, to differing degrees, adopted a similar approach to themes of gender and sexuality. Alain Berliner's *Ma Vie en rose* ((1996) – discussed in this volume by Lucille Cairns), Jean-Jacques Zilberman's *L'Homme est une femme comme les autres* (1998) and Stéphane Giusti's *Pourquoi Pas Moi!* (1999) are but three comedies which reject traditional binaries. This particular slant is becoming culturally associated with French film itself; at the 1999 London Lesbian and Gay Film Festival, a series of French productions were screened, including the last two of the aforementioned films. The caption which accompanied the reviews in the brochure stated: 'This focus on French cinema not only highlights some of the most dazzling work in the Festival, but contains a significant number of films where human sexuality is never as simple as the labels "lesbian", "gay" and "straight"' (London Lesbian and Gay Film Festival Brochure 1999: 5). *Gazon maudit* could be identified as having a strong influence on this new challenge to established conventions of gender and sexuality within mainstream comedy.

Notes

[1] According to Gilles Renouard (1996), *Gazon maudit* sold 600,000 tickets in its first week at the French box office. By 31st December 1995, it had managed to sell 250,000 tickets in Italy, 200,000 in Brazil, 165,000 in Belgium and 140,000 in Switzerland. The film was presented at the festivals of Munich, London, Toronto, Sarasota, Yokohama, Taipeh and Cancun where Alain Chabat received the prize for best actor. Finally, in what constituted a first for a French film on British soil, twenty dubbed copies were released in addition to fifteen subtitled versions.

[2] The *Césars* are the French equivalent of the Oscars.

[3] For a global overview of the portrayal of lesbians on the French screen until the mid-1980s

see Bertrand Philbert's *L'Homosexualité à l'écran*, particularly chapters 5, 6 and 7. According to Philbert, from the early 1960s to the mid-1970s, lesbians were portrayed as murderers (*La Fille aux yeux d'or*, Albicoco, 1960) or vampires (*Le Frisson des vampires*, Rollin, 1970). Jacques Rivette's controversial production *La Réligieuse* (redistributed as *Suzanne Simonin, la Réligieuse de Diderot* in 1966) caused a public scandal involving the then interior minister, Alain Peyrefitte, and was heavily censored for questioning religious values and replacing them with lesbian morals ('*les moeurs saphiques*', Philbert 1984: 9). Subsequent productions saw subtle allusions to the possibility of the existence of lesbian characters or relationships (*Thérèse Dequeyroux* (Franju, 1962); *Masculin-Féminin* (Godard, 1966); *Thérèse et Isabelle* (Metzger, 1968); *Marie-Chantal contre Docteur Kha* (Chabrol, 1969). Traditional clichés of lesbians could also be observed, as in Chabrol's *Les Biches* (1965). For Philbert, French cinema 'continued to take delight in a kind of voyeurism.' (*Et ainsi de suite, le cinéma notamment français continuant à se délecter dans un certain voyeurisme*' (1984: 80). Directors of erotic productions clearly capitalised on this voyeuristic trend. In films such as *Emmanuelle* (Jaeckin, 1974) the traditional sex scene between two women became a central convention purely to titillate the male viewer. Any threat to male subjectivity was avoided by using 'female homosexuality as journey of initiation before the return of the male' ('*Encore et toujours, l'homosexualité féminine [est présentée] comme [un] parcours initiatique avant le retour du mâle*' (Philbert 1984: 152). In an interesting take on the lesbian erotic scene, Chantal Akerman filmed herself having sex with another woman in her own production *Je, tu, il, elle* (Akerman, 1974). The presence of a woman behind the camera, in Philbert's view, intensified the strength of the scene. Veiled hints at the existence of a lesbian relationship can be observed in *Céline et Julie vont en bateau* (Rivette, 1974), and in productions released in the 1980s, including *Coup de foudre* (Kurys, 1983) and *4 Aventures de Reinette et Mirabelle* (Eric Rohmer, 1986), although the identification of such rapports can be said to depend on the viewing position adopted. Philbert highlights the importance of reading strategies when he asserts of Rivette's production that one can 'benefit from a gay reading of the drifting relationship between Dominique Labourier and Juliet Berto and their rejection of heterosexual norms, although nothing is explicit.' ('*une lecture homosexuelle peut être faite avec beaucoup plus de profit à travers la dérive de Dominique Labourier et de Juliet Berto et leur rejet dans la norme hétérosexuelle, bien que rien n'y soit explicite*') (1984: 60).

⁴ As Steve Warren explains, *gazon maudit* literally translates as 'cursed grass'. It is an outdated, familiar expression which signifies a lesbian 'because *gazon* (grass) refers to a woman's pubic hair and it's cursed because it's forbidden to men. The phrase had fallen into disuse until the movie restored its popularity, but it has literary credentials, having been used by Baudelaire in a poem (which was banned on publication) about a lesbian in his masterwork *Les Fleurs du Mal* (*Flowers of Evil*)' (Warren 1996: 2)

⁵ Words such as 'masculinity', 'femininity', 'maleness', 'femaleness' etc. are surrounded in inverted commas as their identity is being challenged by the film.

⁶ '*elle a fait de son héroïne un vrai mec, et de son film un vaudeville en plus*'

⁷ '*ce qui limite la portée du film, c'est le choix de Balasko de faire de l'amante une lesbienne à la limite du travelo ... on a du mal à croire au pouvoir de séduction d'un tel personnage*'

⁸ This point coincides with Karen Hollinger's view that 'the advocacy of a simplistic "positive images approach" to gay representation which suppresses contradiction and results in unrealistic, static, one-dimensional portrayals seems hardly the answer' (1998: 10).

⁹ '*Y a-t-il une culture lesbienne?*'

¹⁰ '*Gazon maudit ... a certainement fait beaucoup pour nous, car c'était la première fois qu'une lesbienne était l'héroïne d'un film sans être ridiculisée*'

¹¹ Where it is true that, prior to the release of the film, the lesbian community lacked the cultural, political and social power of its gay male equivalent, disparity is still in evidence today, almost five years after the film's release. The gay male community has long attracted intense media attention in France, both as a result of the AIDS epidemic, and the ensuing political activism, and

through the glamour pages of glossy, society magazines on which stars are shown to converge on the 'trendy' night spots which occupy Paris' flourishing gay district, le Marais. As the 'scene' is the most visible manifestation of this minority's culture, the absence of lesbian establishments in the Marais is evidence of their exclusion. The most popular lesbian bar of the time, *L'Escandalo*, was situated across the eastern border of the Marais while the principal dance venue, the *Privilège*, which featured as the nightclub in the film, was located to the north. Despite talk of a 'lesbian and gay movement' media interest is still dominated by an overriding focus on gay men. Investigations into the *'franc rose'* (the pink franc) reflect this; in his accurate and informative article entitled 'Financial (Self-) Identification: the Pink Economy in France', Steve Wharton attributes the increasing economical wealth of the community to the *Syndicat national des entreprises gaies* (The National Committee of Gay Businesses). As a group of predominantly male establishments and companies which dominate the Marais, it stands as a testimony to the disparity in power and impact between the gay male and female communities. Wharton's quotation of one of the group's members reinforces this: 'the Marais did not come into existence all by itself; it answered an urgent need: to bring "poofs" out of their anonymity, to free them from their guilt.' (*'le Marais ne s'est pas créé tout seul: il répondait à une urgence: sortir les pédés de leur anonymat, les déculpabiliser'* (Wharton 1997: 77)). In using the 'reclaimed', previously derogatory term for gay men, *'pédé'* or 'poof', without including *'gouine'* or 'dyke', the speaker is clearly demonstrating the perceived dominance of the gay male within the construction of the visual symbols of the community's power. For more discussion about the French gay movement since 1968 see Frédéric Martel (1996, translated 1999).

[12] *'Maintenant on parle beaucoup de nous, parce que c'est la mode, mais on nous considère encore comme des cas. Or nous sommes pas des phénomènes'*

[13] *'Tiens, une erreur'*

[14] Butler adds that 'heterosexuality is always in the process of imitating and approximating its own phantasmatic idealisation of itself – *and failing'* (Rivkin and Ryan 1998: 722 [author's emphasis]).

[15] *'Arrête, parce qu'à force de plaisanter, tu m'excites'*

[16] *'Non merci, on a déjà baisé'*

[17] *'Bon, Ingrid. Si on concluait cette affaire tout de suite. C'est quand même pas une affaire à laisser passer'*

[18] *'Ecoute, Ingrid, on rigole bien, on baise bien, on s'amuse bien mais laisse ma femme en dehors de tout ça. C'est pas du tout le style de se faire draguer à la sortie de l'école en rentrant avec ses mômes'*

[19] *'Engin'*, *'Top Model'* and *'Camioneuse'*.

[20] *'On joue aux mecs mais on a peur de s'en prendre une. Les couilles te manquent?'*... *'Où tu vois une femme, toi?'*

[21] *'On discute entre mecs'*

[22] As Judith Butler has observed, this shift is characteristic of the fluidity which exists in some lesbian relationships: 'a butch can present herself as capable, forceful, and all-providing ... And yet this 'providing' butch who seems at first to replicate a certain husband-like role, can find herself in a logic inversion whereby that 'providingness' turns to a self-sacrifice, which implicates her in the most ancient trap of feminine self-abnegation' (1991: 726).

[23] *'Ce qui m'interesse dans cette scène, c'est son côté masculin, notamment lorsqu'elle le renverse: on a du mal à identifier les deux corps. Je voulais que cette scène soit troublante. Je voulais aussi qu'elle contienne une perte de repère. Elle commence sur le ton de la comédie et finit sur un questionnement. C'est une des scènes les plus érotiques du film. Le voyeurisme n'est jamais satisfait. Pour conclure le marché, comment vont-ils pouvoir faire l'amour tout en se haïssant à ce point? On ne saura jamais s'ils ont éprouvé du plaisir ou non, l'ambiguïté persiste'*

[24] *'Un enfant a besoin d'un père et une mère'*

The representation of childhood in Sandrine Veysset's

Y AURA-T-IL DE LA NEIGE A NOEL?

Lyn Thomas

What are children for?

> In this context of isolation, alienation, doubt and intellectual con-
> flict, it is not difficult to see the attraction of the child as a literary
> theme. The child could serve as a symbol of the artist's dissatis-
> faction with the society which was in the process of such harsh
> development about him. In a world given increasingly to utilitar-
> ian values and to the machine, the child could become the symbol
> of imagination and sensibility, a symbol of nature set against the
> forces abroad in society actively denaturing humanity. (Coveney
> 1982: 44)

This discussion of nineteenth-century literature, originally published in the
middle of the twentieth century, indicates an investment in childhood which is
still prevalent, and increasingly problematised. In recent years anxieties about
the relationships and boundaries between adults and children have been one
of the most striking manifestations of this investment. The success of Sandrine
Veysset's *Y aura-t-il de la neige à Noël?* (1996) may perhaps be indicative of
these investments and anxieties, and of the continuing presence of the dichoto-
mies identified by Coveney in Western European culture. Like Coveney, Jacqueline Rose has been concerned with the nature of adults' investment in childhood expressed through the medium of art – in Rose's case a children's story
written with adults in mind (Rose 1984). Veysset does not pretend that her work
is directed at children: 'In the publicity I made it clear that people shouldn't
turn up expecting Walt Disney. It did happen once – a woman turned up with
two small children. I said "Madame, are you sure you want your children to
see this?" She walked out after 15 minutes' (Romney 1997: 17). Thus, as a
representation of childhood aimed at adults, her film, like Peter Pan, inevitably poses the question of the kind of 'desire for the child' it expresses and constructs (Rose 1984: 3). Audience measures – 829,336 spectators by December
1998 according to the records of the Centre National de la Cinématographie
– positive reviews, and the award of prestigious prizes such as the 1997 *César*
for the best first film and the Louis-Delluc prize for the best French film of the
year, suggest that the film struck a chord with contemporary French audiences
and critics. Many of the reviews concentrated on the depiction of childhood –

seen as realistic on the one hand, and magical on the other.[1] This analysis of the representation of childhood in *Neige* aims to explore this issue. What might be at stake in the need to explore the threats to childhood, whilst at the same time preserving it in magical snow? Why was a 'fairytale' with seven real children a critical and popular success in France in the late 1990s?

Separate spaces and threatening looks

Y aura-t-il de la neige à Noël? opens with a credits sequence which identifies childhood as the film's central theme. The actors' names appear in multicoloured letters on the screen, accompanied by children's shouts and a simple tune played on percussion, reminiscent of a toy musical instrument. Then, as the richer melody of the piano takes over, the camera follows a group of children playing in a haystack. We see the game as if from the point of view of the children inside the haystack, and are drawn into a warmly lit sequence which connects childhood with carefree fun, freedom and camaraderie. The return to the original percussion instruments and appearance of the title itself end this sequence, and the film proper begins. The magical notes of childish music and the lyrical melody of the piano are replaced by the sound of an engine (and in fact there is no more music until the closing shots). The opening shot is filmed from inside the lorry, the restricted point of view that of the driver gazing through the windscreen. The film then cuts to a shot of children playing with a miniature farm they have built in the mud, and this shot ends with one of the children gazing at the lorry through bushes. The lorry driver is identified as the children's father, and he immediately puts them to work, as their mother returns from the fields to offer lunch (it later emerges that this family is less straightforward than it seems, as the father also has a wife and legitimate children in the nearby town, Cavaillon).

This opening sequence develops the theme of the special and separate experience of children which the credit sequence offers in idealised form. Adults, particularly the father, and children are seen to inhabit separate worlds, and the physical space they share is intersected by their threatened or threatening gazes at each other. This motif is repeated throughout the film, which emphasises the separation between child and adult by repeated shots of, and through, windows and the windscreens of vehicles. The father, as the parent who is most excluded from the children's world, and whose obsession with money and work place him at the opposite pole to the children and to the mother, is most often the focus of these images. In the first bedroom scene between the two parents the mother lingers by the window and we see the children playing in the yard from her point of view, as she tells them to protect themselves from the fierce midday sun (each of the three sections of the film – summer, autumn, winter –

was made at the appropriate time of year, and the physical experience of each season is emphasised). We hear the father telling her to 'forget those children for a while'[2] and like her are drawn back into the darkness of the room, the mystery and perversity of adult relationships.

The first conflict between the father and the family is heralded by his arrival in the fields where Bruno, the eldest son, is working; again the father's point of view, as he drives the lorry, opens the sequence, and is contrasted with the images of the children at play which have preceded it. The lorry symbolises his power over the family, since its noisy arrival and departures dictate the rhythms of their existence, but it also symbolises the father's isolation and entrapment in a rigid and unyielding masculinity. The outcome of the dispute with Bruno – a punishing afternoon picking tomatoes for the whole family – emphasises this solitude. The mother and children are at least united in their labours, whereas the father is rejected by a favoured daughter, Blandine, who refuses to go over to the lorry and kiss him goodbye.

Later in the film these contrasts become still more marked. Blandine and Paul, forced by the father to go and stay with his legitimate family in Cavaillon, refuse to travel with him in the alien territory of the cabin of his lorry. They travel in the back with the crates of vegetables picked by their mother and the Moroccan workers, becoming, perhaps like the latter, 'clandestine passengers' ('*les passagers clandestins*') (Richou 1996: 57). The *Cahiers* article on the film found that this moment was the apogee of the children's resistance to their father: 'They reclaim the illegitimate state which the father imposes upon them' (Richou 1996: 57).[3] The possible thematic link between the children's illegitimacy and the immigration question had already been indicated by the scene when the father's legitimate son pays first the Moroccans, and then the mother for their labours in the fields.[4] Given the fact that in February 1997, shortly after the film's release, Veysset was a signatory to the '*Manifeste des 66 cinéastes*' (Manifesto of the 66 film-makers) against the *Loi Debré* (which rendered the act of sheltering immigrants without valid papers – *les sans papiers* – illegal), this parallel is perhaps no accident. However, the politics of the father's exploitation of immigrant workers does not become an overt theme; the focus is on the children whose action represents their refusal to share the father's symbolic and physical space and, significantly, his viewpoint. They refuse to see the world, and most significantly their mother, through his distorted vision, symbolised by the view through the windscreen of his lorry, and this refusal allows them to remain in their own sphere, where, despite material deprivation, warmth, affection and imagination abound.

The father's separation from all of these qualities is brought out again during the 'autumn' sequence of the film. On a wet evening he drinks coffee with the mother as the children play peacefully around them: 'I would stay if

I could'.[5] He leaves, and the film cuts to his point of view, as he gazes from his lorry through the bars of the window at the warm family scene within. He is separated from the children by two physical barriers – the windscreen and the window. In the sequences which follow he attempts to counter his isolation through increasingly intrusive attempts at appropriation of the warm and affectionate world the children inhabit. His final move in this sequence demonstrates the fragility and perhaps the necessity of the boundary between adults and children which the film, and culture more broadly, construct. We see Jeanne, the eldest daughter, as she leaves the school bus with a boy, from the point of view of the driver of a car. Again, the policing gaze through the windscreen is the father's, as we discover in the next shot, which shows him and Jeanne driving home in silence. Jeanne leaves the car in tears, and the father creeps back to his lorry and departs, without saying goodbye. The implications of this sequence, which is characteristically understated, are spelt out in the next scene, when the mother is seen weeping as she works in the fields, and then telling the father she knows about his attempted incest. The vulnerability of the children, and the threat to the childhood world which the father's attempt to cross the boundary between adult and child represents, are expressed in the words of both parents. The first intimations of the mother's despair and suicidal thoughts are present in her comment that it would be better if the baby 'never woke up again in this madhouse', and the father walks away, promising that he will damage them all if they try to leave.

The violence of the dispute between the parents breaks out again shortly after this, and the sequence begins with the father's policing gaze – through the window of his workshop – at the mother as she crosses the courtyard without addressing him. The ensuing row is observed, again through a window, by one of the children, Marie, who is at home because of illness. She sees what she should not have to see, but here the window perhaps represents some slight protection of her world from the chaos of the adults' relationship. If the gaze through the windscreen is a threat, windows more frequently symbolise protection or hope. Thus, at the end of the film, the vision of the snow falling, framed by the window, seems to symbolise the mother's choice to live, and to allow her children to live, just as on a physical level, the fresh air she lets into the room by opening the window perhaps saves their lives. The camera imitates the mother's gaze down through the window at the children playing in the snow, in a shot which is reminiscent of a parallel moment in the summer sequence, when they play under the hot sun. In the final shots of the film the spectator gazes at the mother, through the window on which the children's snowballs explode, leaving silvery traces. The mother holding the baby smiles, perhaps tearfully, and the image echoes the 'white tears' ('*larmes blanches*') of Adamo's song '*Que tombe la neige*' which accompanies it. The mother's benign gaze, unlike the father's solitary and voyeuristic look of surveillance, can be returned – the camera can look back at her and the baby, who links her to the children outside.

Childhood under threat: cruel fathers and ambivalent mothers

The separate spheres inhabited by the children and the adults, particularly the father, are thus visually demarcated in the film by the use of the symbols of screen and window, and of point-of-view shots. This aspect of the film might lead to the conclusion that a process similar to that identified by Patricia Holland in her analysis of still images of children is taking place:

> Above all, the imagery displays the social and psychic effort that goes into the difficult distinction between adult and child, to keep childhood separate from an adulthood that can never be achieved. Attempts are made to establish dual and opposing categories and hold them firm, in a dichotomy set against the actual continuity of growth and development. There is an active struggle to maintain childhood – if not actual children – as pure and uncontaminated. The ultimate, if paradoxical, fear is that children will be deprived of their childhood. (Holland 1992: 13)

Threats to childhood, as we have seen, are omnipresent in the film. The most menacing of them, the loss of innocence and *joie de vivre*, and thus of childhood itself, through some act of violence perpetrated by the father, gradually intensifies as the film progresses. The potential for violence inherent in the situation reaches its ultimate expression in the ambiguous ending, and ironically it is the mother's despairing love which threatens the children's survival (see below). However, in the course of the film the main threat is the cruel and unpredictable patriarch, who alternates shows of affection with meanness and egoism.

The work which he forces the children to do is also a threat to their carefree state, and the film emphasises the back-breaking tedium of rural labour. This aspect of the film was frequently commented on by critics, mostly in positive terms, and the film was seen as an antidote to 'those Cognac ad images of Emmanuelle Béart in cheesecloth frocks gaily tending her goats and Gérard Depardieu raising a glass of his cru to the Panavision skyline' (Romney 1997: 16). In this kind of review Veysset herself becomes a champion of the rural, the southern, the provincial – in a word the non-Parisian, an image which she herself seems happy to collude with: '"I wanted to show how people really live in the country. I wanted to show the work, which you never get to see. Postcard images don't move me at all – pretty pictures of trees in bloom," she practically spits' (Romney 1997: 16–17). Here Veysset, perhaps unconsciously, links her film with Agnès Varda's *Sans toit ni loi* (1985), whose heroine, Mona, counts among her few possessions postcards of Van Gogh's paintings of trees in blossom in the south of France. Varda's film contrasts these images with the harshness of the landscape and the failure of Mona's struggle for survival. Similarly, in *Neige*, in summer, clouds of dust cross Veysset's images; the scene in the tomato field is filmed initially from a distance, as if to emphasise the size of the field, the bent bodies lost in the vast expanse of vegetables, the exposure to the elements – wind and sun. The mother is almost perpetually seen handling vegetables: cutting them, cleaning them, lifting crates full of them. In autumn and winter the harsh and desolate landscape mirrors her increasing despair, which is the most significant threat to the children's survival. We do not then find in this film the juxtaposition of idyllic childhood and rural landscape which Holland (1992: 14–15) observes in the advertising stills she analyses:

> For all its modernisation, the nostalgic imagery of childhood refers overwhelmingly to a harmonious and comfortable world before industrial civilisation, when plenty did not depend on work or wealth. A rural idyll is pictured on milk cartons, bread wrappers, supermarket labels, advertisements for food stuffs, and in high-gloss magazines about country living.

The rural world which these children inhabit is far from idyllic; the images of hard physical work in the fields make the connection between the production of food and labour which is missing from the advertisements. The everyday hardships of living in an old and unconverted farmhouse – the lack of bathroom, the damp and cold in winter – are foregrounded, so that the film differentiates between a holiday and real-life experience of the rural south, and the aesthetic charm of the building's exterior, particularly in the summer sequence, is undermined by the cheap furnishings, cramped conditions and lack of light in the interior.[6] This unidealised image of rural childhood was perhaps one of the main factors in the critical success of the film, linking it to Varda's canonical depiction of the south in *Sans toit ni loi*, and thus to the New Wave, and for many critics to the great cinematic tradition of French realism.[7]

The counterpoint to the gruelling physical labour is the children's ability to play, in the least promising circumstances; thus, for instance, they make boats out of courgettes, adapting the tissue paper used to wrap fruit and vegetables as sails, and sailing them down the irrigation channel. The image of these little boats and the transformation of the materials of work into toys which they represent seem to signify the possibility of escape through the rich resources of the imagination. Similarly, the opening shots of the children playing with the 'farms' they have made from mud demonstrate their ability to make something out of nothing. In this notion there is some similarity to the process noted by Richard Dyer (1993) in his analysis of musicals, where in the utopian solution scarcity is replaced by abundance. These sequences seem to associate childhood with the kind of desire and ability to transcend harsh reality which motivate the forms of entertainment analysed by Dyer. However, in both cases the difficulties of the children's lives reassert themselves. The boats reach the elder brother, Bruno, in the fields and he is enjoying their cargo of sweets when the father arrives, shouting angrily at him about the leaking irrigation pipe. The houses and farms of mud have to be destroyed in the winter sequence, as they are in the way. The mother crushes them herself rather than watch 'big boots' ('*les grosses bottes*') of the legitimate sons trampling them. The image of the houses disappearing under her feet forms part of the general sense of possibilities closing down, and of increasing mental and physical confinement of the autumn and winter sequences.[8]

On the psychic level, despite the unanimity of their resistance to the father, the children are shown to suffer as a result of his behaviour and its effect on the mother. On the few occasions when they are seen outside the farm, they are made aware of their illegitimacy: at Cavaillon a neighbour comments that the family does not have children of their age when they tell her who their father is. At school a classmate calls Paul 'bastard' during an argument. At home, as we have seen, they are subjected to the father's violent rages, and forced to observe his arguments with their mother. However, the pain of childhood is perhaps most poignantly suggested through one of the children, Blandine. Critics have commented that the children are treated as a group, rather than as individuals, and generally speaking, this is true.[9] Blandine nonetheless emerges as a significant character from the start of the film (she is the first child to be addressed by name). She is clearly a favourite of the father – he praises her for fetching his lunch – '*tu es bien brave*' – and wants to kiss her goodbye. The film, like the father, marks her out for special attention by a close-up shot of her face when her mother has walked away from her towards the fields. The mother's anger is clearly directed at the father, not at her, and Blandine states her awareness of this to him – 'it's your fault' ('*c'est ta faute*'). Nonetheless the camera lingers on her disappointed face as her mother walks away, signalling a less overtly stated drama than that taking place between the parents. This drama may be more central to the film than is immediately apparent, and Christiane Olivier's feminist rewriting of Freud's theories of infantile development seem pertinent. Olivier writes of the female child's frustrated desire for her mother, arguing that feminine traits, such as relationality, become a way of counteracting the absence of a desiring maternal gaze directed at her, and of filling the inner void which results from that lack:

If the call and the cry have the function of signalling awareness
of distance from the mother and of re-establishing the link with
her, having cried more during the first months of life, little girls
begin to talk earlier, thus indicating an absence, a distance to be
crossed to reach the mother, which does not exist in the boy of the
same age. (Olivier 1980: 82)[10]

In Cavaillon Blandine shows that she is missing and grieving for her mother
by refusing to eat. In bed on the first night she asks Paul to say goodnight
to her again, as her mother always says a last goodnight to her, and she can't
sleep without this ritual. Paul reluctantly mumbles 'goodnight', and Blandine's
slightly discontented sigh indicates that this was not the nurturing voice of
the mother. Poignantly, at the end of the film, when the mother is contemplat-
ing collective suicide, Blandine speaks after the other children have gone to
sleep, anxious to elicit the precious, final 'goodnight my pet' ('*bonne nuit ma
puce*'). This ritual seems indicative of the kind of struggle to reach the mother
described by Olivier, and Blandine, like Olivier's little girl, uses language to try
to cross the gap created by darkness, physical and psychic separation. Blandine also fits into the classic scenario of Olivier's *Les Enfants de Jocaste* by
trying to win her mother back from the father. She stands outside the closed
door of the bedroom during the mother's afternoon siesta with the father: 'I
want you to come out' ('*je veux que tu viennes*'). The mother emerges, and the
pleasure of reunion with her perhaps leads Blandine to acquiesce to the threatened departure for Cavaillon if it is her mother's wish. In Olivier's schema the
absence (and in this case inadequacy) of the father compound the little girl's
uncertainty about her own desirability and her romance with her mother.

If Blandine is depicted as a needy little girl, there are hints of a similar
neediness in the mother herself, who is '*une fille de l'assistance publique*'
(an orphan) in the father's words and who, by her own declaration, has been
marked by her experiences in the orphanage when she was little. Her father
was even more absent, as we discover towards the end of the film, when she
recounts her childhood to the children: 'My father is my most beautiful childhood memory but I didn't see much of him'.[11] A modern audience, given its
probable exposure to the discourses of psychology, would be quite likely to
make the link between this lost father and her apparently inexplicable attachment to the man who was to become the father of her seven children, and who,
as she tells the children, promised a home and family early in their encounter.
If the mother is depicted as a rather textbook case of emotional deprivation in
childhood leading to a lifetime of dysfunctional relationships, Blandine's drama
is more subtle and more everyday. The mother is present, and her affectionate
behaviour towards all the children is highlighted (the film has been described

by Veysset as *'un hommage à l'art maternel, à la mère'* and is dedicated to her mother (see Chevassu 1996). This is certainly how it was read by critics: the poetic language of the *Cahiers* piece, for instance, suggests the power and resonance of the idea of an infinitely nurturing maternal presence:

> By sacrificing herself as much as possible, she comforts her progeny and creates a space of freedom and protection for them. Harking back to the old imaginary association of countryside, the earth and maternal symbolism: fertility and protection, the film stays throughout with the point of view of a mother who protects her children without knowing them any better for this. The mother – territory, guardian of the process of a shared memory which deposits itself and is fertilised in her. (Richou 1996: 58)

And yet, she is also an ambivalent figure. In the early part of the film she leaves the children in the afternoons to be with the father; the eldest son, Bruno accuses her of forgetting 'everything too quickly', and in an exchange which ends with an awkward silence blames their situation on her inability to leave. Some collusion with the father's cruelty is an inevitable consequence of the fact that despite everything, she stays with him – thus it is the mother's feet which crush the children's toy houses. The ambiguity of the final scene renders ambivalence her most significant characteristic at this point: she is both the giver of life and the greatest threat to the children's survival. The fact that the ending is left open, that we do not know whether the snow is real or a dream (leading to death) intensifies this ambivalence.[12] In the end, the mother's despair, her own unmet needs, which are perhaps the source of the maternal vocation (described as originating in a dream she had at sixteen), also determine its limitations. The case of Blandine highlights this early in the film and serves to link these exceptional circumstances to the inevitable limitations of parental love, and the equally inevitable totality of the child's demands. Blandine's love for her mother cannot be satisfied; the nurturing presence can never give enough, and longing and anxiety are seen as fundamental elements of childhood, or at least female childhood.

Restoring the myth of happy childhood

Despite the omnipresence of the threats of physical work, of the parents' sadomasochistic dynamic, and of the anxieties and fears inherent in childhood itself, the film returns repeatedly to the association of childhood with the kind of euphoric moments typified by the credits sequence. In each season there is a special moment when everyday experience seems to be transcended. At the end of the summer sequence, the mother takes the children to watch a firework display in the nearby town: shots of the fireworks alternate with close-ups of the children's expressions of wonder and amazement, and their comments and cries are the only sounds. The film's structure – the fact that this scene ends a 'season' – lends this moment a heightened significance. In the autumn section, a formal device, the use of slow-motion, highlights a scene where the children shelter under a sheet of plastic which they all hold above their heads as they run to school. Again there are close-ups of smiling faces and the theme of creating something special from the everyday, as well as the notion of the children's collective unity, is reinforced by the image. In winter it is of course Christmas – complete with candles, jokes, songs and shoes of all sizes left under the tree – which provides the magic, culminating in the snow which closes the film. Snow, even more than fireworks or rain, is capable of transforming the landscape, and is associated with exactly the kind of picture-postcard prettiness which Veysset vehemently rejects. Symbolically the children also escape from the dark miasmas of the conjugal bedroom into the fresh air and 'innocence' of enveloping whiteness and their own play. Whilst the summer and autumn moments of euphoria are based in realism, in the final sequence the fairytale element of the film dominates. Veysset has commented on the fact that the number of children in the family is an intended reference to the fairytale, and on the combination of everyday experience and the children's dream world which she hoped to convey:

> I wanted it to be both realistic and dream-like in relation to the children. The idea of the tale was present in my mind as I made the film. There were many moments when I wanted to be in the universe of the children, who can escape from everyday life. The fact that there are seven children for example, was linked to the fairytale. (Quoted in Ostria and Roth 1996: 61)[13]

The parents themselves, as well as constituting threats of different kinds to the 'children's universe', seem part of this fairytale structure. The mother's ambivalence is overlaid by repeated affectionate gestures which link her with archetypal images of nurturing femininity – the good fairy, or as the *Cahiers* critic points out, Snow White looking after the seven dwarfs. The father, on the other hand, is 'the wicked wolf' of the fairytales, who prowls and spies on his 'prey', and who has almost no redeeming features. This structure could be read as a defense against parental ambivalence, a kind of Kleinian splitting, so that all the goodness is concentrated in the mother and all the badness in the father. Graham Dawson, who has used Klein in his analysis of boys' adventure stories comments: 'The internal landscape of images produced by severe splitting, as described by Klein, resembles a fairytale world of benevolent wish-fulfilling fairy godmothers, malevolent and threatening witches, and other 'helper' and 'persecutor' figures' (1994: 36). If this kind of inner landscape is reminiscent of Veysset's film, the notion of narrative as a defence against anxiety, a means of obtaining composure, which Dawson explores may also be relevant here. The film mobilises both desires and anxieties about childhood. Childhood is represented as a separate and special world and, as Jacqueline Rose (1984: 9) has pointed out in her discussion of the adventure story and the fairytale, this corresponds to an adult desire:

> But what I want to stress in both cases is the idea which they share of a primitive or lost state to which the child has special access. The child is, if you like, something of a pioneer who restores these worlds to us, and gives them back to us with a facility or directness which ensures that our own relationship to them is, finally, safe.

The threats to these worlds and resulting anxieties could not be more poignantly presented, and yet in the end both are contained by the fairytale elements, which allow us to believe in the good version of the ending, and by the euphoric moments of play or pleasure in simple things – rain, fireworks, snow.

These moments are particularly powerful because they resemble fragments of memory, or perhaps more accurately, they resemble a common cultural image of childhood memories – the delight in simple pleasures, the ability to transcend the everyday, as Veysset herself suggests. Thus the film's realism, as well as its fairytale qualities, guarantees the containment of anxieties about childhood. Interestingly, the film as a whole, and these sequences particularly, has been read as autobiographical, despite Veysset's vehement denials, and absolute refusal to be drawn on the topic of her own childhood. Thus Pascal Richou, writing in *Cahiers* states confidently, 'They are making a store of happy memories for themselves, memories which of course are those of Sandrine Veysset' (1996: 58).[14] Thus we enter the domain of a kind of universal childhood which all can relate to and recognise, and which in the end is free of the contradictions of social injustice and sexuality. As in Peter Pan childhood in *Y aura-t-il de la neige à Noël?* 'serves as a term of universal social reference which conceals all the historical divisions and difficulties of which children, no less than ourselves, form a part' (Rose 1984: 10). The film successfully balances the expression of anxieties with their containment in the combination of fairytale and a form of 'autobiographical' reminiscence, a collective, mythical memory of childhood, rather than an individual story.

Perhaps, however, the best fairytale of all is the one which is constructed outside the film by the critics, and in which Veysset is both the 'enfant terrible' and the new talent of French cinema. Few critics are able to resist the desire to narrate Veysset's ordinary background, her encounter with Carax and sudden rise to fame. In its perpetual search for a new 'new wave' of French cinematic genius, the critical establishment is drawn to a story reminiscent of that of François Truffaut: the deprived childhood and the benign patron and father-figure (Bazin in Truffaut's case). Thus, despite Veysset's denials, the film comes to represent her suffering, that of a rural childhood, just as *Les 400 coups* became the story of Truffaut's own life, and of urban deprivation. The 'rags to riches' narrative,[15] the belief in the inevitable recognition of talent by benign helpers, and the individualism and happy faith in current industrial arrangements which it implies, are perhaps as important to contemporary French cinema as the myth of childhood is to modern audiences.

Notes

[1] In this reviewers took their cue from Veysset herself who commented, 'I wanted it to be realistic and dream-like at the same time in relation to the children' (*Je voulais que ce soit à la fois réaliste et onirique par rapport aux enfants*') (Ostria and Roth 1996: 59). Thus the *Cahiers* article on the film concludes, 'A "fairytale" effect: Snow-white, the ogre, and the seven dwarfs to conclude this stark, deep first film which is as exciting and tough as the countryside itself can be' (Richou 1996: 58).

[2] '*oublie un peu ces enfants*'

[3] '*Ils reprennent à leur compte cet état illégitime que leur impose le père*'

[4] The presence of Moroccan workers on the farm emphasises the colonial and patriarchal structure of exploitation on which it is based. It is also reminiscent of Varda's *Sans Toit ni loi* (1985).

[5] '*Je resterais bien si je pouvais*'

[6] The darkness of the interior is emphasised, along with the father's avarice, by his habit of systematically switching off the lights when he enters the room.

[7] Darke comments, for instance, 'It derives from a particularly French brand of realism that stretches across the films of Maurice Pialat, Jean Renoir and Marcel Pagnol' (1997: 10). He also recognises the parallels with *Sans toit ni loi*.

[8] Veysset has commented on this trajectory towards claustrophobic confinement: 'After the summer scenes I wanted to move towards something more sober. This fitted in well with the film because the idea was that in summer there are lots of people around, going in and out, and everything is open. Then, little by little, the film shrinks into a smaller space and into more brutal movements, which become non-movement.' ('*Après les scènes d'été, je voulais aller vers quelque chose de plus sobre. Ce qui collait bien avec le film parce que l'idée était qu'en été, il y ait beaucoup de monde, qu'on rentre, qu'on sorte, que tout soit ouvert. Ensuite, petit à petit, le film se reserre dans l'espace et dans la brutalité du mouvement, qui devient non-mouvement*' (Ostria and Roth 1996: 61).

[9] Richou comments, 'As a result these children are not treated as separate characters in their own right. At most we have retained their names and a few details about them by the end.' ('*Du coup, ces enfants ne seront pas traités chacun comme des personnages à part entière. Tout au plus aurons-nous à la fin retenu leurs prénoms et quelques indications sur eux, mais guère plus*')

(1996: 58).

[10] '*Si l'appel et le cri ont pour fonction de signaler la perception de l'écart avec la mère, et de rétablir le lien avec elle, après avoir pleuré davantage dans les premiers mois de la vie, voilà que les filles se mettent à parler plus tôt, témoignant d'une absence, d'une distance à franchir pour rejoindre la mère, qui n'existe pas chez le garçon du même âge*'

[11] '*Moi mon père c'est le plus beau souvenir de mon enfance, pourtant je ne l'ai pas beaucoup vu*'

[12] Veysset has explained how she kept the end open to avoid people arguing: 'I had treated the story in such a way that the ending is open, it's possible to think the mother dreams the end or that it's reality.' ('*J'avais traité l'histoire de façon à ce que la fin soit ouverte, qu'on puisse penser que la mère rêve la fin ou bien que c'est la réalité.*') (Ostria and Roth 1996: 60)

[13] '*Je voulais que ce soit à la fois réaliste et onirique par rapport aux enfants. L'idée du conte était présente à mon esprit en tournant le film. Il y avait plein de moments où je voulais qu'on soit dans l'univers des enfants qui s'échappent de la vie courante. Le fait qu'il y'ait sept enfants, par exemple, était lié au conte*'

[14] '*Ils sont en train de se fabriquer des souvenirs heureux, qui sont bien sûr ceux de Sandrine Veysset elle-même*'

[15] If the 'rags to riches' narrative is compelling, the subsequent fall from favour with the second film, released in 1998 – *Victor ... pendant qu'il est trop tard* also has a certain inevitability.

Space, place and community in CHACUN CHERCHE SON CHAT
Lucy Mazdon

Chacun cherche son chat (Vertigo Productions/France 2 Cinéma) was released in France on 3 April 1996. The third full-length feature of director Cédric Klapisch, the film achieved both relatively healthy box-office figures (435,196 admissions in France in its first two months of exhibition) and a generally positive critical response (it won a prize at the Berlin Film Festival in 1996 and Garance Clavel was nominated *meilleur espoir féminin* in the *Césars* of 1997). Klapisch's earlier full-length films were *Riens du tout* (1992) and *Le Péril jeune* (1994), both of which were comedies. The latter won the *Grand Prix* at the Chamrousse Film festival in 1994. Klapisch has also directed a number of short films, notably his works for *3000 Scénarios contre un virus*, a series of shorts produced in 1994 as part of the French AIDS campaign. He followed *Chacun cherche son chat* with *Un Air de famille* (1997), an adaptation of the popular stage play written by Jean-Pierre Bacri and Agnes Jaoui. This film enjoyed immense success at the French box office and went on to win a *César* as well as two awards at the Montreal Film Festival. His most recent work is *Peut-être* (1999), a science fiction film set in a Paris of the future and made with a budget of 75 million francs. Ironically, Klapisch's growing status as a French film-maker is perhaps best illustrated by the fact that Miramax is currently remaking *Chacun cherche son chat* for the American market. This can certainly be attributed to the film's reception in France and its rather more surprising success in the United States. Twenty-three French language films were released in the American market in 1997. *Chacun cherche son chat* was distributed by Sony Classics who had purchased the rights to the film at the Sundance Festival. A limited release on 20 June 1997 was gradually extended until sixty copies had been made and the film had attracted around 330,000 spectators and 1.5 million dollars in box-office takings, making it the most successful French language film in the United States that year. Evidently the impact of the film should not be overstated. The total number of spectators for the twenty-three French films shown that year stands at only 2.4 million, a derisory figure when compared to audiences for indigenous productions. Interestingly, one of the major success stories in the American market that year was another French film, Luc Besson's *Le Cinquième élément*, which earned over 65 million dollars and attracted around 14 million spectators. Nevertheless, this is perhaps the exception which proves the rule. Besson's film was made in English, employed Hollywood stars and was distributed according to the norms of the Hollywood blockbuster with 2,500 copies released in its opening weekend, thus underlining the prominence of the American 'super-production' and the extremely marginal place accorded to the vast majority of foreign films.

The success of *Chacun cherche son chat* is rather surprising if we consider its remarkably slight plot. It tells the story of a young woman, Chlöe (Clavel), living in the Bastille area of Paris. Chlöe's attempts to find someone to take care of her cat Gris-Gris while she goes on holiday are unsuccessful until someone suggests she try Madame Renée (Renée Lecalm), an elderly neighbour who is very fond of cats. Chlöe returns from her holiday to discover that Gris-Gris has disappeared. The rest of the film chronicles her attempts to find her cat with the help of her gay flat-mate, Michel (Olivier Py), Renée, another neighbour, Djamel (Zinedine Soualem), and a vast number of other local residents. Chlöe's search for Gris-Gris seems to coincide with a search for a partner. She sleeps with a young man she meets in the area (Romain Duris) and the film ends with the promise of some form of relationship between Chlöe and another neighbour, Bel Canto (Joël Brisso).

Plural appeal and multiple pleasures

However, the film appeals on a number of levels. Klapisch initially intended to produce the story as a short film, yet he claims that while shooting he came across so many fascinating people and ideas he decided to improvise them into his script. This sense of the film's location actually giving rise to its narrative and thematic concerns is revealed in the focus on the area in which it was shot and in the naturalistic acting style of many of the principal characters. Most of the actors were new to cinema and many of them, notably Renée Lecalm, were non-professional actors. The use of non-professionals, coupled with a clearly recognisable social and geographical setting recalls the work of British directors such as Ken Loach and Mike Leigh.[1] A number of contemporary French film-makers, for example Erick Zonca, director of the critically acclaimed *La Vie revée des anges* (1998), have described their debt to the work of these directors, work which forms a marked contrast with the so-called *cinéma du look* so prominent in French production of the 1980s and 1990s.[2] Klapisch's espousal of these particular cinematic traits thus positions him within a discernible body of contemporary French (and European) production. Nevertheless, the film also looks back to its cinematic antecedents. Its very precise Parisian locations recall a number of other filmic representations of the city: *A Bout de souffle* (Godard, 1960), *Les 400 coups* (Truffaut, 1959) and *Bob le flambeur* (Melville, 1956) to name but a few. Perhaps most strikingly the film recalls the work of Eric Rohmer. Its slight plot, focus on the experiences and emotions of a female protagonist and precise locations echo Rohmer's *Contes et proverbes*. Indeed, this connection was apparently seen to be a useful marketing tool by the film's British video distributors as the video copy is preceded by a trailer for Rohmer's *Conte d'été* (1996). In many ways, then, *Chacun cherche son chat* typifies much contemporary French production through its nods to the various histories of cinema. Like many recent French films it combines the stylistic features of the New Wave with the social comedy of both French cinema of the 1930s and 1940s and the work of Leigh, Loach *et al*. In contrast to the work of directors such as Besson (notably the aforementioned *Le Cinquième Élément*), Klapisch's film is very clearly and deliberately rooted in a certain construction of French 'national' cinema and a specific portrayal of French (or at least Parisian) life.

Paradoxically, it may be these very specifics which enabled the film's relatively broad appeal. To an American audience the film almost certainly corresponded to a notion of 'French' life and 'French' cinema. The work's focus on dialogue and character and its romantic concerns typify much of what is frequently claimed to distinguish French production from the action and spectacle of its Hollywood counterparts. For example, on 30 November 1998 an American correspondent to the Internet Movie Database described *Chacun cherche son chat* as 'a lovely, light, pointless film ... A few days in the life of a young woman framed by the search for her missing pet. I was charmed'.[3] The Parisian location incorporates sufficient iconic images of 'France' (the *boulangerie*, the local bistro, the gossiping concierge) to construct a generalised 'Frenchness' easily accessible to an American audience.[4] However, the ability to function on this level does not reduce the extreme precision of the film's cultural and spatial references. It is almost certain that French audiences would interpret the film according to these specifics (and this is surely Klapisch's intention), thus suggesting that the film becomes something rather different via these shifting modes of reception. For American audiences it is a typically 'French' light romantic comedy. For French audiences it is both this and a far more specific exploration of spatial and social concerns.

This multiple appeal is extended through the film's musical soundtrack, incorporating a variety of musical forms but dominated by contemporary popular music, much of it French in origin.[5] This combines with the fashionable Bastille location, the young stars and the featured clubs and bars, to appeal to a youthful audience familiar with contemporary French popular culture and the various venues in which it is enjoyed. However, the film also uses non-French music, notably salsa and other forms of so-called 'world' music. These musical styles are certainly popular in France where the failure of indigenous pop/rock music to achieve the prominence of its British counterparts has enabled space for 'other' musical forms. Nevertheless their presence also indicates an attempt to extend the film's appeal beyond a narrowly defined concept of France or French audiences. This is underlined during the film's closing sequence when we hear Portishead's '*Glory Box*', a commercially and critically acclaimed song whose trip-hop origins extend well beyond specific national boundaries.[6] The film also makes use of traditional French *chanson*, most strikingly in the closing scenes in the local bistro. Indeed, the juxtaposition of the clientele's rendition of '*Ça c'est Paris*' and the aforementioned '*Glory Box*' provides a strong example of the film's attempt to address different audiences via its articulation and representation of a number of musical tropes and themes.

Using 'small things' to talk about 'big things'

Despite these different layers of appeal and interpretation Klapisch's emphasis on the specifics of geographical and temporal location is readily apparent. The film is set in the eleventh *arrondissement* of Paris, in the Bastille area also known as Popincourt. Traditionally frequented by artists and the working classes, the area has recently been transformed as new bars, fashionable shops and restaurants have opened around the Bastille Opera House and rent increases have forced out many of the inhabitants. The film opens with a long shot over the rooftops of the *quartier*, firmly anchoring the narrative in this particular space. Cranes tower over the buildings suggesting the twin processes of development and demolition to which Klapisch returns throughout the film. Indeed, a central motif is the demolition of the church Notre Dame de l'Éspérance and the resident's response to its gradual disappearance. The film's setting is explicitly contemporary. This is revealed both in the previously described soundtrack, the clothes of the young protagonists and in a number of other signifiers. For example, as Chlöe, Michel and Djamel distribute fliers asking for information about Gris-Gris, we see posters calling for votes for Lionel Jospin in the ongoing presidential elections.[7] Later in the film we see Chlöe waking up to the radio announcement of Chirac's election victory. Klapisch's insistence upon such details reveals his ambition to represent a very precise socio-historical milieu. This is extended in his other full-length films, which similarly reconstruct very specific locations. Describing *Un Air de famille* and the ways in which it differed from its theatrical source, Klapisch stated:

> I also tried to add social background because I show where it takes place. You see the city where these people live, the kind of apartments they live in and their society ... I wanted this single family to represent their society. I wanted to show people of authority, people of intellect, successful people and unsuccessful people, and show how they feel with each other, and how this is organised. Even though the family is small scale, it represents the whole society, and I wanted to highlight this because I think

what's interesting in a movie is to talk about big things with small things.[8]

This use of 'small things' in order to talk about 'big things' lies at the heart of *Chacun cherche son chat*. Via the minutiae of the *quartier* and Chlöe's search for her cat Klapisch describes shifts in traditional Parisian communities and the impact of an increasingly insistent consumerism.

Tradition and transformation, community and isolation

Chlöe's life-style epitomises the transformations which threaten the traditional way of life of the area. Her job as a make-up artist, subject to the whims of an arrogant and superficial designer, her precarious position as lodger in Michel's apartment, and her relationships all bear witness to a rootlessness and isolation which contrast markedly with the solidarity of the older community. The very fact that she is unable to find anyone to look after her cat reinforces this isolation. At the beginning of the film she asks Michel to care for Gris-Gris. He refuses and suggests she dump the cat at the side of the motorway 'like everyone else'. Michel is her flat-mate and supposedly her best friend and yet he not only advocates the cruel abandonment of her principal object of affection but is also unwilling to help her out. Indeed, later in the film he moves his partner into the apartment without consulting Chlöe, thus revealing a disregard for their friendship and undermining her position in the home.

The opening scenes merit a closer look as they very explicitly set up this sense of fragmentation and loneliness which will be developed throughout the film. A long shot over the roofs of the Bastille area is accompanied by the sound of Chlöe's voice on the telephone and the insistent sound of traffic and drumming. The scene then cuts to the interior of Michel's apartment, where we see Chlöe on the telephone and hear Michel and Jean-Yves (his lover) arguing. Jean-Yves leaves, slamming the door in Michel's face. Chlöe gets up and closes the window in order to shut out the sound of the drumming, which she describes as 'a pain in the arse'. The scene then cuts to an open window from which emanates a much louder drumbeat. This short sequence provides a very succinct representation of the diagetic space and Chlöe's position within it. As we have already seen, the shots over the rooftops dominated by cranes locate the film in the Bastille area. Chlöe's lone voice and vain attempts to find a carer for her cat reveal her isolation. This is reinforced by another phone call later in the film. As the local residents join the search for Gris-Gris, Chlöe receives a number of phone calls from friends of Madame Renée to inform her of their progress. A shot of Chlöe on the phone cuts to the view over the rooftops which opens the film. However, this time her lone voice is replaced by a cacophony of voices suggesting her gradual entry into the local community and underlining her isolation at the film's outset.

Michel's violent argument with Jean-Yves and his claim to have ended their relationship because his lover was getting too serious suggest transitory, superficial couplings which correspond to Klapisch's subsequent portrayal of the transformations in the *quartier*. The incessant drumming is also significant. It invades the area and thus dominates the space in a manner denied to the film's heroine. Its invasion of the *quartier* is offensive (both Chlöe and Madame Renée complain about the noise) and initially anonymous (Chlöe does not know where the noise comes from). This is striking as its overwhelming presence in the area contrasts with the similarly ubiquitous but ultimately positive presence of Madame Renée and her tight-knit group of friends. Moreover, it is Madame Renée who is able to locate the source of the drumming and who unashamedly tells its perpetrator that his musical efforts are 'a pain'. While Chlöe takes the anonymity and inevitability of the drumming for granted, Madame Renée is fully aware of where it comes from and does not hesitate to express her annoyance. Dialogue, communication and respect for others are central to her understanding of life in the neighbourhood in contrast to Chlöe's passive acceptance of the noise and the drummer's selfish persistence. It comes as no surprise to discover that the drummer is the man with whom Chlöe has a brief fling. He typifies the new aspects of the area: fashionably dressed and present in the trendy bars of the *quartier*, his speech consists of little more than exclamations of '*ouiah*' and '*mortel*'. While Chlöe believes their coming together to be based upon numerous fleeting encounters in the area, he claims never to have seen her before and, having slept with her, lies about her identity to a friend on the telephone. In his character Klapisch embodies the selfishness and the superficiality of a contemporary culture which favours image over substance, an incessant and invasive drumbeat over true communication.

Finding a place in the community

This move from isolation to community, from fragmentation to solidarity, is perhaps the film's key theme. Klapisch explores and represents this shift in a number of ways: in the contrast between Chlöe's short-lived fling with the drummer and her developing closeness to Bel Canto; in the juxtaposition of Renée's helpful and dependable group of friends and the petty cruelties and insincerities of the bar culture frequented by Chlöe; in the familiarity of the traditional commerces (the baker and the bistro) and the over-priced superficiality of the new boutiques and the trendy Pause-café. Particularly interesting is the manner in which the film explores these shifts via its broader negotiations of space and the social framework of the Popincourt area. We have already seen that Chlöe's initial isolation is revealed by scenes of her lonely attempts to find a home for Gris-Gris. This is extended as we see her venture outside the apartment. She passes Bel Canto as she leaves the building. He is her neighbour and yet at this point she knows nothing about him (it is of course Renée who reveals his true identity). She argues with the sharp-tongued concierge (an extremely negative image of Parisian life) and proceeds to walk past the hoardings which disguise the demolition and rebuilding of the quartier accompanied by the sound of drumming. Thus her movement through the neighbourhood is shown to be fraught with tension (the argument), solitary (she does not know her neighbours) and surrounded by noise and upheaval.

As the search for the cat begins and she gradually joins the community of local residents, her movement through this space alters. In a scene which follows the series of phone calls described earlier, we see Chlöe walking through a local market. A travelling shot follows her through the stalls and the crowds of people and her relaxed progress through this busy space contrasts with her lonely journey at the beginning of the film. This is reinforced when her walk is interrupted by an elderly woman who, although unknown to Chlöe, is familiar with her and her plight, thanks to yet another elderly resident we see waving from across the street. This self-proclaimed 'cat expert' takes Chlöe to a nearby street map. This map, of a kind found throughout Paris for the use of visitors and tourists unfamiliar with the geography of the city, becomes something quite different as Madame Clavo personalises and transforms its one-dimensional representation of space, describing who lives where and explaining how they can help in the search for Gris-Gris. This move from map to lived experience typifies the film's treatment of the area in which it is set. Rather than use the location as a mere backdrop for the narrative (a means of 'mapping' more important themes and characters), Klapisch sets out to show the *quartier* in all its complex, mobile reality (it is perhaps the film's most important theme and character). Chlöe's new relationship with the area in which she lives culminates in the film's closing sequence. She joins Bel Canto in the local bistro as he says his farewells to his friends. Unlike her earlier visits to the bar during which the locals' mockery of Djamel provoked her anger as she failed to understand the affection it concealed, she is now at ease in their company. Bel Canto kisses her goodbye and, having watched his van depart, her face revealing her growing surprise and pleasure at the possibility of a future relationship with her erstwhile neighbour, she turns and breaks into a run. The film ends with a long travelling shot of a joyful Chlöe running through the streets that she has finally made her own. She has not only found her cat and a potential partner but also a place in the area and amidst the community from which she was previously so alienated.

Peopling the quartier

As we have seen, the Bastille location is perhaps the film's principal protagonist. It is in this *quartier* that Gris-Gris goes missing. Chlöe's search for her cat takes place in the neighbourhood and through this activity she meets the residents who will transform her existence. It is striking that the holiday which necessitates the temporary home for Gris-Gris and thus sets in motion the film's narrative is reduced to two brief shots of Chlöe walking towards and away from the Gare de Lyon and an even shorter image of her in the sea. The film is entirely anchored in its chosen Parisian location. However, this is not to deny the importance of the human protagonists. Indeed, the spatial location and the transformations it has to endure are also developed through the various characters who reside in its apartments and frequent its shops and bars.

Klapisch's portrayal of the film's characters is somewhat simplistic. In contrast to his complex rendering of the geographical location, many of the human actors seem little more than stereotypes which correspond to the oppositions he establishes between the traditional way of life and the encroaching commercialisation. Thus we see the eccentric but extended conversation of the various old ladies involved in the search for Gris-Gris and the affected banalities of Chlöe's colleagues, the meaningless posturing of the selfish drummer and the inarticulate stammering of the kind-hearted, generous Djamel. In other words, the traditional residents are generally well meaning and capable of true feeling while the trendy newcomers are self-obsessed and spiteful. However, although it is undeniable that some of the protagonists are little more than caricatures, the film moves beyond such one-dimensional portraits in its development of its main characters. This is essentially due to the fine performances of the actors. The very fact that the film developed out of Klapisch's involvement with the area and its inhabitants suggests that the credibility of his protagonists will depend far more upon their performances than upon narrative, dialogue and so on. Renée Lecalm is particularly remarkable for her extremely naturalistic style and her rootedness in the film's chosen location.

The relationships which develop between these characters extend the themes of urban transformation and the impact on traditional communities already discussed. We have already examined the contrast between the true community of local residents and the superficial relationships of Chlöe's 'friends' and colleagues. A key element of Chlöe's isolation is her failure to find a partner and the disappointments provoked by these unsatisfactory friendships. This is perhaps best exemplified by the sequence in which Chlöe, after criticism from a colleague for her scruffy, unattractive appearance, dresses up and goes to a bar. Her attempts to choose an outfit (advised by Michel) reveal her lack of self-confidence and the need to project an image which lies at the heart of the culture to which she seems to want to belong. The visit to the bar proves disastrous as her friend fails to join her, she is harassed by a man and then verbally attacked by his girlfriend and finally has to extricate herself from an attempted seduction on the part of the female bar-tender who has accompanied her home. She ends this disastrous evening by sharing Michel's bed. He resists her attempts to sexually arouse him and tells her that she is afraid of men. While Michel's assessment is to some extent corroborated by Chlöe's nervous demeanour, the unpleasantness of the bar culture which she attempts to infiltrate suggests instead that her isolation is due to the unavailability of true friendship and affection. In contrast, the relationships she forms with Djamel, Renée and later, Bel Canto, prove fulfilling and authentic. She is initially angered by the casual mockery of Djamel in the local bistro but comes to realise that it is based upon real feeling, unlike the false compliments of the bar seducer, which disguise nothing but contempt.

This opposition between false friendship and true feeling is demonstrated in the sequence which follows Chlöe's discovery that Michel has moved his partner into their shared apartment. After an extremely hostile encounter with Claude, she approaches Michel to ask how long he will be staying. As they both profess their affection for each other and for Claude the evident hypocrisy of their affirmations is represented by the fact that we see their faces reflected in the mirrors which Michel is polishing in preparation for a sale. The duplicity of the conversation and thus the limitations of their friendship are revealed by this doubling of their images; it is not their 'true' selves speaking but rather a simulacrum of self upon which their rather partial relationship is based. This scene is followed by Chlöe's visit to a waste ground in the company of Renée and one of her friends. Her discovery that the dead cat they have brought her to see is not Gris-Gris provokes joy and gratitude very different to the feigned happiness previously expressed to Michel.

Contemporary nostalgia: having it both ways?

It is very clear where the film's sympathies lie. As the preceding remarks demonstrate, Klapisch is quite categorical in his critique of the impact of urban 'development' upon the traditional way of life of this particular Parisian *quartier*. The negative results of this process are underlined by the eviction of Bel Canto and Gisèle, the numerous locks and graffiti on Madame Renée's front door (indicating a potential violence far removed from the solidarity of her friends) and the closing of traditional shops in favour of boutiques (such as that opened by Chlöe's designer colleague, which is held up to unrelenting ridicule by Renée and her friend). Chlöe finds happiness in the traditional community, not in the trendy life-style to which she initially aspires. Her search for her cat leads her from superficiality, artifice and solitude to true feeling and a sense of belonging. Nevertheless, it would be unfair to accuse Klapisch of an entirely hagiographic account of this community. The racist comments of the concierge who helps Chlöe look for Gris-Gris problematise the solidarity which dominates its representation (the exclusion of non-white 'others' is obviously a less positive aspect of the traditional life-style). Bel Canto's departure is shown to be a positive form of progress. The move from traditional *chanson* to 'Glory Box' in the closing sequence suggests the possibility of a social formation which will combine elements of both the traditional community and the new life-styles (and avoid the pitfalls of each). As we have seen, Chlöe does finally belong to the *quartier* in which she was previously so isolated, and yet she remains alone (the relationship with Bel Canto is a possible future). In other words, rather than simply re-affirming traditional ways of life, *Chacun cherche son chat* can be seen to be positing a way of living in the city in which the networks and sociability of earlier communities hold at bay, but do not entirely encapsulate, the overwhelming isolation of modern urban dwelling.

This leads to a potential problem in the film's treatment of these themes of modern urban life. Klapisch could be accused of trying to have it both ways. He criticises the impact of development on the traditional community and yet ultimately seems to embrace some aspects of it. His film certainly seems to embrace the *quartier* as it was before the advent of the bars and boutiques it mocks. However, the music and fashions so central to these same bars and boutiques are a distinctive feature of the film and indubitably a key part of its audience appeal. Despite the naturalistic acting styles and the recognisable locations the film is quite stylised. A series of binaries organises many of the central moments and themes: for example, the previously described cut from Chlöe and Michel to Chlöe, Renée and Blanche; the cut from the racist remarks of the concierge to Chlöe's embarrassed conversation with three black workers; Chlöe's first futile visit to a bar and her trip to the local bistro with Djamel. This use of opposing scenes evidently reinforces the film's ideological positions but it also suggests a certain aesthetic self-consciousness which could be seen to sit somewhat uncomfortably with its generally naturalistic feel. This is particularly evident in Chlöe's dream sequence which was much criticised by reviewers of the film. It does strike a rather jarring note and perhaps reveals the 'work in progress' aspect of the film. *Chacun cherche son chat* does occasionally smack of an extended short film and the work of a young director developing the tools of his trade. The sense of 'having it both ways' should thus perhaps be seen as symptomatic of this process and of the film's plural identities. Certainly the tensions and paradoxes it provokes create a number of potential pleasures and prevent the film from becoming little more than a rose-tinted vision of 'traditional' Parisian life.

Much more could be said about this film. Indeed, its apparent inconsequence belies a wealth of meanings and pleasures which help to explain its box-office success. The film is paradoxical, criticising the impact of commercialisation – notably 'youth culture' – while simultaneously exploiting this very culture for its own subsequent commercial career. However it should not be condemned for this. Indeed, it is the trap which any film-maker must face. If a film wants to find an audience it must inevitably embrace the commercial processes it may aesthetically and ideologically censure. Klapisch's film is both explicitly contemporary (in its soundtrack, its representation of fashionable parts of Paris and in its aesthetic and narrative choices) and decidedly nostalgic (in its account of fast-disappearing ways of life and in its references to earlier cinematic styles). This duality locates it very firmly in the 1990s French culture from which it emerged, a culture in which an unproblematic turning to the past[9] goes hand in hand with the mythologising of the millennium and the possibilities of technological progress. *Chacun cherche son chat* is not part of these discourses. It is far too sensibly small-scale for that. Nevertheless, its contemporary nostalgia is not unfamiliar and ultimately the film should be applauded for its finite and detailed narration of a specific story, a specific moment and above all, a specific space.

Notes

[1] Both directors have had very long and productive careers. Loach's recent work includes *Riff-Raff* (1990), *Raining Stones* (1993), *Ladybird Ladybird* (1994) and *My Name is Joe* (1998). Leigh's recent films include *Life is Sweet* (1990), *Naked* (1993), *Secrets and Lies* (1996) and *Career Girls* (1997).

[2] Examples include *Diva* (Beineix, 1980), *Le Grand Bleu* (Besson, 1988) and *Les Amants du Pont-Neuf* (Carax, 1991).

[3] Internet Movie Database, http://uk.imdb.com (1 September 1999).

[4] Useful comparisons can be made with American representations of France and French identity in films such as *Gigi* (Minnelli, 1958) and *Green Card* (Weir, 1990). The specifics of place and social class are effaced in favour of a generalised, stereotypical portrayal of France (consider Depardieu's garlic-crunching, wine-drinking character in the later film).

[5] Examples include '*Food for Love*' performed by Ceux qui marchent debout and '*J'veux du soleil*' performed by Au Petit Bonheur.

[6] The term 'trip-hop' was coined to describe the music of the likes of Massive Attack, Portishead and Tricky. It has proved popular in France partly thanks to marketing and perhaps also due to the markedly multi-racial identity of both its exponents and its musical references.

[7] These elections took place in 1995.

[8] Cited by Beth Williams on the British video release of *Un Air de famille* (Tartan Video, 1998).

[9] For example, in popular 'heritage' films such as *Germinal* (Berri, 1993), *Le Hussard sur le toit* (Rappeneau, 1995) and *Le Colonel Chabert* (Angelo, 1994).

Screening the past: representing resistance in UN HEROS
TRES DISCRET
Howard Seal

During the latter years of the twentieth century the role the French played during and immediately after World War Two underwent rigorous reappraisal. The controversy created by the publication of Pierre Pean's *Une Jeunesse Française: François Mitterrand 1934–1947* (1994) became evidence of the complexity and sensitivity with which this period was still viewed, arousing distant anxieties which post-war France had endeavoured to suppress. Equally telling are the circumstances surrounding the trial of Maurice Papon, who on 2 April 1998 was found guilty in a Bordeaux court of complicity in the deportation of 1,500 Jews. The trial had a major impact on wider French society, motivating large sections of the population to confront a period in their history which they had previously approached ambivalently.

It was within this context that Jacques Audiard made *Un Héros très discret* (1996), a film set in the years following the end of World War Two. The film concerns the story of Albert Dehousse, played at different stages of his life by David Fernandes, Mathieu Kassovitz, and Jean-Louis Trintignant, and recounts his personal narrative as he transforms himself from under-achieving travelling salesman into celebrated war hero. As such the central character can be readily understood as a metaphor for the French experience more generally, as Dehousse strives to reinvent himself not in opposition to the interests of the newly established Fourth Republic but rather in complicity, or even, perhaps ironically, in *collaboration* with it.

However, the film is of interest not just in the way it examines specific aspects of contemporary French history but also in the way it examines the cultural production of history more generally; in particular the way in which it brings into focus the contradictions and incongruities implicit in the process of making the events of the past known in the present through conventional narrative and realist forms.[1] Before we consider such matters in more detail it is worth examining further the political and cultural context into which this film fits, particularly because it directly informs the film-making strategy employed by Audiard as he attempts to grapple with a period from the past which he has described as one in which 'the biggest lie of our generation was created ... the lie of France as a war resister' (Darke 1987: 24).

The publication in 1994 of *Une Jeunesse Française: François Mitterrand 1934–1947* created huge interest in France. Not only did it draw attention to the controversial life of the first Socialist President of the Fifth Republic, but it also drew attention to post-liberation France and the political intrigue which the end of the war instigated. From the myth developed by De Gaulle that he foiled a Communist plot to the myth that surrounds the *épuration*, post-liberation France became a time in which what was known and what was remembered remained obscured by false recollections, self-delusion and personal and political necessities. Above all the period is marked by the myth of *la France résistante*, a tale of national heroism regarded as an essential precondition for national unity and post-war reconstruction and regeneration. The heightened interest in Mitterrand's wartime record, and the political machinations which followed the liberation, were also brought under close scrutiny as a result of the trial of Maurice Papon. The life of Papon, and the story that surrounds him, is particularly relevant in a discussion of this film. Not only was the film released shortly before Papon went to trial, but – as we shall see – for a film whose central themes depend upon personal reinvention and the relationship between the requirements of the State and private self-interest, the life of Maurice Papon seems particularly appropriate.

The circumstances which lay behind other events which had emerged from the dark days of World War Two, in particular the trial of Klaus Barbie, the Gestapo Chief, and the exploits surrounding Paul Touvier, head of the wartime collaborationist militia in Lyon, could conveniently be dismissed by the French as aberrant and outside the French experience. The trial of Papon, however, a man whose life mirrored the French history of the twentieth century, could not be so easily dismissed and proved to have reverberations throughout France. During the trial the media became increasingly engrossed in French wartime activities, reflecting widespread concern. Revelations of wartime activities led to an impression that France, rather than being *résistante*, had in fact been entirely collaborationist. During this time expressions of regret regarding their wartime activities were offered by the Catholic Church, as well as the professional associations of the police department, lawyers and doctors. Furthermore, the decision to put the innovators of cinema, the Lumière Brothers, on the 100-franc note was reversed when it became known that they were Vichy sympathisers (Fenby 1998).

As with the fictional Albert Dehousse, a brief account of the real life of Papon demonstrates his particular penchant for reinvention, pragmatism and survival. Early in his life Papon aligned himself with the Radical Socialist parties, securing a job working within the Air Ministry for the Popular Front Government. During the war he joined the Vichy administration, rising quickly to become Secretary-General of the Prefecture based in Bordeaux where Jewish Affairs and other matters arising out of the Occupation were among his responsibilities. In mid-1944, just a few months before the liberation of Bordeaux, he made contact with the local Resistance leader and soon after became his Chief of Staff. Amongst his post-war offices he was a senior Official at the Interior Ministry, later becoming chief of the Paris police, and was in command when it was responsible for the death of hundreds of Algerians protesting against French activities in the North African colony. In 1968 he was elected to the National Assembly where he headed the Parliamentary Finance Committee, soon to become Minister for the Budget under Giscard d'Estaing. His personal story is thus appropriate here not just because his trial supplies the cultural and political background for the film, but also because, as a man able to adjust to the circumstances which surround him, he displays all the characteristics of the film's main character. Not only do we see both these men transform themselves with chameleonesque ease but they do so to the requirements of the French State.

Like Papon, Dehousse also manages to align himself with the new administration. In the film we see him leaving his small town and moving to Paris and there recreating an alternative version of his, to date, unremarkable life. As a result of some fortuitous encounters he decides to reinvent himself as a member of the Resistance, spending a great deal of time analysing their behaviour, scrutinising their manners as well as purchasing their various publications and mastering the details of their recent history. Once he feels comfortable with his new-found knowledge, he successfully infiltrates the *anciens résistantes*. Now on the inside he is rapidly accepted into its ranks, culminating in the offer of a post as Lieutenant Colonel and being sent to French-occupied Germany to manage psychological and propaganda operations. In Germany, Dehousse is again a great success, skilfully carrying out his illusion. Eventually, however, he begins to suffer under the weight of his own deception, in which his life has become a lie, and he confesses to his lover. Following an incident in which he mandates the execution of seven French Wehrmacht volunteers, he chooses to denounce himself to the authorities. Partly to conceal their own incompetence, and partly to safeguard the myth of resistance, the French administration treat him with leniency and we are given to believe that an eventful and gleaming career continued, appropriately shrouded in mystery, suspicion and debate.

Throughout the film Dehousse demonstrates his growing expertise and shows himself to be both a consummate liar and a skilled master of reinvention, adept at imitation and creator of artifice. He is also forced to recreate himself, to make himself something he is not. Our 'self-made hero', the English title for the film and one which seems particularly appropriate, must – like France – reconfigure his identity and become something other than he was. For each new Republic, for each new administration, Papon changes his colours to become representative of what is required, whatever the State demands. Like so many others, when Papon argued in his defence that he acted in accordance with the requirements of the State and that he was merely following orders it seems no matter how odious his crimes may have been he sincerely believed that he worked in the service of his country. Indeed, according to Jonathan Fenby, to distinguish between the interests of the French State and the interests of a French-trained civil servant is a fallacious distinction. Thus he writes about Papon that 'he as much as any man can be taken as a symbol of devoted service to the state – thus, to himself' (Fenby 1998: 278).

Dehousse had no such training but his post-war transformation and the manner in which he achieves his new reality mirrors not only Papon but the very transformation which an entire nation underwent. However, unlike Papon he was no collaborator, and thus his experience of the war years was perhaps more in keeping with that of the majority who were neither collaborators nor resisters but who were indifferent and detached from the severity of the world around them. To this extent Audiard seems conscious of the need to redress the balance which had characterised many of the French films which dealt with the war, in particular the Gaullist myth of *la France résistante*.

The immediately post-war French cinema was particularly sensitive to the need to serve the interests of the 'new' state through reinforcing the myth of the Resistance. For example, the film *Boule de suif* (1945), set during the Franco-Prussian War, functions at an unambiguous allegorical level in which a prostitute brings about her own death when she refuses to entertain the Prussian soldiers. Many other films, such as *La Libération de Paris* (Chanas, 1944), *Le Jugement dernier* (Chanas, 1945), *Jéricho* (Calef, 1946), *Les Clandestines* (Chotin, 1946), *Le Père tranquille* (Clément, 1946), and *La Bataille du rail* (Clément, 1946), combine to provide a collective impression to corroborate the notion that the French were unified in their resistance. While on one hand a number of these films merely celebrated acts of resistance, there were also more complex ideological operations at work, which sought to bind post-war French society to the activities of the Resistance. *La Bataille du rail* is typical in that it shows ordinary railway workers actively sabotaging the railway system. Not only are we never shown collaborators but, rather, it seems that the whole population is participating in the act of resistance. Furthermore, in contrast to more formulaic and familiar representations, particularly those associated with classical Hollywood, the film does not emphasise the acts of one heroic character in particular but rather focuses on the collective, thereby inviting different forms of identification. The film's realism, which is partly accomplished through a documentary style, lends *Un Héros* even greater authenticity, further affirming its ideological project. A feature of these films was also to broaden those exploits, which constituted an act of resistance. This approach can be best seen in *Le Silence de la mer* (Melville, 1949) in which the act of resistance is extended to the refusal to talk to a German soldier. The ideological project of these films was not limited to associating post-war France with *la France résistante*; they also played a role in unifying the French people under a single banner for the difficult years ahead. Thus in *Jéricho* the Resistance is characterised by a broad cross-section of society, while in *Le Père tranquille* not only are the Resistance members on display drawn from the common people but they are also seen to be from the entire family and spanning a broad age range.[2]

Thus cinema played an important role in developing and sustaining the national myths developed following the end of the war. Furthermore it should be remembered that during this time a censorship committee, the *Commission Militaire Nationale*, was in place, responsible for situating the image of the Resistance as a key player in generating national unity. Clearly these films were not interested in investigating difficult questions and it seems that French cinema, like the French nation, was eager to put the past behind them. Certainly questions of collaboration, anti-Semitism and French guilt were not explored, and it was not until 1969 that an alternative history of the French experience of German occupation was explored from a new critical stance. Two films in particular, *Le Chagrin et la pitié* (Ophuls, 1969) and *L'Armée des ombres* (Melville, 1970), were responsible for going some way in redressing the balance, although the hostility of their reception (it was well over a decade before *Le Chagrin et la Pitié* was shown on French television) demonstrates the unease with which this period was still viewed. Since then a number of other films have been made dealing with this period, most noticeably *Lacombe Lucien* (1973) and *Au Revoir les enfants* (1987), both by the director Louis Malle. While both of these films, and their popularity, suggest maturity on behalf of the French in dealing with uneasy and complex issues, it is a period of history which remains inadequately explored in French cinema.[3]

Audiard's approach is influenced not just by a need to reconsider this painful period in history but to do so while acknowledging that to represent a past, particularly a past which is contentious and fragmented, is a precarious endeavour. His intention to use conventionally contradictory modes of representation to address the complexity of portraying the past is signalled right from the start, when we are told that 'the best lives are invented'. Soon after, distinctive techniques are introduced aimed at sustaining the paradoxical effect whereby history is regularly undermined in contrast to fiction which is typically privileged. Thus we see the departed father of Dehousse, clad in military attire, coming to life within a framed picture, laughing and singing, and ironically declaring *'Vive la France'*. Only later do we learn that he died a drunk rather than a hero of the Great War – as the Young Dehousse had been lead to believe. Throughout the film our faith in the historical narrative is further undermined by a battery of cinematic and discursive techniques which throw into disarray the reality privileged in more traditional historical re-enactments. Thus we witness the recurring and arbitrary sequences in which musicians perform the soundtrack, deliberately drawing attention towards the artifice and away from any attempt at historical verisimilitude.

Other techniques are also employed to bring into question the history on display – indeed Jacques Audiard said he wanted 'everything to be false'. This is further achieved through the use of contradictory recollections: historians, sociologists, Vichy apologists and those who knew the real Dehousse who offer conflicting testimony about the man and the period in which he lived. We are naturally suspicious of these documentary-style talking heads, because throughout the film we have come to learn that Dehousse is indeed a fraud. However, things are a little more complicated than this, since they are no more or less fraudulent than the man they seek to unmask. For Audiard they merely represent another layer of confusion, bringing forward more questions over the history on display. This is equally true of the way in which Audiard has introduced documentary footage into the film. He cleverly uses both original documentary material as well as footage which appears to be original but which Dehousse has managed to infiltrate. While we may get pleasure from the way in which he has bluffed his way into photographs he has no right to be in, the result is to throw into question more generally the authenticity of the historical document itself, further blurring the boundaries between fact and fiction, between reality and falsity.

Audiard's film is also valuable in the way he has endeavoured to find the appropriate form to account for complex historical events which have already been severely altered through layers of additional representations as well as the fragmentation of memory itself. In 'The Modern Event' Hayden White discusses what he believes to be those unique events, which characterise the history of the twentieth century. He argues that these events are distinctive in that they challenge the familiar historiographic narratives which strive for verisimilitude and coherence, and can be found through more traditional renderings. These changes, he argues, are as a result of two significant developments. Firstly, he suggests that the twentieth century has witnessed events of such horror and magnitude that they were hitherto unimaginable and thus lay outside the representational strategies characterising the forms of realism developed in the previous century. These events, he argues, function within society in a similar way as infantile traumas operate in the psyche of neurotic individuals. The force of these events and the ways in which they are articulated mean that they cannot be simply forgotten, nor can they be readily recalled and made meaningful, and they certainly cannot be mastered. Rather, they remain within our consciousness, bearing down on contemporary social arrangements, memories and experience. However, what particularly structures these 'modern events' as radically different from what has taken place previously are the modes of representation which have accompanied them and made them visible. So significant are the new technologies of representation that it is alleged that these events have been fundamentally transformed through the act of representation itself. Cinema, television and the visual media have granted these events unprecedented prominence and, by narrating them in ways which have made the act of narration visible, these events are said to be acted upon and consequently fundamentally changed. The possible manipulation of events through representation and narration, their potential to be trivialised or magnified, exaggerated or distorted, means that it is impossible to ever accurately depict what has gone before. Instead we are left with circumspections, interpretations, and manipulations, often with the intention of trying to make sense of things which ultimately cannot be fully understood or satisfactorily represented.[4]

As a period of the past replete with painful memories and unanswerable questions, the events addressed in this film are consistent with the 'modern event' as described by White. As such it is also a period which defies simple narrativising within a purely realist mode of representation. Coupled with the knowledge that there can be no objective truth, as we would have previously understood the terms, other approaches to representation must now be sought. Thus, for Audiard, a conventional approach to the history on display would not have sufficed and it was necessary to find an approach which would also capture the confusion and uncertainty. Contradictory voices go some way to achieving this, as does the random use of documentary images selected indiscriminately from both the Resistance and Vichy. One of the most telling moments where such an effect is successfully realised is at the end of the film when our identification with Dehousse is intentionally undermined. In a rare self-referential flash, the elderly Dehousse looks into the camera to address the spectator and then with disarming candour asks us, 'What do you think, was it good? Did I look natural?' In doing so he throws the narrative into referential chaos, forcing us to rummage through our recent memories of the film in an attempt to salvage what we think we may know from what was merely portrayed. However, this moment is almost unique within the film in which the spectator is placed in relative comfort from the outset. Indeed, while the film is clearly intended to be an examination of the relationship between deception and authenticity and between the fabrication of historical truth and the construction of historical myth, this is seldom achieved. When Dehousse asks 'Did I look good?' he is directing us towards his own performance as an historical player, and we are forced to confront the bonds of identification which have been nurtured throughout, perhaps wondering whether we may also have been duped.

Other issues of ambiguity are also explored. For example, Dehousse's sexuality is brought to our attention. Thus we are led to question his ability as a heterosexual and it is interesting, for example, that his self-destructive confession takes place in bed. This also contrasts with other testimony provided within the film in which his sexual prowess has become severely inflated. Interestingly, his failure as a lover contrasts sharply with his mysterious mentor, who appears to be both a successful gay member of the Resistance and openly promiscuous. Bearing in mind the film's allegorical significance, we can only speculate on the meaning of these codings. A further ambiguity can be seen with regard to the question of 'otherness' – in this case absent otherness within the text. At a particular point in the film Dehousse, in need of yet another disguise, is forced to assume the role of a Jew, Rozinsky, who he knows has been transported to a concentration camp. Given the parallels already suggested regarding the role of Dehousse and his affinity with the French, this opens up an interesting exploration of the value of the Jew in French society as well as the treatment of the Jews during the war more generally. Cleverly introduced into the film, the audience is perhaps prodded into reflecting upon not just what happened to Rozinsky, but also how his fortuitous absence is now being exploited by Dehousse, ironically played by a Jewish actor, as he attempts to recreate himself.

Although at an individual level the experience of Dehousse is sensational, at a communal level at which the French did come to identify with De Gaulle, it is remarkably prescient. At an early stage in the film we are shown clearly that he occupies this middle ground. Not only is his mother identified as a collaborator, his wife, we learn, spent the war in the Resistance, while Dehousse stands in between, ignorant of both. Dehousse is also shown as marginal in that he occupies the place as a spectator of history rather than as an active participant; a point made manifest as we share his voyeuristic interest in tennis and the humiliation he suffers when he is forced to participate. As with most French people, only after the war ends can Dehousse begin to take up a position. This is achieved, however, by deception and lies, which culminate in his acceptance into the world of the Resistance as well as the creation of a myth around his character.

The various witnesses brought in to provide testimony offer a range of stories which are both contradictory to what we see as well as often ridiculously exaggerated. The myth of Dehousse runs in parallel with the more general myth of *la France résistante* that developed around the nation as a whole. Just as the 'new' Dehousse was forged on lies and deceit, we should be in no doubt that Audiard is suggesting a parallel pattern for France and, just as Dehousse was forced under pressure to reveal his truth, Audiard seems to be suggesting that the time has arrived for contemporary France to be able to talk openly about what happened during these years, no matter how painful this may be. However, by focusing on a character who is also an innocent, who does little more than fulfil the demands set out by De Gaulle, manufacturing his story only in response to the requirements of the new administration, Audiard falls short of a complete examination of the period. Since Dehousses' wife and family were active in the Resistance and he was never given the opportunity to support them, we could see the film as merely suggesting that France was ignorant rather than guilty. Certainly the film does not enter into a thorough interrogation into what Vichy represented and what collaboration signified. In interviews Audiard has asked the damning question 'What did our fathers do during the war?' and, while the question suggests issues of guilt, cover-up and terrible secrets, the film neither satisfactorily answers the question or sheds any further light on its corollaries.

Indeed the task Audiard has set himself falls short in a number of ways. Audiard has stated that he wanted the themes of 'fakery and fabrication' to be fully integrated into the *mise-en-scène* (Drake 1987: 24). However, even the formal strategies referred to earlier, which indeed do encourage the audience to be more sceptical about the nature of the history on display, fail to produce a film which fully explores the part film may play in creating the historical illusion. The problem arises because the central portion of the film still follows a broadly realist narrative pattern which encourages identification with the main character and which has the overall effect of situating the audience firmly within a position of knowledge. Thus those techniques, which may appear to be producing a distancing effect or a critical approach, act only to support the notion that we are watching a resourceful but nevertheless traditional fiction. Indeed the overall effect produced is one which is more likely to bring pleasure rather than cynicism. Thus the diverse documentary styles, rather than mystifying the audience or pushing them towards a feeling of alienation, merely suggest how documentary film may be used in the reproduction of history more generally. Although Michael Temple has argued that specific effects are introduced into the film that are intended to 'remind us of our present position as spectator, disrupting our identification and undermining our judgement' (1977: 48), this is in fact rarely achieved. From the start we are fully implicated within the narrative, always at one with the hero and his dominant position therein. Indeed we become implicated in his deceit, sharing with Dehousse, sometimes uncomfortably, his pain as well as his pleasure and, unlike almost every character in the film, we are never excluded from knowledge. Indeed we are always in on the joke. For example, we are never convinced by the talking-heads – we know we are watching a fiction of which they are a part.

This is a film which is never ambiguous about its intentions. However, the techniques employed are, in general, used solely to focus our critical attention towards the formation of historical narratives while, ironically perhaps, the cinematic illusion remains altogether intact. Perhaps one of the best examples of this during the film is when we watch Dehousse as he somewhat awkwardly infiltrates a Resistance ceremony in order to be filmed and photographed shaking the hands of Resistance fighters. Later we see him again, this time in black and white film footage at the ceremony, now a matter of documentary 'fact'. He has become an element within recorded history. Thus his transformation from a non-person, outside of history, to participant, is clearly and unambiguously presented. While the forgery plays its part within the film as a key moment in his construction of a hero, thus substantiating his position, the spectator is granted full understanding, a privileged position. In this example Audiard has shown how the historical record can be manipulated, while the knowledge granted the spectator ensures that the integrity of the cinematic edifice remains stable.

These concerns aside, Audiard does succeed in his attempt to re-evaluate a particularly difficult moment from the past, and has done so through an imaginative use of the potential of cinema. To achieve this the director has chosen to move beyond the binary opposition associated with the historical film, which places the real and the imaginary on opposite sides. Instead, he has moved away from an opposition between fiction and fact and the question 'What documentary evidence do we need in the pursuit of establishing the truth?' has brought to our attention important questions around matters of French history and identity which remain unresolved. By effectively blurring the boundaries between fact and fiction, between subjective memory and objective truth, and between personal experience and general knowledge, he has forced the audience into questioning well-established truths about the past and to approach official forms of history with more scepticism. Although Audiard has refrained from carrying out a thorough examination of the way in which film renders truth, the history on display has been more thoroughly scrutinised, and by employing an approach which draws together private fantasy and public history, the film also succeeds in making difficult questions regarding the cultural production of history accessible and meaningful. At this level people can understand and identify with it, making way for a greater awareness of how historical texts are constructed and become fastened to the public imagination. Audiard has said he wanted the film to be 'a purely fantastic vision of history' (Drake 1987: 24). Fortunately for us he has not succeeded in this. Indeed, what makes this film so potent is the way it touches our lives so intimately, stimulating doubt and perhaps encouraging us to ask what action we would take if we had been placed in that position.

Notes

[1] Alternative ways in which the past has been explored through cinema have been discussed in R. Burgoyne (1991) *Bertolucci's 1900: A Narrative and Historical Analysis*. New York: Wayne State University Press; M. Ferro (1988) *Cinema and History*. New York: Wayne State University Press; R. Rosenstone (ed.) (1995) *Revisioning History: Film and the Construction of a New Past*. Oxford and Princeton: Princeton University Press; A. Kaes (1989) *From Hitler to Heimat: The Return of History as Film*. Harvard: Harvard University Press; M. Landy (1997) *Cinematic Uses of the Past*. London and Minnesota: University of Minnesota Press; R. Rosenstone (1995) *Visions of the Past*. Harvard: Harvard University Press; L. Hutcheon (1989) *The Politics of Postmodernism*. London: Routledge; B. Nichols (1994) *Blurred Boundaries: Questions of Meaning in Contemporary Culture*. Indiana: Indiana University Press.

[2] For a fuller discussion of resistance films see Sorlin (1991: 183–99).

[3] See Katheryn M. Lauten's 'Dusting of Dehousse: *Un Héros très discret*', in Powrie (1999: 58–68).

[4] See Hayden White 'The Modern Event', in V. Sobchack (ed.) (1996) *The Persistence of History: Television, and the Modern Event*. London: Routledge, 23–4.

Gender trouble in MA VIE EN ROSE
Lucille Cairns

Ma Vie en rose: reception and analysis of success

First released on 28 May 1997, the Franco-Belgian co-production *Ma Vie en rose* was directed and co-scripted by Belgian director Alain Berliner. Berliner's debut feature has proved to be a phenomenal international success. It has been sold in no less than 33 countries since its projection in Cannes, where it was reportedly, 'one of the most popular and, in fact, longest applauded films',[1] and in Los Angeles. For a first full-length film, this is some achievement.[2]

Predictably, it has not received unalloyed praise from the critics, but, by a slight majority, reviews which have appeared in the French press have tended towards reasonably positive appraisal. Of the ten French reviews of the film included in the bibliography, a rough typology may be established: three were very laudatory, two were fairly so, three mixed praise and reservations, and two were negative. The two negative reviews came from *L'Humanité* and *Cahiers du cinéma*, which slam the film for, respectively, its perceived puerility ('A little story for television to be watched at teatime on Wednesday afternoons [when the children are off school]')[3] and superficiality ('*Ma Vie en rose* doesn't say anything, it sounds out everyone in an educational, consensual fashion and from time to time watches a benevolent, promotional fairy flying above the block of houses. You come out from it both dulled and appalled, as you would from a meeting of flat-mates').[4] As will be argued, the perception of such alleged weaknesses is simply the negative obverse of the film's strategically ludic and conspicuously postmodern style, a style which has, on the whole, elicited positive responses in other, not always populist, fora.

A number of reasons might be advanced for the film's huge commercial success. Firstly, we should acknowledge the sheer hard work of Berliner in response to the perfectionist demands of his producer, Carole Scotta, 'who insisted on thirteen successive drafts of the screenplay before the current version'.[5] Yet mere diligence does not, of course, guarantee success. What other factors might have contributed to Berliner's coup? Most obviously, there is the exceptional talent and uncontrived charm of his central actor, Georges du Fresne, who plays seven-year-old Ludo with consummate skill.[6] Then there is the novelty value of the subject-matter within the context of Francophone film, signalled explicitly by at least two reviews: '"The story of the little boy who wanted to be a girl", rather an original theme in cinema';[7] 'the doubtful sexual identity of a child is something society talks about but is rarely treated in cinema'.[8] The fact that there is as yet no satisfactory means in French of translating the English-language distinction between gender and sex (the single word 'le sexe' serving, inadequately, to designate the two different concepts) highlights just how relatively fresh the key theme of *Ma Vie en rose* still is in the French context.

Other reasons for the film's success may include its self-consciously postmodern attunement to popular culture. The meaning of the term 'postmodernism' is diffuse and labile; I use it here to refer to a late twentieth-century reversal of traditional aesthetic values, a revelling in surface as opposed to depth, in low as opposed to high culture, in the fragmentary and the unstable as opposed to the coherent and the stable.[9] Before the action even begins, French pop-star Zazie is appealing to a youth audience in the theme song '*Rose*'.[10] From a poststructuralist perspective, which questions authorial authority and emphasises the instability, plurality and the deferral of meanings,[11] '*Rose*' provides an ironic self-reflection on the film, which invites – and not infrequently gets – a superficial interpretation. *Ma Vie en rose* is, after all, eminently susceptible to being read like one of the 'sentimental novels'[12] referred to in the song's opening lines: the film is structured by fantasy (Ludo's literal fantasies, but also the fantasy which is gender), and two of the song's subsequent lines, 'I'm neurotically obsessed by happiness',[13] could almost have been spoken by an older, more self-aware version of Ludo. Berliner's revelling in the low-culture icons of Barbie and Ken dolls (here presented as Pam and Ben), together with the film's saturated, almost psychedelic colours in its fantastical scenes portraying the parallel universe into which Ludo periodically escapes, all richly conveyed by extravagant special effects, generate a gloriously kitsch-camp atmosphere. Such an atmosphere can appeal to a wide range of viewers, from the child, to the passive consumer of escapist fiction, to the hip postmodernist critic. Yet the overall tenor of the film is far from tacky; rather, it conveys a wistfully whimsical, child-like vision, which belies the highly politicised interpretations to which the text is open.

Central themes

Whatever the factors explaining the film's popularity – and only the most obvious have been mentioned – its huge popularity among a mainstream audience may also be regarded as something of a paradox. Notwithstanding all the aforementioned features selling it to the consumer of entertainment artefacts, *Ma Vie en rose* can in fact be said to constitute an implicit assault on one of the basic structures of sociality as the Western world (along with most other parts of the world) knows it: conventional binarised gender. Popular belief would have it that Berliner's film is a film about homosexuality. Despite the obvious gay connotations of the colour pink, which is foregrounded in both the film's title and the opening song of its soundtrack, such a belief is flawed. *Ma Vie en rose* deals less with homosexuality than with heteronormativity. Most crucially, it is a film about gender, about the transgression of a quasi-sacred equation of biological sex – male or female – with one, and only one, of the two culturally-sanctioned gender identities: masculinity and femininity. The force of this cultural imperative, the ideological and material viciousness with which it polices the frontiers between masculinity and femininity, is powerfully conveyed in this narrative of a seemingly model French family's ostracisation by, and eventual elimination from, a community of other apparently model French families.[14]

Opening

Ma Vie en rose opens on a deceptive idyll, presenting three heterosexual couples celebrating the virtues of conjugality either in enjoyable flirtation or in dignified solidarity. Soon afterwards, the camera focus widens out and its angle rises in an establishing shot, giving us a bird's-eye view of the community setting and its cultural specificity. This is typical *petit bourgeois* suburbia, a relatively new, squeaky-clean, and green residential development for that basic foundation of our heteronormative society, the nuclear family. Yet even while this illusion is being constructed its subtle subversion is beginning. This ostensibly ideal, family-friendly neighbourhood – praised by one of its residents, Albert, as a 'fantastic area',[15] and by another, Thierry, as a theft-free zone – into which Ludo's family has recently moved, just outside Paris,[16] has just been flippantly critiqued by unconventional grandmother Elisabeth, who stresses its conformity and uniformity by implying that all the houses are (boringly) interchangeable. Far from an idyll, this neighbourhood is, as one reviewer has remarked, a 'spick-and-span suburb where each house spies on the other'.[17]

Initially, the Fabre family, comprising mother Hanna, father Pierre, eldest son Tom, middle son Jean, daughter Zoé and youngest son Ludo (Ludovic), is also configured as admirably consonant with nuclear-family norms. It is lauded by Pierre's boss Albert as a 'fantastic [family]. They've got four children',[18] a comment reflecting the extraordinarily high value placed by France for over a century, and for a variety of reasons (chiefly military, demographic and political), upon the large, traditional family. Yet very soon into the action, this illusion of familial exemplarity is undermined, and, as the film progresses, the whole myth of the heterosexual family unit as a matrix of compassion, unconditional love, and unity is to be demolished. The catalyst of this demolition is, curiously, an eminently endearing, gentle, and objectively inoffensive child, who is constructed by the prevailing ideology of this family community as an undesirable freak because, quite simply, he deviates from hegemonic rules of

gender. In this context, hegemony is the mobilisation of the consent of the dominated to the social order in which they are dominated, as opposed to more
brutal and direct forms of coercion (see McLenan, Held and Hall 1984). Unlike
the use of the term by Italian Marxist Antonio Gramsci, who is most widely
associated with theorisation of hegemony, in this instance gender, rather than
social class, is alluded to as the basis of domination.

Gender play

Ludo's entrance onto the scene immediately challenges popular concepts of
gender as a natural, transparent and stable property. Our first full vision of
him is of a girl, elaborately dressed in his 'princess's dress' ('*robe de prin-
cesse*'), as he puts it, and applauded for his prettiness by the beguiled crowd of
neighbours. The narrative sets up the conditions for this telling misapprehen-
sion through preceding his entrance by a series of close-up frames which desist
from fully revealing the child's face, and artfully generate an expectation in the
spectator that s/he is about to see a girl – Zoé, Ludo's sister, whom the mother
had called to come down just before the camera zoomed into these close-ups.
When Ludo finally makes his entrance, his attire and make-up, enhanced by
the striking androgyny of his face, are so convincingly feminine that the gath-
ered families, with the obvious exception of Ludo's own, are all completely
taken in. Thus, the families of the diegesis (that is, of the spatio-temporal universe constructed by the narrative) and the 'real-life' spectators are very early
on given an ideological jolt. The confounding of their uninformed, thus unbi-
ased perception – what a sweet little girl! – subtly incites the inference that
gender is not an innate, immediately recognisable given, but rather a performative spectacle, a series of signs inscribed on the mutable surface of a body.

The model of gender as performance rather than as a substantive property
is now well established in (largely Anglophone) theoretical discourses, but its
original and most cogent exposition in the work of Judith Butler (1990: 24–5)
should be acknowledged:

> Gender is not a noun, but neither is it a set of free-floating
> attributes, for we have seen that the substantive effect of gender is
> performatively produced and compelled by the regulatory prac-
> tices of gender coherence. Hence, within the inherited discourse
> of the metaphysics of substance, gender proves to be performa-
> tive – that is, constituting the identity it is purported to be. In
> this sense, gender is always a doing, though not a doing by a sub-
> ject who might be said to pre-exist the deed ... There is no gender
> identity behind the expressions of gender ... identity is performa-

tively constituted by the very 'expressions' that are said to be its results.

The title of the present chapter pays a form of theoretical homage to the inspiring, if in more recent years slightly modified, theory of gender propounded by Butler. The inference that gender is not an innate, immediately recognisable given, but rather a performative spectacle, a series of signs inscribed on the mutable surface of a body, is unintentionally supported by the embarrassed response of Ludo's father, who introduces the youngest member of his 'tribe' ('*tribu*') to the new neighbours as 'the joker' ('*le fort en farce*'). While the father's remark is meant to render his son's flouting of appropriate gender behaviour innocuous by passing it off as a harmless joke, the polysemy of language (that is, its capacity to generate a plurality of meanings), the non-unicity (correspondingly, the lack of a single meaning) of the signifier 'farce', also promote the interpretation of gender identities as a form of performance. It is even worth considering the connotations of play, of acting, in the etymology of Ludo's name: was this name chosen to signify ludicity? On the question of language, its central role in the inculcation of gender norms is clearly established at this early point. When Ludo explains his cross-dressing for the garden party by saying that he wanted to look 'beautiful' ('*belle*'), even the one slightly unconventional adult in the diegesis, Elizabeth, calls him gently to order, decreeing that at his age one says 'handsome' ('*beau*'), not 'beautiful', of a boy.

However, Ludo will have none of it, for he very clearly identifies with the feminine side of the sacred binary division. This identification is almost instantly established by the camera's extreme close-up shots lingering on his careful application of make-up, by the soundtrack's evidence, through his humming, of his contentment in being dressed in women's shoes and earrings and a girl's fancy dress, and most of all by his transparent pleasure in both the whole stylisation process and his convincing the new neighbours that he is indeed a girl. He appears to have formed a concept of gender as nomadic, for although he knows he is currently a boy, he believes he will later become a girl ('when I'm no longer a boy').[19] The norm of gender unicity (namely, that a human subject is always only one gender) has not yet disciplined him, and he later defines himself as 'a boy-girl' ('*un garçon-fille*'). He consciously eschews masculinity: when his mother tries to coerce him into having his hair cut by asking if he doesn't want to look like his father and brothers – that is, masculine – he answers firmly in the negative. Granted, after his first visit to a psychologist, Ludo obediently tries to adopt conventional traits of masculinity, such as toughness and aggression. Yet his discomfort in this imposed gender identity is painfully obvious, and correspondingly invites pity on the part of the spectator – even if such a response is very likely to be in tension with anxiety about just what Ludo's exemption from conscription to masculinity might mean.

Ludo is not the only character to question the normative view of gender as a fixed, pre-determined essence. The randomness of gender, its non-essential character, is also adumbrated in his sister Zoé's pedagogy: 'XY you're a boy, and XX you're a girl. It's like playing poker.'[20] This provokes Ludo's whimsical fantasy of his other X chromosome, the one which would have made him a girl, having mistakenly fallen into the trash can when God threw them down from the heavens. 'Instead a Y slipped itself in. Scientific error!'[21] Yet Ludo is confident that God will fix the mistake by sending him his missing X chromosome, and that he will then be able to marry Jérôme. And Jérôme is not entirely resistant to this (homoerotic?) scenario, saying 'Depends what kind of girl you turn out to be'.[22]

Gender war

If Ludo's first cross-dressing initiative is met with bemused tolerance, his second foments marked hostility. Wearing a pink dress belonging to Jérôme's sister, Ludo stages a wedding scene with himself as bride, Jérôme as groom, and, to considerable comic effect, a teddy bear as the priest administering the fantasised marriage sacrament. When Jérôme's mother Lisette sees them, she faints through the shock of what is presumably perceived as a vision of her daughter, who, unbeknownst to Ludo, is in fact dead. This incident creates severe problems for Ludo's father, who, being professionally subordinate to the dead girl's father, Albert, is in a highly delicate position. His sense of professional vulnerability is thoroughly understandable. What is less so is the aggression of his response to the news that his son has been dressing as a girl: he shouts violently at Ludo, 'It's bad, what you did, very bad!'[23] And for him, this is the main point in the whole scandal, rather than the offending of a bereaved parent's sentiments: when Ludo defends himself by saying he didn't know Jérôme's sister was dead, Pierre replies curtly, 'But that's not the point. And for a start why don't we cut this kid's hair?'[24] As for Albert, while we may indeed expect him to have been offended as a bereaved parent, the film supplies no evidence of this. What appears to revolt him is Ludo's perceived travesty of a sacred Christian and heterosexual rite, and, by implication, the homoeroticisation of his son Jérôme, for Albert is clearly the source of Jérôme's sudden fear that he will go to hell if he continues to sit next to Ludo at school.

After this incident, Ludo's gender aspirations are pathologised: his parents take him to a psychologist in the hope of having him 'cured', as if crossing gender boundaries constituted mental illness. The normativising prejudice to which he is subject manifests itself in many other guises. One of its milder forms is his father's effort to erase his son's gentle, pacific disposition and to launch him into a harrowing apprenticeship of masculinity: getting the little boy to play rough competitive sports, urging a shorter haircut on him against his obvious wishes, and so on. Another, more traumatising, guise is ostracism at school, when, as mentioned above, his erstwhile friend Jérôme asks if he can move away from his seat next to Ludo, explaining that he does not want to be damned. Through the child's bluntness, the viewer is made aware of the ideological uses and abuses of religion, which are here responsible, through the agency of the Catholic father Albert, for transforming cross-dressing and, by dubious association, homosexuality, into a sin. Cross-dressing and homosexuality, two quite distinct phenomena, are here erroneously conflated. Other equally, if not more, disturbing guises of this normativising prejudice are teasing, emotional and physical bullying, expulsion from school due to a petition signed by all the other parents, and being labelled a 'poof' ('*tapette*') in one of the most humiliating and distressing ways possible (seeing graffiti demanding 'Poofs out' ('*Dehors tapette*') scrawled over his family's garage door).

The entire community is mediated as at least nominally Christian: references are made by Pierre and Albert to God; the children have a crucifix in their bedroom. But it is also exposed as being fully complicit with the policing of bodies and minds in the interests of binarised gender, and as hypocritical to boot.[25] Even the sympathetic character of the young, attractive, and caring primary-school teacher ('institutrice') defends gender norms in taking for granted, when Ludo produces Ben and Pam dolls, that he wants to be like the male doll and thus that he aspires to masculinity, from which assumption he shows his dissent by shaking his head. Minutes earlier the same normativising reaction had occurred when, after Jérôme had produced an earring (the one Ludo had lost at the party in the opening sequences), she had said prescriptively that he would be giving it back to his mother, as if an anatomically male child could have no possible use or desire for a feminine-connoted accessory. To give her her due, it should be observed that the young teacher does later try to help Ludo by pleading for tolerance of difference, saying to the children who have been mocking him for effeminacy: 'In any case you're all different and you have to learn to accept everyone, whatever they do, and to respect your friends'.[26] However, hers is rather a lone voice in the wilderness, where difference is precisely what this community cannot accept: in the succinct terms of one reviewer, *Ma Vie en rose* is a 'terrifying film about the rejection of difference'.[27] It is a voice considerably weakened by its inconsistency with her earlier inculcation in the same children of conventional constructs of gender.

The workings of moral cowardice and of hypocrisy are more tellingly exposed in two other forms. Firstly, there is the skilful juxtaposition of two scenes, the contrast between which reveals the gap between social etiquette and private, individual ethics. The first of these scenes is a big neighbourhood party at which, after an initial appalled silence, the revellers had appeared to welcome Ludo dressed in a skirt – and only a kilt at that; perhaps this was the biggest concession his parents could stomach, given the kilt's association with men, albeit foreign men. A camera wipe brings us to a deceptively similar, mediating scene of Ludo dancing and general enjoyment amongst the Fabre children, which is abruptly curtailed when Pierre rolls in drunk and delivers a bombshell. He has been fired, despite Albert's earlier reassurances that his job is safe. Thus, the narrative gives us to understand that the neighbourhood's earlier embrace of Ludo and family at the party had been a hollow sham serving purely to avoid embarrassment, and that Albert's hypocrisy can no longer be in any doubt. Hanna later emphasises and renders graphic Albert's duplicity in adopting the moral high ground: when she kisses him seductively in full view of his wife Lisette, he does not exactly recoil.

Trans-gender, heteronormativity and homophobia

Let us return to the conflation of trans-gender and homosexuality. As we have seen, and as is often the case outside the diegesis of this film, the two are confused, being seen at the very least as mutually entwined. The feeling that one's sexual genitalia and socially-assigned gender do not correspond to one's inner sense of gender is, self-evidently, something different from a feeling that one is erotically attracted to members of one's own sex. However, such a discontinuity has only gradually been acknowledged in the twentieth century, after many decades of intellectual enthralment to the nineteenth-century theory of homosexuality as spiritual hermaphroditism. This model of homosexuality, known as the 'man-woman' or the 'Zwischenstufen' theory, is thought to have originated in Karl Heinrich Ulrichs's Memnon (1868), where the male homosexual character is defined as 'the soul of a woman enclosed in the body of a man', and the female homosexual character as the converse. Ulrichs's theory-cum-fiction widely influenced sexologists and the lay public, including such prestigious and subtle-minded thinkers as Marcel Proust, who presented homosexuals as accursed men-women ('homme-femmes') in his celebrated cycle A la Recherche du temps perdu. In more recent times, it has become obvious that gays may well be entirely comfortable with, and even celebrate, their sex: witness, for example, the hyper-femininity of the lesbian constellation centred around Natalie Clifford Barney in early twentieth-century Paris, or, in the late twentieth-century Western world, the cult of muscularity, leather, and at least aesthetic machismo among some gay men who plainly make no identification at all with the feminine.

However, having established this, let us briefly consider whether it is at all possible to locate homosexuality in Ma Vie en rose. Is it in any sense plausible to

posit sexual attraction between Ludo and Jérôme? Is there any sexual significance in the fact that when Sophie invites Jérôme to play, he brusquely rebuffs
her in favour of Ludo? Or in the fact that when Ludo talks about their getting
married, Jérôme does not so much resist as pose conditions? But if Jérôme is
envisaging marriage to a girl, as he evidently is, in what sense can one be dealing with homosexuality? With respect to such young children, it may be more
appropriate to speak of homoerotic attraction, rather than homosexuality. To
follow the reasoning of (often misinformed) disciples of Freud, it is by no means
indisputable that children of such a young age 'possess' a sexuality at all, or, to
adopt a constructivist view of sexuality, that any one possesses a sexuality, if
sexuality is conceptualised as some kind of innate and fixed essence. While *Ma
Vie en rose* provides material which gives rise to these questions, it would not
appear to provide sufficient evidence to support a cogent 'gay' reading.

However, three points at least are plain: the film does encode the popular
conflation of trans-gender and homosexuality, it does expose both the mindless-
ness and the viciousness of homophobia, and it does reflect the stranglehold of
heteronormativity in which France, as much as any Western country, is caught.
The first point needs no further illustration. As for the second, we need only
refer to the distressing inscription of homophobic graffiti, or to the scene of
heated exchange between Albert and neighbour Thierry, and to that which follows it. Albert is angry because Sophie, Thierry's daughter, has called Jérôme
a '*tapette*', presumably because of his closeness to Ludo. Having overheard the
two men talking, Ludo guilelessly asks his parents what a '*tapette*' is; the degree
of homophobia present in his father is amply evinced by the father's explosive
rage at the thought that his own son has been slandered as a '*tapette*'. For sub-
stantiation of the third point, it is tempting simply to give the reference passim;
but let us take just one example amongst the numerous available. At school, an
institution meant to instruct rather than indoctrinate, heteronormative codes
are assiduously foregrounded by the apparently liberal teacher's scripting of
a romance between Ludo and Sophie ('Sophie and you, you could make a nice
little couple!').

To summarise: the combined and interdependent forces of homophobia and
transsexphobia produce a form of communal, organised hostility towards both
the little boy, with the whole community signing a petition calling for Ludo's
transference to a different school and a group of schoolboys beating him up,
and towards his family, with the father's boss Albert eventually laying him
off, contrary to previous promises, and each member being humiliated by the
offensive graffiti (at seeing the message, brother Tom exclaims in horror 'Oh the
shame!'). Blaming Ludo for the latter, discursive aggression, Hanna decides to
expunge the offending feminine traits from her son, and cuts his hair in a symbolic shearing scene. This scene is likely to have a special cultural resonance

for the French, whose collective historical memory may well correlate it with the humiliation inflicted at the Liberation upon female 'collaborators' during France's German occupation during World War Two. And if this seems like a far-fetched analogy, it should be noted that the cutting of Ludo's hair is contrived as, precisely, a retributive spectacle, with all the family looking on, and, significantly, shame being invested in Ludo's role through the mother's cold words just before she begins shaving him: 'A poof is ... a boy who likes boys. Like you'.[29] Just what is she punishing him for? For his assumption of femininity, or for his having been the medium of her family's defilement by association with a '*tapette*'? Certainly the poignancy of the scene invites the interpretation that such shearing is a deeply upsetting ordeal for its subject, with aural and visual images combining to signify marked distress: the (non-diegetic) mournful music on the soundtrack, the close shot revealing Ludo's discreet tears.

After this forced physical masculinisation, Ludo becomes depressed and withdrawn, alienated from the identity imposed upon him against his nature, as he sees it. In the safety of his own mind, however, he re-runs the fantasy of his wedding with Jérôme. And after the family's move to Clermont-Ferrand, he meets a child similarly resistant to the gender role assigned to her according to her anatomy: Christine, alias 'Chris', who looks just as much a boy as Ludo had a girl before his parents intervened, and who is manifestly unhappy in the girly frock she is obliged to wear at her own birthday party.

It is Chris's determination to appropriate Ludo's masculine clothing which triggers the climax of the film, its uneasy catharsis and, finally, a fragile reconciliation. Chris forces Ludo to exchange his masculine clothes with her feminine ones. Wrongly assuming that Ludo's frock signifies his persistence in crossdressing, Hanna lashes out violently, causing him to flee in fear; she follows him in panic, momentarily and oneirically enters into his Pam and Ben universe, and then awakens surrounded by her anxious family. It is unclear whether this fantastical flight from the social order is intended to be read literally or as a hallucination/dream on Hanna's part. While a literal reading may appear an absurd proposition, the elliptical narrative provides no account of precisely what has happened to Hanna. What is clear, however, is that the figure of the flight serves a particular moral function. It 'teaches' Hanna to understand something of her child's inner world, and, most importantly, to accept and love him for what he is. In a gratifying but rather implausible happy ending, the two parents finally express their love for Ludo as their child, regardless of gender. This does wonders for the viewer's mood, restoring faith in the milk of human kindness and so on, but it somewhat fudges the important issues Berliner's film has powerfully raised and intelligently explored. With respect to Ludo's future as a social subject, as opposed to his reintegration within the bosom of his family, this happy ending leaves the probing viewer somewhat frustrated.

As one reviewer objects, there is an absence of 'any concrete questioning of Ludovic's real future (will he be a closet homo, a straight queen, a trendy gay, a transvestite, a transsexual, or "cured"?!)'.[30]

Conclusions

Ma Vie en rose exposes the discursive forces working to reify gender, a cultural, ultimately immaterial, construct, into a natural property inherent in human beings and determined by their genitalia. Ludo is anatomically male but 'feels' feminine, and this contradiction of the normative sex-gender equation alienates and antagonises his community to the point where it is prepared to eliminate the transgressor, perceived as sinful and sick (just as were, and in some discourses still are, homosexuals). The director brings out the injustice of such prejudices by showing their damaging effects on a young and extremely sympathetic child and on his family, who suffer both from their own internalisation of such gender norms and from society's alienation of the family unit, perceived as responsible for Ludo's putative aberration. The most telling of all the dialogues is that between Ludo and his grandmother Elizabeth apropos his behaviour and his parents:

> Ludo: It's true I don't want to change, but ... I do want them to love me.
> Elizabeth: It's for your own good.
> Ludo: It's not true that it's for my own good![31]

Ma Vie en rose also exposes the notorious conflation of transsexualism and homosexuality: those in his neighbourhood make no distinction between an anatomically male subject's identification with the feminine gender role on the one hand, and homosexuality on the other. Thus a 1990s community is seen to have preserved intact Ulrich's fanciful nineteenth-century fiction of the '*Zwischenstufen*'. Nil progress, at least on some social levels, in 130 years.

Notes

[1] '*L'un des films les plus courus et, finalement, longuement ovationné.*' 'Entre drame et comédie', in *Télérama*, 28 May 1997.

[2] Berliner's previous cinematic work had been confined to scriptwriting and to the '*court-métrage*' (short film). See Agnés Brunet and Michel Pascal, '*Cinéma français: le réveil*', in *Le Point*, 2 June 1997: 102–6; Brigitte Baudii, '*Alain Berliner: vive la différence*', *Le Figaro*, 29 May 1997.

[3] '*Un Petit Conte pour la télévision à regarder au moment du goûter, le mercredi après-midi.*' Pierre Barbancey, *L'Humanité*, 13 May 1997.

[4] 'Ma Vie en rose ne raconte rien, fait son tour de table pédagogique consensuel et regarde voler de temps en temps une fée publicitaire bienveillante au-dessus du pâté de maisons. On en sort à la fois assoupi et révolté, comme d'une réunion de colocataires.' 'Ma Vie en rose', in Cahiers du cinéma, 514, June 1997, 80.

[5] 'qui a exigé treize moutures successives du scénario avant la version actuelle.' Brunet and Pascal, op. cit., 104.

[6] Michael Temple, extolling du Fresne's 'extraordinary performance', goes so far as to claim that 'without Du Fresne at the centre, none of it would work'. (Michael Temple, 'Ma Vie en rose', Sight and Sound, November 1997, 48.)

[7] '"L'histoire du petit garçon qui voulait être une fille", thème plutôt in édit au cinéma.' Olivier Séguret, 'Ludovic, sept ans et toutes ses robes', in Libération, 22 May 1997.

[8] 'l'identité sexuelle incertaine d'un enfant est un sujet de société peu traité au cinéma'

[9] For fuller discussions of postmodernism, see Lyotard (1987); McHale (1984).

[10] Rose was written by Alain Berliner and Dominique Dalcon, and performed by Zazie.

[11] The term 'poststructuralism' designates an intellectual approach which emerged partly from within, but represented a reaction against, French structuralism in the 1960s, rejecting the latter's claims to objectivity and comprehensiveness. Poststructuralism embraces various particular strands of thought, including the philosophical deconstruction of Jacques Derrida, the later work of Roland Barthes, the psychoanalytic theories of Jacques Lacan and Julia Kristeva, the historical critiques of Michel Foucault, and the politico-cultural analyses of Jean-François Lyotard and Jean Baudrillard.

[12] 'romans à l'eau de rose'

[13] 'Le bonheur m'obsède à la névrose'

[14] The contestatory nature of Ma Vie en rose is evinced in Berliner's own comments to a journalist: '"I was won over by the originality and the tone of Chris Vander Stappen's screenplay," explains Alain Berliner. "She raises existential and social issues that particularly interest me, like the right to difference ... I make films in order to tell fundamentally human stories that lead to a questioning. This is what happens with Ma Vie en rose. I receive many personal accounts from people who've seen the film. They feel the need to confide and to enter into dialogue as if all of a sudden they could free themselves from a taboo. That's precisely the function of cinema for me"'. (' "J'ai été séduit par l'originalité et le ton du scénario de Chris Vander Stappen, explique Alain Berliner. Elle soulève des questions existentielles et sociales qui m'intéressent particulièrement, comme le droit à la différence ... Je fais du cinéma pour raconter des histoires foncièrement humaines qui débouchent sur une interrogation. C'est ce qui se passe pour Ma Vie en rose. Je reçois beaucoup de témoignages de gens qui ont vu le film. Ils prouvent le besoin de se confier et de dialoguer comme si tout à coup ils pouvaient se libérer d'un interdit. Voilà bien pour moi la fonction du cinéma."') (Brigitte Baudii, op. cit., 48)

[15] 'quartier formidable'

[16] In or near Mennecy, the administrative centre of l'Essonne, part of the Paris region, created in 1964.

[17] 'banlieue proprette ou chaque pavillon épie l'autre' M.P., 'Ma Vie en rose', in Le Point, 2 June 1997, 120.

[18] '[famille] formidable. Ils ont quatre enfants'

[19] 'quand je ne serai plus un garçon'

[20] 'XY c'est que t'es un garçon, et XX c'est que t'es une fille. C'est comme un poker, quoi'

[21] 'A la place il y a un Y qui s'y est mis. Erreur scientifique!'

[22] *'Faut voir ce que tu seras comme genre de fille'*

[23] *'C'est mal, ce que tu as fait, c'est très mal!'*

[24] *'Mais la question n'est pas là. Et d'abord pourquoi qu'on ne lui coupe pas les cheveux à ce gosse?'*

[25] This is a point remarked upon in several reviews of *Ma Vie en rose*. For instance, *Cahiers du cinéma* refers to 'the neighbours, ghastly and incredible pharisees' (*'les voisins, affreux et pharisiens à souhait'*) (514, June 1997, 80); *Positif* gives a lapidary definition of the film as a 'fable on the hypocrisy of supposedly advanced societies' (*'fable sur l'hypocrisie des sociétés dites évoluées'*) (*'Ma Vie en rose'*, in *Positif*, 437–8, July/August 1997, 132).

[26] *'De toute façon vous êtes tous différents et il faut apprendre à accepter tout le monde, quoi qu'il fasse, à respecter ses copains.'*

[27] *'film terrifiant sur le rejet de la différence'*. *'Ma Vie en rose'*, in *Jeune cinéma*, 244, Summer 1997, 50.

[28] *'Sophie et toi, vous pourriez faire un joli couple tous les deux'*

[29] *'Une tapette c'est un garçon qui aime les garçons. Comme toi'*

[30] *'toute interrogation concrète sur le devenir réel de Ludovic (sera-t-il homo planqué, hétéro-folle, gay dans le vent, travesti, transsexuel, ou "guéri"?!)'* Olivier Séguret, op. cit.

[31] Ludo: *C'est vrai que je ne veux pas changer, mais ... je veux qu'ils m'aiment quand même.*
Elizabeth: *C'est pour ton bien.*
Ludo: *C'est pas vrai que c'est pour mon bien!*

MARIUS ET JEANNETTE: nostalgia and utopia
Phil Powrie

My film is my way of dealing with things, of making small utopias, because the big ones are no longer on the agenda – Robert Guédiguian[1]

Marius et Jeannette was one of the more successful films of the 1997–1998 French film season. Originally produced for television (the channel Arte) on a small budget, it was written by the director Robert Guédiguian and his usual script-writer, Jean-Louis Milesi, in three weeks, and shot over thirty days in August and September 1996. It was chosen as part of the *'Un certain regard'* section of the Cannes Film Festival in May 1997, which it won, receiving the *Prix Gervais*. As a result of this success, Guédiguian decided to give the film theatrical release. It was released in almost 200 cinemas in November 1997, winning a clutch of prizes. In November 1997 Guédiguian and Milesi were awarded the *Prix Henri-Jeanson* for the script-writing. In December 1997 the film won the *Prix Lumière* for Best Film,[2] and the *Prix Louis-Delluc*,[3] and Ariane Ascaride (Jeannette) was awarded the *César* for Best Actress at the 1998 Cannes Film Festival. Over 500,000 spectators had been to see it through-out France by Easter 1998, rising to 2,627,827 by the end of the year. This, in French terms, makes it a popular film, quantitatively speaking. The subject-matter is also popular, although in a different sense.

The film is the story (literally, indeed, since it is subtitled a *conte*, or fairy-tale) of a closely-knit group of characters. Jeannette, the single mother of two children, works in a supermarket, from which she is sacked after complaining about the working conditions. She meets Marius when she goes to a disused cement-works which is being pulled down and where he is the site guard. She tries to steal some paint; Marius stops her, but stung by her taunts that he is a fascist, he takes the paint to her house, and paints her kitchen. He gradu-ally becomes integrated into the small community of which she forms a part, where two other couples live along with Jeanette in houses facing onto a small enclosed courtyard: Caroline, a Communist who survived the Nazi concentra-tion camps, and Justin, a radical retired school-teacher, who live apart, but sleep together; and Monique and her husband Dédé, who once voted for the National Front, and who is constantly taunted by the others for it. The story focuses on the couple formed by Marius and Jeannette, her fears of losing her independence, and his fears of losing her children in an accident, as he had lost his own and his wife. The characters are fundamentally working-class or radical middle-class, and they – as Guédiguian suggests in the foreword to the screenplay – 'allow us to speak of Castro, Le Pen, deportation, strikes, football' (Guédiguian and Milesi 1997: 5).[4] As *Le Monde*'s critic noted on its theatrical release, the film's concerns are 'the nostalgia for a revolutionary utopia, the conflict between generations, the will to preserve a spirit of resistance and a sense of community' (Frodon 1997a).[5] At the same time, this apparently dour subject-matter is vehicled, as is proper to a 'fairy-tale', in a light-hearted way, where, as we shall see, even the villains are presented sympathetically. As another critic says, it is a film which combines the real and the utopian, and which is 'working-class without an ounce of demogogy. A film which makes you happy to belong to the human race' (De Bruyn 1997).[6] The tension between the real and the utopian is one of several in the film, whose success, and whose tensions, are encapsulated in its opening shot.

To the accompaniment of the traditional-sounding 'Il pleut sur Marseille' ('It is raining over Marseilles'), a large transparent inflatable globe floats upside down, apparently from nowhere, past ships at harbour, and past a submerged road-sign indicating the globe's direction, L'Estaque. The globe comes to rest in the harbour of L'Estaque, the northernmost suburb of Marseilles. L'Estaque would be familiar to those spectators who had seen Guédiguian's six previous films as the location for those films, as indeed it is for this one. Even those unfamiliar with Guédiguian's films would recognise L'Estaque as an iconic Provençal location, the subject of several of Cézanne's paintings (a copy of one of which hangs in Jeannette's kitchen). There are at least two types of tension in this opening shot: the tension between universalist aspirations (metaphorised by the globe) and regionalist inspirations (the visual and aural emphasis on location) is paralleled by a similar tension between utopia (the globe, literally the transparent 'no-place') and realism (the very real harbour, with large ships at anchor). It is a tension of which Guédiguian is very aware; in his view he produces films which are 'more allegorical than realist, while being interested in being between the two' (Anon. 1997a).[7]

There is a third tension, however, within the notion of utopia, floating transparently on the surface of the film: utopia, for many, might seem to be forward-looking, and to look outwards rather than inwards. Paradoxically, however, the globe comes to rest on a muddy sand-flat, signalling that in this case at least, utopia is as nostalgic as it is dynamic. That nostalgia is a nostalgia for a very real place, steeped in a sense of the past, a nostalgia for a particular film period, and for a particular style of political action – which could be called a community politics, which was thrust into the limelight in the same year as the appearance of this film, 1997. The film's ideology, then, is, like the globe itself, transparent and upside-down, simultaneously superficial, like the globe floating on the surface of the harbour, and yet effortless. This is a fairy-tale for modern times, which leaves spectators, unlike Guédiguian's previous films and indeed many of the films of the current 'new cinema', feeling good.

This article locates Guédiguian's film in its local context before explaining how the call for civil disobedience by a group of film directors in February 1997 – of whom Guédiguian was one – helped this film become more than a regional phenomenon. The tension between nostalgia and utopia will be explored, showing how that tension is to some extent hidden, firstly by topical issues, such as immigration and redundancy, and secondly by the form of the film, which is a sort of Brechtian fairy-tale.

The local hero

Part of *Marius et Jeannette*'s appeal lies in its regional identity, much like the films of Pagnol had done some fifty years before. Indeed, the title is a transparent reference to Pagnol, whose trilogy *Marius* (1931), *Fanny* (1932), and *César* (1936) are good examples of the hallmarks not just of Pagnol's cinema, but of Guédiguian's: Provençal types, a close-knit local community, theatricality (a reliance on typically exuberant 'southern' dialogue rather than on exuberant cinematography). We shall return to this connection, which is not as simple as it seems; suffice to say that reviewers accordingly insist on placing the film within an auteurist trajectory which is firmly regional. Almost all reviews mention Guédiguian's six previous films, the fact that all of them are located in the same part of Provence, and that all of them use the same troupe of actors. This seemingly banal contextualisation is so obvious that we do not realise to what extent it frames the expectations of spectators, inserting those expectations within a framework of regionalist auteurism which determines responses: this film, like the six which preceded it, is about regional working-class types, with an emphasis on local colour, and will speak to us of the importance of regional identity and, in all probability, about an even more clearly defined local community.

Guédiguian made his first film in 1980, the same year that the very different *cinéma du look* took off with Beineix's *Diva* (1980). It is a contrast he is keen to emphasise. He points out that the typical 1980s discourse, in film or more generally, was one of compromise, which sought to minimise class conflict (Baecque and Toubiana 1997: 59). In this respect, the young cinema of the 1980s produced 'totally evanescent films' (60), [8] and he criticises the clear lighting most closely associated with the *cinéma du look* as 'lighting without shadow, giving a sharp image, where things are very clearly defined, where matter does not exist any more, there is no body, no face, no expression' (Derobert and Goudet 1997: 46).[9]

Guédiguian's films, on the other hand, are the opposite of what he seems to mean by 'evanescent', being politically committed. The subject matter of Guédiguian's six films before Marius et Jeannette – *Dernier été* (1980); *Rouge*

Midi (1983); *Ki Lo Sa* (1986); *Dieu vomit les tiédes* (1989); *L'Argent fait le bonheur* (1992); *A la vie, à la mort* (1994) – is much the same: 'all of them speak of redundancy, poverty, exploitation, and more often than not finish badly. And yet, one value survives: friendship. All of Guédiguian's films could have the title of the sixth: 'To life, to death' (Trémois 1997: 275).[10] For example, *Dernier été* tells the story of an unemployed youth who has decided to leave L'Estaque – he dies in a bungled burglary; and *L'Argent fait le bonheur* explores how local mothers put an end to gangland turf wars and racism in their community.

The local community, which forms the basis of Guédiguian's films, is also evident in the fact that he has used the same actors in many of his films, and who are nearly all friends from his younger days. He lives with Ariane Ascaride (Jeannette), and Gérard Meylan (Marius) is a childhood friend, who was active with Guédiguian in the Young Communists. Ascaride, Meylan, Jean-Pierre Darroussin (Dédé), Frédérique Bonnal (Monique), and Pierre Banderet (Monsieur Ebrard) all went to the Paris Conservatoire to study with Antoine Vitez and Marcel Bluwal, both of whom were members of the French Communist Party. Interviews with the actors as well as with Guédiguian stress how the group form a kind of 'family', closer in many respects because of both their political allegiances and their family ties than many repertory companies. As Ascaride points out, 'we have become a family in the concrete sense. Jean-Pierre Darroussin met his wife on one of Robert's sets. Malek [the production director] and Gérard were the witnesses for our wedding' (Rigoulet 1997b: 21).[11]

The sense of community which emanates from Guédiguian's films, and which is also clear in his working environment, extends to other aspects of his film-making, such as the financial structures. After his first film, Guédiguian established a production company in Paris, Agat, which financed several of the younger generation of film-makers, mostly for television projects. These included Pascale Ferran, Cédric Kahn, and Gérard Mordillat,[12] all of whom – along with Guédiguian and others – were signatories to a text which was a key moment for the 'new cinema' of the 1990s.

The return of 'community politics'

On 12 February 1997 a petition signed by fifty-nine film directors, including Guédiguian, appeared in *Le Monde* and in *Libération* asking for support in opposing the government's proposed immigration laws. The details of this petition and its importance are described elsewhere in this piece (see also Powrie 1998), and here it is necessary to simply recall that this movement generated a return to politics for many intellectuals and artists during 1997, even though the film directors' involvement was relatively short-lived. The group of directors dissolved after a large demonstration on 22 February.

Twelve of the signatories, including Guédiguian, published short reflections on what had happened in *Le Monde* on 19 March. The common thread running between these brief pieces is that nearly all, with the exception of Guédiguian, claim to have no party-political experience, and all, Guédiguian included, speak of the collapse of traditional left-wing party politics. This is coupled with a renewed sense of 'something having to be done', and that film-makers are as well-qualified as anybody else to do this. What this meant in practice was an awareness of non-party-political action, 'the invention, or re-invention of a political practice',[13] according to one (Goupil 1997: 25), or a 'community politics',[14] according to Guédiguian (1997: 25). Guédiguian's notion of what might be meant by 'proximity' is – and this returns us to the parochial setting for his films – a community politics based on an authentic local dialogue of which his films form a part, as opposed, in his view, to a less authentic and probably less sincere 'national' dialogue, represented by the traditional party system. Referring to the character Dédé in *Marius et Jeannette*, who once voted for the National Front, Guédiguian says that 'demonstrations and petitions by intellectuals are useless. You have to play on issues of community, in a hand-to-hand struggle. I must speak to my neighbour who lives and does his shopping in the same place as I do, because I won't give him a politician's spiel' (Anon. 1997b).[15]

Yet, although Guédiguian's pitch is for a politics of community apparently rooted in parochialism, it is clear that *Marius et Jeannette* tackles issues which are just as much part of a national discourse. The foremost of these, given the context of the February petition, is racism, a particularly acute issue in Marseilles because of the large proportion of National Front voters (35 per cent, as opposed to 65 per cent Communist in Guédiguian's own ward (Baecque & Toubiana 1997: 58)). It is hardly surprising that it surfaces throughout the film, both in the constant taunting of Dédé for having voted National Front (and the ensuing joke of his head injury caused by his throwing a stone at a National Front poster), and in the ex-school-teacher's explanations to the children of why fundamentalism is blind to the richness of diversity. There is also the issue of job shortages, as illustrated in what *Libération*'s critic, following Guédiguian, labels the 'moral' tracking shot of a long line of women waiting to be interviewed for a job (Guédiguian had said, citing an aphorism by Godard, that 'tracking shots are a moral matter' (quoted in Rigoulet 1997a)).[16]

It is clear, then, that *Marius et Jeannette* gained considerable popularity from the context of the February petition, because it reflected a return to a long-lost political commitment, and an authenticity guaranteed both by its local setting and by the impeccable radical credentials of Guédiguian. It is no less clear that the renewal of political commitment represents a nostalgic return.

That nostalgic return is underscored and doubled by the nostalgic return to the popular cinema of the 1930s.

Nostalgia

In its sympathetic focus on what the French call *'petites gens'* (lower-class characters), the film is indebted as much to Renoir as to Pagnol. Renoir is a key reference point for Guédiguian, although this is more evident in his previous film, *L'Argent fait le bonheur*. This film features a bank robbery staged by the Estaque community in order to dig themselves out of a financial hole; the robbery is inspired and morally supported by the local priest, suggesting Renoir's *La Marseillaise*, where the priest hides in the foothills with other outlaws; and the bridge from which Toni leaps in Renoir's film appears in *L'Argent fait le bonheur*. Indeed, Guédiguian is ambivalent about Pagnol, saying that while he acknowledges Pagnol's strengths (the emphasis on dialogue and exterior scenes (see Derobert & Goudet 1997: 48)) and admires the films Pagnol made using Giono novels, he does not like the *Marius* trilogy, for several reasons. The trilogy, he feels, misrepresents the multiculturalism of Marseilles in the 1930s – there are no working-class characters, as it is firmly located in the petite bourgeoisie; and it creates a stereotypical Marseilles 'folklore' (see Baecque and Toubiana 1997: 60). (However, Guédiguian can be said to fall into much the same trap with his folkloric panegyric to that eminently Provençal dish, the aïoli.) Furthermore, Guédiguian, despite the obvious references to Pagnol, does not like being called a 'regional' film-maker, which he feels is 'too belittling, scornful' (Guédiguian 1996: 155).[17]

Whatever his reticence concerning Pagnol, Guédiguian is well aware that the Pagnol connection is what endeared the film to the public: 'It is because there is the Pagnol reference that the public can accept the other things that I am doing'.[18] Therein lies the nostalgic appeal of *Marius et Jeannette*, as opposed to its positioning within the context of the radical politics of 1997: it harks back not just to a radical politics associated with the late 1960s but also further, both in time and nature, to the 1930s film culture which represents what many see as the 'classic' French cinema as a 'regional' variant of that classic cinema.

The nostalgic connotations of the film are evident in the discourses which surround it, whether produced by Guédiguian himself, by his troupe, or by reviewers. For example, Ariane Ascaride comments on the importance of Gérard Meylan for the director in terms which are crucial to a nostalgic positioning: 'He is the guardian of the past, memory of an 'archaic' function, he is an important figure in L'Estaque, the son of the headmaster, who was a key figure' (Rigoulet 1997b).[19] When one puts this statement next to Guédiguian's affirmation that making a film about the working-class in L'Estaque was a way to be on his parent's wavelength (see Baecque & Toubiana 1997: 58),[20] it is clear that the film functions as an evocation of village or small-town life which has more or less disappeared, with its focus on local notables reminiscent of pre-Second World War and pre-urbanised France.

The nostalgia vehicled by the film is not only associated with the connotations attached to people, but also with technique. Guédiguian speaks of his attachment to the iris shot, frequent in Chaplin's films (as the film script reminds us (see Guédiguian and Milesi 1997: 121), because, in his view, 'it is a closure which is softer and which is connected with memory or disappearance' (Derobert and Goudet 1997: 44),[21] and he is scathing where the very mobile Louma camera – so frequently used by the *cinéma du look* – is concerned. In his view the contrast between the sophistication of the equipment and the world of the worker is too wide (46).

Disappearance and memory, then, are key themes of the film, whether it be the disappearance of working-class fathers (Jeannette's two husbands and her father), working-class mothers (Marius's wife, killed in a car accident), or the working class in general. The latter is illustrated by the dismantling of the cement factory where Jeannette's father met his death, and which, as Toubiana astutely points out, 'functions as the cemetery of a working class which does not count for anything any more, and from whose loss the characters in Guédiguian's films seem not to have recovered' (Toubiana 1997: 25).[22] Correlatively, disappearance is mirrored by the work of memory which the film celebrates, as more and more of the personal histories of the two main characters are brought reluctantly into the open, just as the film celebrates the demise of the working class by the activities of a small but vibrant community in the immensity of the disused cement-works. As the *Cahiers du cinéma* critic pointed out, what is likely to have attracted many spectators is the combination of melancholy and utopia: 'in this combination of utopia and melancholy resides the true beauty of the film' (Cohen 1997: 57).[23]

Utopia

Turning now from nostalgia to utopia, it is clear that a number of features encourage utopian aspirations. The major location of the film, the courtyard, is doubly utopian, firstly because it functions as a microcosm of French society, and secondly because it appears to be idealised. As one reviewer suggests, it is like a paradise from a 1930s popular film, to which Guédiguian responds that although the area of Marseilles in question has changed, he wished to idealise it: 'The place has a whiff of paradise, as if it came straight out of a popular 1930s film'. Isn't it a bit idealised? 'I recognise that it is, it is my own private

Estaque', confesses the film-maker. 'In twenty years, the area has changed a lot, just as Marseilles has, and I have made some choices' (see Royer 1997).[24]

A second major example of utopia, much commented on by reviewers, is the fact that potentially unsympathetic characters are presented sympathetically. Monsieur Ebrard, who is responsible for Jeannette losing her job, turns up later in the film as a door-to-door lingerie salesman with a patter which makes the assembled women laugh to tears; and Dédé, who voted National Front, is constantly made fun of, but in a clearly affectionate way. *Cahiers du cinéma* and *Le Nouvel Observateur*, indeed, commented unfavourably on this aspect, saying that the film refuses to engage with the Other: the characters 'stay amongst themselves, in their class, which does not need to mix with others, or rather with the Other, that of the wealthy' (Mérigeau 1997).[25]

Another example of utopianism, echoing the microcosmic function of the courtyard, this time at the level of *mise-en-scène*, is the very conscious play on colours, with Marius dressed in red and smoking blue Gauloises, and Jeannette wearing blue and drinking red Martini, the two of them painting Jeannette's house in white. The colours clearly suggest the colours of the French flag, and point to a desire for universalism. This emphasises the refusal of the Other (since it is only working-class characters who represent 'France'), but at the same time, it out-manoeuvres that particular criticism, firstly by making it clear that the particular is there to ground the universal, and secondly by making visible a class which some may believe has vanished, or changed beyond all recognition, thus giving the universal its utopian force. As Guédiguian points out in an interview, 'it is from the particular that you reach the universal' (Guédiguian 1996: 155).[26]

Finally, it is not true to say that the characters stay amongst themselves, with all the regressive connotations that this might suggest. The film, perhaps with too overt a political correctness, has a multi-ethnic family at its core (Jeannette's children have different fathers, one of whom is of Algerian descent), but more important is the fact that much is made of upward mobility through education, while at the same time there is emphasis on an awareness of one's roots and a commitment to the working class, reflecting Guédiguian's own politics, but being no less utopian for it. Jeannette's son becomes a teacher of Arabic, and her daughter a journalist with a penchant for left-leaning conceits: she will write, we are told, that 'the walls of the Estaque poor are painted by Cézanne in paintings which inevitably finish up on the walls of the wealthy'.[27]

Guédiguian's response to criticism that his film refuses to engage with the Other is to emphasise the utopian aspect of this modern fairy-tale: 'The film, from the very start, is presented as a fairy-tale. It is something which is very conscious, asserted. The film in no way wished to be the sociological or political portrait of an area of Marseilles' (Baecque and Toubiana 1997: 58).[28] Furthermore, he stresses that all he wants to do is 'say that there are things which are going well in the working-class world' (59).[29] It is on this feature of the fairy-tale that we shall conclude.

A Brechtian fairy-tale

So far, we have examined how *Marius et Jeannette* manifests a tension between nostalgia and utopia. That tension is to some extent hidden by topical, social-realist issues – such as immigration and redundancy – which place the film's concerns firmly in the France of the 1990s. Paradoxically, however, it is precisely because that social-realist streak is presented to us so simplistically that, while being at odds with the gritty present which so many of the new generation of film-makers exhibit in their films, and which Guédiguian himself showed in abundance in his previous films, it still manages to hide the tension between nostalgia and utopia by playing on both. The film tries to anchor a hopeful future based on community and class solidarity, but by presenting those values in a class vacuum, and in elegiac mode, the film's tense is a kind of melancholic future anterior tinged with a moral piety and clichés familiar in social realist texts.

What prevents the film from sinking completely into social-realist moral piety, and which also manages to negotiate the tension between nostalgia and utopia, is the Brechtian edge. Guédiguian's interest in Brecht dates from before his film-making days. Darroussin recounts how he first met Guédiguian at the Conservatoire where Darroussin was studying with Ariane Ascaride. Guédiguian, who was writing a thesis in history at the Ecoles des Hautes Etudes, came to the Conservatoire to give a talk on Brecht which, says Darroussin, was 'such a pain in the arse that I fell asleep' (Rigoulet 1997b: 21).[30] Responding to a question about the theatrical nature of his films, Guédiguian confirms that this is his Brechtian side, saying that he 'thinks a lot about Brecht when writing ... scripts and when shooting' (Baecque and Toubiana 1997: 60).[31] Brecht is most obviously an influence in the theatrical nature of the film, with its contained central location of the courtyard, its wordiness (extending to Justin and Marius reading from written texts, a strategy familiar in Godard's work as well), and its frequent addresses to the audience, the most striking of these being Justin's invective against fundamentalism which begins with a close-up on his face speaking direct to camera, before the camera pulls back to reveal that he is talking to the two boys as they sit on the promenade wall. A less obvious, but still powerful Brechtian effect is the contrast in the restaurant sequence between the yuppie couple, with their almost incomprehensible discussion centring on exchange rates, and the simple pleasure of Marius combined with the bewilderment of Jeannette as they order from the menu.

The desire to provoke critical distance in the spectator, which is the hallmark of the Brechtian *Verfremsdungeffekt*, or defamiliarisation effect, is evident in such a contrast, as it is in one of the more minor cinematographic effects, but no less striking for that, the curious zoom-in and zoom-out from Marius as he faces the mechanical digger, gun in hand. Guédiguian's explanation of this effect is typically disarming, but founded in a Brechtian discourse: 'To get people to ask me about it; so that people speak to each other when they are leaving. I like clumsy things in films. I like to denounce the cinema' (Derobert and Goudet 1997: 47).[32]

The form of the fairy-tale allows Guédiguian to mix styles – 'from melodrama to burlesque', he says (Anon. 1997a)[33] with, for example, a fight in the café towards the end of the film, which Guédiguian makes clear is intended to be a parody of the Western (see Frodon 1997b). Such a mix of styles allows him to maintain a balance between the pleasure of fantasy and the moral force of the cautionary tale: 'With the fairy-tale, I maintain a balance between the desire to make people wonder or to re-enchant, to give people their courage back, to say that the world could be better and that we can look at it differently' (Anon. 1997a).[34]

The film, then, is nostalgic in its regret for the passing of a simple (although not naïve) way of life, based in solidarity and community, key elements of the *appel* which rallied the new generation of film-makers in February 1997, and in its parallel hankering for a cinema which exhibited precisely those characteristics. It is utopian in its appeal for a multicultural and tolerant society. What prevents it from becoming a sentimental appeal, swamped by the mawkishness of nostalgia, is the Brechtian effects to which it so often has recourse, one of which, as mentioned above, is the reading of texts. It is fitting then that this exploration should finish by citing Marius's dictation of a poem to Jeannette's son Malek, which manages to combine fantasy and moral message, instruction and entertainment. The poem's last line begins and closes the scene in which it appears, and it could act as a metaphor for the film itself:

> Just as tears well up in the eyes then are born and swell, so words do the same. We must only prevent them from splattering like tears, or repressing them deep inside us. A bed first welcomes them: the words glow. A poem will soon take shape, it will, on starry nights, roam the world, or console reddened eyes. But it will not give up. (Guédiguian and Milesi 1997: 66)[35]

Notes

¹ *'Mon film est ma manière à moi de m'en sortir, de fabriquer de petites utopies puisque les grandes ne sont plus à l'ordre du jour.'* This, and many of the quotations in this chapter, are taken from texts available on the newspaper database of the BiFi in Paris; most of these online texts are unpaginated. My thanks to Keith Reader for collecting part of this material, and for his comments on a first version of this chapter.

² Prizes awarded by foreign press correspondents working in France. Best Director went to Luc Besson for *Le Cinquième Elément*.

³ Where it was in competition with six other films, including Manuel Poirier's *Marion*, and Bruno Dumont's *La Vie de Jésus*.

⁴ *'Nous permettront de parler de Castro, de Le Pen, de la déportation, des grèves, du foot'*

⁵ *'La nostalgie de l'utopie révolutionnaire, le conflit des générations, la volonté de perpétuer l'esprit de résistance et le sens de la communauté'*

⁶ *'Populaire sans une gramme de démagogie. Un film qui rend heureux d'appartenir à l'espace humaine.'* Some took against what Christophe Honoré, writing in *Cahiers du cinéma*, called 'the human warmth thing' (*'le coup de la chaleureuse humanité'*) (Honoré 1998: 4).

⁷ *'Plus allégorique que réaliste, tout en étant intéressé par le fait d'être entre les deux'*

⁸ *'Des films totalement évanescents'*

⁹ *'Ces lumières sans ombre, donnant une image très pétante, des chose très pointues, très définies, où il n'y a plus de matière, plus de corps, plus de visage, plus de regard'*

¹⁰ *'Tous parlent de chômage, de misère, d'exploitation, et le plus souvent finissent mal. Pourtant, une valeur surnage toujours: l'amitié. Tous les films de Robert Guédiguian pourraient porter le titre du sixième: A la vie, à la mort'*

¹¹ *'Nous sommes devenus une famille au sens propre … Jean-Pierre Darroussin a rencontré sa femme sur un tournage de Robert. Malek et Gérard sont nos témoins de mariage'*

¹² Ferran, *L'Age des possibles* (TV fiction for Arte, 1995); Kahn, *Le Point de vue du piéton* (TV fiction for France 3/Arte, 1996); Mordillat, *Architruc* (TV fiction for Arte, 1996).

¹³ *'L'invention, ou la réinvention, d'une pratique politique'*

¹⁴ *'Militantisme de proximité'*

¹⁵ *'Les manifs et les pétitions d'intellectuels ne servent à rien. Il s'agit de jouer de la proximité, de lutter au corps-à-corps. Je dois parler à mon voisin, qui vit et fait des courses au même endroit que moi, car, moi, je ne lui raconterai pas de salades'*

¹⁶ *'Le travelling est une affaire de morale'*

¹⁷ *'Trop dévalorisant, méprisant'*

¹⁸ *'C'est parce qu'il y a la référence Pagnol que le public peut accepter ce que je fais par ailleurs'*

¹⁹ *'Il est le gardien du souvenir, la mémoire d'un fonctionnement 'archaïque', il est une figure importante à L'Estaque, le fils du directeur de l'école, qui était un personnage de référence'*

²⁰ *'En phase avec mes parents'*; the phrase *'en phase'* also means *'in phase with'*, which is more complex than simply being on the same wavelength.

²¹ *'Ce sont des fermetures plus douces, qui ne sont pas sans rapport avec la mémoire, ou la disparition'*

²² *'Cette cimenterie vaut comme cimetière d'une classe ouvrière avec laquelle on ne peut plus compter, et dont les personnages des films de Guédiguian semblent ne pas s'être entièrement remis'*

²³ *'Dans ce mélange d'utopie et de mélancolie réside la vraie beauté du film'*

²⁴ *'L'endroit a un parfum de paradis, comme tout droit sorti d'un film populaire des années 30. N'est-il pas un peu idéalisée? 'Je le reconnais, c'est mon Estaque à moi', avoue le cinéaste. 'En vingt ans, le quartier a beaucoup changé, comme Marseilles du reste, et je fais des choix'.'* It is worth pointing out that in another interview Guédiguian makes it clear that the courtyard in ques-

tion exists, even if it is no longer typical: 'Malek (his childhood friend who has become his director of production) has lived there since 1988. I have spent hours there, and in the summer, whole nights drinking' (Loiseau 1997) ['*Malek (son ami d'enfance devenu son directeur de production) y habite depuis 1988. J'y ai passé des heures et, l'été, des nuits entières à boire des coups.*']

[25] '*Ils restent entre eux, dans leur classe, qui n'a pas à se mélanger aux autres, ou plutôt à l'autre, celle des possédants*'

[26] '*C'est à partir du particulier qu'on fait de l'universel*'

[27] '*Les murs des pauvres de l'Estaque sont peints par Cézanne sur des tableaux qui finissent fatalement sur les murs des riches*'

[28] '*Le film, d'emblée, se présente comme un conte. C'est une chose très consciente, revendiquée. En aucun cas, le film ne voulait être un portrait sociologique ou politique d'un quartier de Marseille*'

[29] '*Dire qu'il y a des chose qui vont bien dans le monde populaire*'

[30] '*Tellement casse-couilles que je me suis endormi.*' Fumaroli, in his wilfully provocative analysis of the culture industry in France, points out how the notion of state-supported 'Culture' was developed by a kind of post-war Brechtian mafia, rooted in the theatre, but extending beyond it, especially in the Mitterrand years under Jack Lang as Minister of Culture (see Fumaroli 1991: 43–4 and 182–5). Guédiguian's Brechtianism, therefore, is not as unusual as it might otherwise have seemed, and indeed the Brechtian context may just as well account for the film's popularity as the formal Brechtian effects within the film to which I shall be turning. My thanks to Keith Reader for pointing out this parallel.

[31] '*Je pense beaucoup à Brecht en écrivant mes scénarios et en tournant*'

[32] '*Pour qu'on me pose la question: pour que les gens en parlent entre eux à la sortie ... J'aime bien les choses maladroites dans les films. J'aime bien dénoncer le cinéma*'

[33] '*Du mélo au burlesque*'

[34] '*Avec le conte, je balance l'envie d'émerveiller ou de réenchanter, de redonner du courage, de dire que le monde pourrait être meilleur et qu'on peut le regarder differemment*'

[35] '*Comme les larmes montent aux yeux puis naissent et se pressent, les mots font de même. Nous devons seulement les empêcher de s'écraser comme les larmes, ou de les refouler au plus profond. Un lit les accueille: les mots rayonnent. Un poème va bientôt se former, il pourra, par les nuits étoiles, courir le monde, ou consoler les yeux rougis. Mais pas renoncer*'

Deforming femininity: Catherine Breillat's ROMANCE
Emma Wilson

'*Dévore-moi. Déforme-moi jusqu'à la laideur*'
Marguerite Duras – *Hiroshima mon amour*

In Marguerite Duras' screenplay to the film *Hiroshima mon amour* (Resnais, 1959) a woman voices her desire to be deformed and destroyed by her lover. Duras' work, and other recent films and texts by women in France, have worked to raise crucial issues about female sexuality, violence and masochism. Such works take risks in exploring images of women in sexual roles that are potentially degrading, painful and humiliating. Readers and viewers are called to ask themselves whether it makes a difference if these images are presented in films and texts created by women. Is such a liberal exploration of female sexuality crucial to an understanding of women's identity and their independence? Is it liberating for women as both authors and consumers of such films and texts to acknowledge the possible pleasure of the victim position? Can such works open up the way we think about active and passive roles? Most simply, how do we judge films and texts that seem to perform female sexual fantasies?

These are crucial issues for the viewer of Catherine Breillat's 1999 film, *Romance*. The film offers an explicit and transgressive account of a young woman's erotic encounters and her desire to be dominated. Marie, Breillat's patient and pliable heroine, undergoes a series of deformations in the course of the film, as the co-ordinates of female sexuality are remapped across the territory of her body. The politics of this rethinking of female sexuality will be explored here. Much critical discussion of the film in the year following its release has centred on the way it disturbs boundaries between art cinema and pornography. The film transgresses certain codes of sexual representation, in particular in its shooting of full frontal male nudity and seemingly non-simulated sex acts. Despite this, by virtue of its art – its stylisation – the film was considered to merit certification and was passed uncut in France and the UK. The issue of art cinema versus pornography is important in considering questions of censorship and sexuality on screen, in particular in the fairly novel context of a female-'authored' erotic film. However, exclusive focus on questions of the illicit and the sexually explicit diverts our attention away from the potential innovation of Breillat's art, from its re-forming of representations of the body and its troubling, at times brutal excavation of female masochism. It is in these terms, in thinking the body, both surface and interiority, form and deformation, and in linking sexuality and degradation, that *Romance* may be seen to reflect and perpetuate broader French-specific investigations of female sexuality which, for feminists, have proved at once ethically troubling and politically charged.

Romance is Breillat's sixth film and the first to bring her wide-scale notoriety in France, the UK and the US. The film is part of a larger and sustained project in Breillat's art to consider, challenge and reinvent female sexuality. A brief overview of her earlier work will help establish the context of *Romance*. In particular this will draw attention to two crucial issues for Breillat's viewers and critics. On the one hand we can begin to appreciate her constant interest in the erotic and pornographic, and its source in the libertarian 1970s. On the other hand we gain an insight into the ways in which feminist critics have from the start seen Breillat as a film-maker with the potential to challenge and open up conventional (sexist) views of female sexuality.

Breillat began her career as a writer, not a film-maker, writing prose fiction in her teens. She published her first novel, *L'Homme facile*, at the age of 17. She continued writing (erotic) novels during the 1970s, and also began to work in cinema, notably writing the screenplay for photographer David Hamilton's soft-porn film *Bilitis* (1975). For Kathleen Murphy, this Breillat sounds like one of her own heroines: 'Breillat was a wild child who matured early' (1999: 16). Having begun work in cinema, Breillat attempted to make her directorial debut with *Une Vraie jeune fille* (1976), an adaptation of one of her own novels. The film's production company went bankrupt, however, and the film could not be released (Lejeune 1987: 96). Breillat continued to write the script for her second film, *Tapage nocturne*, nonetheless, and after two years in search of finance she shot the film in 1979 and it was released in the same year. Paule Lejeune quotes Breillat summing up the subject of *Tapage nocturne* (in terms which might apply also to *Romance*): 'It's a film about desire and seduction; the heroine always goes to the limit of her desires. She accumulates experiences because desire is quickly spent' (1987: 96).[1]

After this start to her film-making career, Breillat encountered certain problems. Lejeune notes in her volume *Le Cinéma des femmes*, in 1986, that Breillat had given up film-making for the time being to devote herself to screen-writing. René Prédal offers a bleaker gloss on this. Commenting on funding difficulties faced by French women film-makers in the 1980s, he notes: 'Breillat took ten years to move from *Tapage nocturne* (1979) to *36 fillette* (1988)' (1996: 621).[2] In this period Breillat returned to screenwriting, most famously authoring the script to Maurice Pialat's *Police* (1985).

36 fillette, Breillat's third film, was her first international success, securing distribution in the US and critical interest in France. Continuing Breillat's exploration of female sexuality, yet inserting itself amongst a number of other French films that analyse, expose and exploit relations between young girls and older men, *36 fillette* narrates the relations between a 14-year-old girl, Lili, and a 40-year-old man. Theirs is, in Susan Hayward's words, an 'almost-affair', while 'the film works to deromanticize virginity and its loss' (1991: 258). Kathleen Murphy begins her analysis of the film in typically racy, overblown terms: '*36 fillette* is a bra size, and Delphine Zentout's ripe breasts, bursting out of a tight black corset, seem to have a life of their own in Breillat's third film' (1999: 16). But her tone has become more sober, her observations more distanced and objective as she moves towards a reckoning with Breillat's film-making as a whole. Alluding both to and beyond *36 fillette*, Murphy muses, 'Breillat's passion plays unfold in emotional bell jars almost entirely insulated from the concerns of the mundane world. In the hermetic atmosphere of these movies, both lovers and those of us marking time in the dark lose sight of any horizon but that of the flesh' (1999: 18). Murphy marks out the ways Breillat's films are concerned primarily with a space of eroticism removed from everyday reality. This hermeticism does not reduce their political impact, however. For Hayward, Breillat's sexual politics, at least in *36 fillette*, are certainly subversive. She concludes that Breillat's preoccupation with female nubile sexuality is distinguished from the work of contemporary male directors. She argues that *36 fillette* de-eroticizes desire by 'keeping men out as beholder of the gaze' (1993: 258), in other words by disrupting the assumption in narrative cinema that men will look and women will be looked at.

Breillat followed *36 fillette* with *Sale comme un ange* (1991) and *Parfait amour!* (1996) both of which return again to questions of sexuality, its gender encoding and its cinematic fixing. Implicitly emphasising the integrity of Breillat's *auteur* corpus, making her almost a feminist Truffaut, Murphy comments that in *Parfait amour!*, 'Frédérique might be Lili, three decades along' (1999: 18). *Parfait amour!*, drawing on a *fait divers*, shows the influence of Breillat's work with Pialat on *Police*. For Claire Vassé, reviewer in *Positif*, the film is an 'anatomy of a sexual affair' (1996: 29).[3] Vassé draws attention to aspects which we will see recur in *Romance* and which enhance a sense of the continuity of Breillat's work. She identifies one of the key stylistic features of Breillat's work as film-maker: her painstaking attention to visual detail and pace. For Vassé, 'Catherine's Breillat's gaze is clinically precise' (1996: 30).[4] Vassé also alludes to the denaturalisation of language in Breillat's films. *Parfait amour!* (like *Hiroshima mon amour*) depends largely on dialogue between a pair of lovers. Yet, as Vassé says, 'all through the film, one witnesses a succession of long monologues rather than real conversations' (1996: 30).[5] This effect is brought to the fore all the more in *Romance* where large sections of the film's soundtrack are made up of Marie's hesitant, sometimes clichéd, sometimes disarmingly frank interior monologue. As we see from this example, and evidence above, Breillat seems in *Romance*, her most recent film, to pursue her attempt to place female subjectivity on screen, amplifying still further the features of her previous works.

In discussion of *Romance*, and her own role as director, Breillat emphasises her place within the context of contemporary French women's film-making. In an interview in *Cinéaste*, she comments: 'For French spectators, women are taking power to talk about sex in a way that men don't' (Sklar 1999: 25). In *Cahiers du cinéma*, Breillat was interviewed by her sister, director Claire Denis, whose work, particularly in *Beau travail* (1999), also attempts to represent the body on film. Breillat's work has been compared elswhere with that of the new director Brigitte Rouän; for Ginette Vincendeau, it bears comparison with works by Tonie Marshall or Jeanne Labrune (Vincendeau 1999: 52).

More insistently still, critics have been keen to locate Breillat's work within a context of sexually explicit film-making and writing. The film most frequently mentioned in reviews, and certainly a point of reference in *Romance*, is the Japanese film, *Ai No Corrida* (*In the Realm of the Senses*) (Oshima, 1976). This film offers a sexually explicit account of an affair between a servant girl and the master of the house. It ends with the murder and mutilation of the master by the servant girl. (The film was not given a certificate or cinema release in the UK until 1991). *Romance* has also been considered in the context of Buñuel's *Belle de jour* (1967), in which Catherine Deneuve plays a bourgeois wife who begins working in a brothel. *Belle de jour*, like *Romance*, makes its viewers question the relation between reality and fantasy, unsettling faith in the veracity of the images shown. Within this erotic, yet high art, tradition, comparisons have also been made with the novel *Histoire d'O*, an account of female masochism. Vincendeau goes further, alluding to the context in which she sees *Romance* fitting: 'Culturally it belongs to a French tradition that goes back to de Sade and encompasses the writings of Apollinaire, Bataille, Klossowski and Pauline Réage (author of *Histoire d'O*), in which eroticism is cerebral matter' (1999: 51). The latter point is important since it draws attention to the way in which *Romance* can be seen, like its literary forbears, as a philosophical exploration of eroticism, raising questions about relations between sexuality, transgression and representation. In her fairly abstract preface to *Romance*, Breillat writes, 'what matters to me is not ... cinema's morals, it would only then be about morality, but making a *moral cinema*. Namely without compromise' (1999: 8–9).[6] She makes a distinction here between a cinema that would be moralising and a truly ethical cinema: in her terms this ethical cinema would be a cinema which would be uncompromising in its exploration of sexuality, and not hide-bound by questions of right and wrong, moral and immoral.

Such abstract thinking about her cinema is typical of Breillat's interviews and her attitude to her film-making as a whole. It infects the very soundtrack of *Romance*, where Marie's voice over sometimes appears to ventriloquise the director's thoughts on sex, desire and female sexuality. Ironically the supposedly cerebral nature of the film has served in helping it be seen more widely, at least in the UK. As Leslie Felperin explains, the press release signed by BBFC (The British Board of Film Classification) president Andreas Whittam Smith and director Robin Duval explaining the decision to pass *Romance* uncut as an '18', states: '*Romance* is a serious work ... With its overly philosophical commentary, it is a particularly French piece. It is also very French in the frank way it addresses sexual issues' (1999: 13). If *Romance* owes its seriousness, its 'Frenchness', to its place in a high-art philosophical tradition, does this rescue the film from risks of exploitation and exposure?

Romance opens surprisingly with an image of a man's face being made up with white powder. A young male model is being dressed up to play the role of a toreador. This opening focuses immediately on performance and on the intersection of love and death (implicitly alluding to sources such as Almodóvar's *Matador* (1988)). Marie is absent from the first shots. When she is first seen, she is seen from behind, her profile at the edge of the frame. She is framed as viewer of the scene. From the start, the film aligns the external viewer with Marie's angle of vision: we view the events of the film through the filter of Marie's consciousness. This knowledge serves to unsettle our understanding of the status of the images viewed. Do we see the film's scenes as events in the life of its protagonist Marie, or as scenarios that she imagines? For Breillat, 'the words of *Romance* are like Marie's soul, the image is like her body' (1999: 23).[7] The episodic structure, the inclusion of 'classic' sado-masochistic encounters and the dream-like fantasy sequence with which the film closes, seem to de-realise the narrative. Yet perhaps one of the implications of the film is to make us aware of the inter-relation between fantasy and desire. As the cultural theorist Slavoj Zizek comments: 'Fantasy constitutes our desire, provides its co-ordinates; that is it literally "teaches us how to desire"' (1997: 7). Breillat's film shows us the ways in which a woman learns to desire, and indeed perceives her affective and sexual life, in the terms of a set of classic fantasy scenarios. Reality and fantasy are utterly fused. The course of the film follows Marie through these fantasy scenarios in a line which leads ultimately to the production of a new identity, the explosion of the past and a new autonomous future.

On this course, the film leads us to question the relation between Marie's mind and her body, between what she thinks (and we hear in voice-over) and what we see. This relation between mind and body is complex and challenging. Our attention is drawn to this in the first scene in which we hear Marie's interior monologue. The scene is in the glacial white interior of the flat Marie shares with her boyfriend, the male model we have seen in the opening shots. The setting is at once antiseptic and aesthetically startling, starkly beautiful (like much of the film). Marie is herself fashioned to fit her surroundings with clinical, short white frocks, simple underwear, hair tied back. She seems a product of her surroundings, as the rooms themselves seem a reflection of her state of mind, at once cold yet iridescent. As Marie cleans her teeth – a mundane act rendered a precise ritual – we see her side view from the back, repeating the earlier frames of her profile watching, and we see her image reflected in mirrors in front of her. The *mise-en-scène* works to fracture our image of Marie and to make us see her, even at this early stage in the film, metaphorically in pieces, broken up.

This effect of severance is further enhanced by the relation between word and image. Philosopher and film theorist Gilles Deleuze has drawn attention to the ways in which modern (art) cinema is definied by a *'va-et-vient'* between word and image (1985: 322); he cites film-makers such as Godard, Resnais and Duras in this context. Breillat is true to this cinematic innovation where the words and images of *Romance* appear two parallel modes of expression. The abstraction of the words seems at times at odds with the fleshy reality of the images, this effect of distance still further achieved by the fact that much of the soundtrack is voice-off or voice-over, grafted onto the images, rather than monologue or dialogue recorded at the time of shooting. Relations between word and image underline the potential experimentalism of Breillat's cinema, yet simultaneously reveals its expressivity, as the very distance and split between word and image seem to tell us something of the division between Marie's thoughts and sensations (realised at its most extreme in her brothel fantasy).

In interviews Breillat emphasizes the cerebral nature of her work and indeed of her understanding of sex and sexuality. In the filmed interview which appears on the French DVD of *Romance*, she claims, 'sex is totally in the mind'.[8] Her protagonist Marie offers a series of drifting thoughts which, in isolation, have the portentousness of philosophical pronouncements on desire (most notorious, perhaps is her line: 'Love between men and women is impossible'.[9] The film runs the risk of taking itself too seriously as a (quasi)philosophical work and in so doing alienates in particular some anglophone reviewers. Yet the greatest risks it takes, and with most effect for the viewer, come in its filming of the body. Contrary to Breillat, then, I suggest that the visceral, not the verbal, is what is most important and innovative in *Romance*. Sex may be conceived in terms of a set of fantasy structures, as Marie, like a fairy-tale heroine, contends with an imaginary world, a world of 'romance', fit for an enactment of 'Beauty and the Beast'. Breillat may show us how sex is lived and understood as mental construct. Yet her achievement in *Romance*, nevertheless, is to show how sex can be filmed as wholly tactile, sensory experience.

Conventionally, cinema depends on visual pleasure. The spectator is seen as both viewer and voyeur who is distanced from the object viewed and who has control over what he sees (and desires) (Metz 1982). Feminist film theory has sought, variously, to look at the ways in which such roles are gendered, working from a consideration of the ways 'looking' is gendered masculine and 'being looked at' is gendered feminine (Penley 1988). Breillat's film disrupts this economy of vision in various ways. She shows a woman, Marie, actively looking: the subject of her own desire. Yet she also shows her making herself an object of desire, putting her body on display and allowing it to be put on display. This exhibitionist complicity itself works to trouble active and passive roles in viewing relations. Beyond this, Breillat works to disrupt the relations of distance and control, on which viewing has been seen to depend, by her emphasis on the tactile. She refuses merely to offer us images of the body's surface, of its integrity and wholeness. Breillat is concerned to bend the body into new shapes, to make the viewer question the relation between inside and outside, to make us feel, as much as see, the images displayed. In so doing she renews cinematic art, unsettles the composure of the body of her actress and, all the more disturbingly perhaps, of her audience. *Romance* is a difficult film to watch and it has drawn an emotional, both positive and negative, response in the press (as we shall go on to see). One of the challenges for students of the film is to account for the trouble it causes. Central to this is the extraordinary work of the actress Caroline Ducey.

Even the most vehement critics of *Romance*, and there have been a number, are unanimous in their praise for the work of Caroline Ducey. Her casting as Marie is such an achievement that her body becomes entirely identified with the film's ethos and its success. Ducey's style of acting is languid and under-stated. Although she is more self-contained, her work as Marie is reminiscent of Chloë Sevigny's impassive sensuality in her roles in *Kids* (Clark, 1995) and *Boys Don't Cry* (Peirce, 1999). Caroline Ducey's body is filmed in such a way as to be pliant, yielding and passive. She is repeatedly viewed in the frame knocked off her vertical axis. Such a shot is first seen as she leans over her boyfriend's bed and becomes sexually intimate with him. The scene follows her lead, against his resistance. It is a scene about unveiling as Breillat sets out her film's agenda. Marie insists Paul removes his cotton T-shirt, and, under the covers slips her hand inside his cotton shorts. The scene imitates the conventional double bind of narrative cinema where the sex act is produced partly from perception, partly from suggestion. But then *Romance* goes further, transgressing the codes of such cinema, as in full view Marie holds Paul's penis in her hand and leans forward to take it in her mouth. Breillat's very still camera merely observes as Marie's mouth works on the penis. The camera seems to record the mechanical rhythm of her motion; attention is paid to the contact between mouth and penis, testing both internal and external sensation. Marie's act, of utmost intimacy, draws attention to the ways she constructs herself as porous, suppliant and open.

This first scene of contact, of the unsettling of the body from its axis, fore-shadows others which follow in the film. Marie's sexuality constantly unfolds through the film, her appetite for sexual encounter virtually insatiable. Marie remains unsatisfied, manifestly, by Paul. Indeed Paul's own sexual ambiva-lence is hinted at in his solitary viewing of muscle-bound men on the television screen, and his insistence that a male friend accompanies himself and Marie on dates. In an inversion of the male fascination with lesbianism, prevalent in erotic and pornographic material, Breillat seems to stage Marie's fascination with a (repressed) gay man.

Marie leaves the intimate space of her non-relation with Paul to seek out sexual favours from strangers. This nocturnal wandering leads her into the arms of Paul's macho alter ego, Paolo, whom Marie picks up in a bar. Paolo is played in the film by the real-life Italian porn star Rocco Siffredi. His presence in the film flags the film's unabashed contact with the exploitation genre of por-nographic cinema. On the one hand *Romance* seems to show that desire and the sex act are never 'real', are always conducted with reference to a set of given cultural and personal fantasies. Yet, on the other hand, Breillat attempts to break through the tasteful veils that have dissimulated the erotic in art-house cinema by inserting the 'real' presence of a porn star in her film. The encoun-ters with Paolo, and the more humiliating near-rape scene with an unknown man on the steps of Marie's apartment block, seem to work to break a taboo on women's pleasure in casual sex. The scenes offer images of Marie's body again in new contortions, bending into each new position her fantasies, rather than her male partners, require of her.

These scenes are, however, incidental to the major scene of erotic and somatic (bodily) invention which is a scene of bondage that falls at the centre of the film. Bizarrely, Marie is a primary school teacher. There is a scene in the classroom where Marie teaches her tiny pupils the difference between the verbs 'to have' ('*avoir*') and 'to be' ('*être*'), saying, 'Having is not at all the same thing as being. One can be without having. And one can have without being'.[10] Marie acts out this split between having and being in sadomasochistic relations with the school's headmaster, Robert. Her role as schoolteacher, as feminine and innocent, seems reminiscent of the role of Pomme (a hairdresser) in *La Dentellière* (Goretta, 1977) or Véronique (a music teacher) in *La Double Vie de Véronique* (Kieslowski, 1991). Breillat, however, partially disrupts this cin-ematic investment in an angelic female passivity: Marie's passivity is pushed to the limits where she will be bound and gagged by her boss in after-school recreations. The film seems to follow its ethical imperative of an uncompromis-ing exploration of sexuality. Does this work to critique the hidden sadism of male fascination with pliable women? Does this allow for the possibility that masochism, the breaking down of her bodily limits and the bounds of her tolerance, becomes a means to metamorphosis and liberation for Marie?

There are two bondage scenes in the film: the first largely serious and transformative in cinematic terms, the second parodic and ritualistic. It is the first that will be discussed. Here Marie is dressed in her signature white dress. She becomes like a doll or a child in the scenario that opens out in Robert's apartment (a space delineated by Japanese screens, dark wood and blood red drapes). Breillat's style of filming is stark and pointed. A first indication of the power relation of the scene comes in a close-up of a hand on a wrist. As in the opening shots of *Hiroshima mon amour*, the body is filmed in parts, severed from the faces which mark its identity. Yet Breillat cuts from these framed body shots to close up images of Marie's face. Between agony and ecstasy it is reminiscent of Bernini's statue of St Theresa. This statue has, in particular since its evocation by the psychoanalyst Lacan, become an icon of female *jouissance* (sexual pleasure). For critical theorist and feminist Barbara Johnson, it is significant that our culture sees the archetypal embodiment of female sexual pleasure in a silent and lifeless statue. She writes: 'There seem … to be two things that women are silent about: their pleasure and their violation. The work performed by the idealization of this silence is that *it helps culture not to be able to tell the difference between the two*' (emphasis in original) (1998: 137). I argue that in this bondage scene Breillat is precisely breaking that silence and breathing life into the white marble statue that has been, for so long, an icon of ideal femininity. She does this by returning to the very images of women's immolation and humiliation in order to make them felt and heard differently. In *Romance* we move from the very confusion of pain and pleasure in the bondage scenes through to rebirth in a new whole form, and new embodied imagery of female presence and identity.

The first bondage scene in particular is painful in the way it makes the viewer undergo – feel as well as visualise – the constraints of Marie's bondage and the perverse release in it which she finds. Marie suspends her agency and control in the scene. When she acquiesces to Robert's desire to tie her up she enters a somnambulistic state. We see his hand on her neck, moving her like a puppet. She seems literally to be hung up, her body hanging flaccid. Robert gags her, enforcing the type of silencing of which Johnson speaks. While the rope, the constraint of her female passivity and of her sexual need, are literally bound around her, her image seems to be reconstructed as an obscene work of art. The image of the Saint in ecstasy gradually mutates into an image of one of Hans Bellmer's contorted surrealist dolls or mannequins. Robert seems to treat Marie like an image; he appraises the posture he has created, saying, 'It was very pretty for me, really very pretty'.[11] Within this aestheticisation of her body, in which both male protagonist and film-maker seem to indulge, one part seems to escape representation and disrupt the scene of possession. Throughout the scene, Marie's dress is uncomfortably hitched up, her tights and underwear are pulled down to thigh level so that her vagina is on show, like a stain or a shadow in the centre of the screen. This visibility disrupts the order of the image, reminding us of Marie as living, visceral human being. The film again pulls back the veils of sexual representation in cinema, making Marie's sex visible, and finding ways to make it tactile too.

The bondage scene perpetuates the rewriting of the body I am charting in *Romance*, showing both the film's cinematic innovation and its attention to female bodily identity. The most significant part of the scene, with respect to both these issues, is its closing moment and Marie's emergence from the bondage she has suffered. Here the scene makes us uncertain of further boundaries between the 'real' and the staged. As Marie is untied, it has suddenly become too much for her, we witness what seems the literal untying of Caroline Ducey. The actress' eyes are wet, her hair dishevelled and her skin flushed. Her body seems to be quivering involuntarily as she lies prone on the bed. Her tears seem genuine. In surprisingly long takes, by pushing her actress to the limit, or by extraordinary artistry, Breillat manages to convince her audience that, as in various of the scenes of intercourse, and in the scene where Marie masturbates, we are witnessing 'real', unstaged physical responses and reactions. This lack of mediation is shocking for the viewer (as in the extreme example of snuff movies) and promotes the film's immediacy, its tactile presence.

This is achieved still more surely in the filming of Marie as medical object, after she has become pregnant (by Paul) towards the end of the film. As we saw above, critics have commented on the clinical precision of Breillat's gaze. Her interest in *Romance* in particular appears to be in testing the limits of the erotic and the pathological, showing how these inverse discourses of the body at times coincide. Hence the move from images of the penetration of Marie's vagina as sexual object through to images of its invasion in medical procedures. The scene which perhaps most fully convinces us that film can be a tactile and proximate as well as visual and distanced medium comes where Marie submits to medical investigation by a doctor and a series of medical students. Each gloved hand pushing up her vagina – the film does not stint in showing the image repeated – seems a further reminder of the female body as tactile presence, as porous and penetrable surface. The body in Breillat's film-making is humid, viscous, hairy. She seems to break through the white marble ideal of femininity (and the bloody reality of the female body is shown materially as Marie moves from virginal white to scarlet and black).

The end of the film is explosive, breaking with an old patriarchal order and confirming the sense that bondage has been, inversely, a means to future liberation and self-fulfilment for Marie. Very pregnant, she finds the courage literally to blow up her boyfriend. The blast is intercut with equally transgressive shots of childbirth. Again Breillat eschews cinematic euphemism letting us see and feel every biological detail of the birth scene. This is read by many as a symbolic scene of Marie's own rebirth. The film seems to suggest that acting out her masochistic fantasies releases her from her psychological bondage to Paul and lets her discover her own autonomy as female desiring subject, as fertile mother and heroine of a female-scripted drama. Some may dispute the film's investment in masochism as therapy in a process of personal renewal. What tempers the trouble with this investment, however, is the film's uncompromising engagement in transgression and its challenge to fixed views of female sexuality. Breillat rewrites the body in cinema, offering a new vivid dimensionality. Her visceral art does not fail to make an impact, requiring its critics to find words to speak of both its pain and its pleasure.

Responses to *Romance* have, unsurprisingly, proved intense and divisive. The film triggers strong reaction, touching a nerve in its viewers. A blueprint of this polarised critical position can be found in the April 14 edition of *Télérama*, the French arts and television magazine (Remy 1999). The piece is headed by the comment 'Opinion is divided'.[12] This division is explained further: 'Catherine Breillat's boldness either seduces you or bores you'.[13] Two film critics take up the case; one for, one against. Vincent Remy defends the film whereas Aurélien Ferenczi takes it apart, finding it full of cliches'. Remy's defence rests on the film's treatment of female identity and sexuality. He finds in the film an important feminist achievement: 'if it fails to reconcile men and women, this film will have reconciled a woman with her body. And perhaps some men with women's bodies too'.[14] Remy finds a virtue in the film's ability to challenge its audience and disrupt our responses: 'Certainly, Madam Breillat is going to stir things up even in this magazine and amongst its readers. Let's test it out'.[15]

Ferenczi, by contrast, is less impressed by the film's ability to challenge its audience. He writes, 'One of the film's motivating forces is undoubtedly provocation. But what if, paradoxically, *Romance* didn't go far enough?'.[16] Ferenczi remains unconvinced by the film's innovation and remarks, however: 'the film is quickly reduced to a series of scenes which we've seen before now and then, such as an attempt at fellatio or a condom being put on, et cetera. A sort of catalogue, exhaustive but hackneyed, of what can be shown on screen without crossing the boundary dividing "normal" cinema from porn'.[17] Ferenczi's worldweariness with the erotic in *Romance*, his sense that we have seen it all before, may be surprising to British audiences and here the national specificity of the reception of *Romance* may be significant. *Film Français*, the French cinema trade journal, heads one article on the film with the title: '*Romance* censored in Dorset (GB)'. We learn that: 'Bournemouth town council asked to see *Romance*, the first film showing an erect penis to come to British screens'.[18] (The same town council was responsible for banning Cronenberg's *Crash* in its cinemas.)

Despite the BBFC passing the film uncut, its reception in the UK has fared rather differently from that at home. To suggest, however, that the film acquires or loses value as a result of the novelty of the images it presents – fellatio, a condom being put on etc. – as Ferenczi does, does much to minimise the importance of the film's means of representation, and of its embedding of sexual imagery in a drama of female liberation (as Remy seems more inclined to concede).

Interestingly both Remy and Ferenczi are male critics, leaving it difficult to draw any simple conclusions in this instance about whether the film appeals more to men than women. It is notable, however, in the international reception of the film, that female film critics such as Ginette Vincendeau, Linda Ruth Williams, Claire Vassé and Kathleen Murphy have taken the film seriously in terms of its cinematic innovation and exploration of female sexuality. Few male critics offer a firm defence of the film, with the exception of the dispassionate analysis by Thierry Jousse (1999) in *Cahiers du cinéma*. Most have been quicker to make fun of the film; perhaps most forthright is Jason Caro writing in *Film Review* (1999: 34):

> Breillat's extremely explicit French movie was apparently greeted with much acclaim on its domestic release. Why, I'm not quite sure, since her warts 'n' all exploration of a woman's sexual needs seems more preoccupied with its heroine's front bottom than any insights into the cogs and wheels of female desire. Then again, I'm a man so what do I know? Well, the difference between bold cinematic expression and pretentious French porn masquerading as art, since you ask.

What to make of these strong reactions? In the first place, doubtless the film's largely less incendiary, more intellectual reception in France is evidence of precisely the way *Romance* seamlessly fits and extends a French cinematic (and literary) exploration of the erotic. The terms of the debate are already set for the film's appreciation. It wins or loses acclaim in artistic terms and as an aesthetic product. In the UK in particular, and in the US too, the film's content is perceived as more excessive and obtrusive (indeed in Australia the film was denied a certificate, though this decision has latterly been revoked on appeal). The film's too excessive material seems to invite knee-jerk and macho derision (perhaps the film's high seriousness about female sexuality cannot avoid this). Yet the political feminism which has saturated serious film criticism in the UK and the US rather more than in France, has rendered other Anglophone film critics particularly sensitive to the subversive effects of the film's thinking on female pleasure.

The intensity of debate around the film testifies to its power to generate response. It is a trail-blazing film, with the courage and stridency to take itself seriously, to deform and rethink the female body on screen. The cinema trailer throws up a series of words: 'shocking, provocative, sexual, perverted, troubling, lucid, sincere, sexual, cruel, erotic, crude, exciting, aggressive, tender, free, forbidden'.[16] *Romance* frees up the forbidden, for women. The viewer may not share Marie's fantasies, but the experience of sharing her vision, through her sexual metamorphosis, lets sex, cinema and being female feel different. Breillat wants to make an impression. She claims that she likes to make people accept what they deem unacceptable. The challenge for the viewer of *Romance* is to question how far the violence we undergo in watching the film can itself be a source of pleasure and expiation.

Notes

[1] 'C'est un film sur le désir et sur la séduction; l'héroïne va toujours au bout de ses désirs. Elle cumule les expériences parce que le désir s'épuise vite'

[2] 'Catherine Breillat met dix ans à passer de Tapage nocturne (1979) à 36 fillette (1988)'

[3] 'anatomie d'une histoire de sexe'

[4] 'le regard de Catherine Breillat est un regard médicalement minutieux'

[5] ëtout au long du film, on assiste plus à une succession de longs monologues qu'à de véritables conversations'

[6] 'ce qui me tient à coeur, ce n'est [...] pas la morale du cinéma, il ne s'agirait alors que de moralisme, mais de faire du cinéma moral. C'est-à-dire sans compromis'

[7] 'les mots de Romance sont comme l'âme de Marie, l'image est comme son corps'

[8] 'le sexe est totalement mental'

[9] 'L'amour des hommes et des femmes est impossible'

[10] 'Avoir, c'est pas du tout la même chose qu'Etre. On peut Etre sans Avoir. Et on peut Avoir sans Etre'

[11] 'Pour moi c'était très jolie, vraiment très jolie'

[12] 'Les avis sont partagés'

[13] 'L'audace de Catherine Breillat séduit ou ennuie'

[14] 'à défaut de réconcilier les hommes et les femmes, ce film aura réconcilié une femme avec son corps. Et peut-être quelques hommes avec le corps des femmes'

[15] 'Assurément, dame Breillat va jeter grand trouble jusque dans ce journal, et parmi ses lecteurs. Qu'on en juge'

[16] 'L'un des ressorts du film, c'est évidemment la provocation. Et si, paradoxalement, Romance n'allait pas assez loin?'

[17] 'le film se réduit vite à un collage de scènes déjà vues ici ou là, telle qu'une ébauche de fellation ou la pose d'un préservatif, etc. Une sorte de catalogue, exhaustif mais usé, de ce qui est montrable à l'écran sans que soit franchie la frontière séparant le cinéma "normal" du porno'

[18] 'Le conseil municipal de la ville de Bournemouth a demandé à voir Romance, premier film montrant un pénis en érection à sortir dans les salles britanniques'

[19] 'choquant, provoquant, sexuel, pervers, troublant, lucide, sincère, sexuel, cruel, érotique, cru, excitant, agressif, tendre, libre, interdit'

DIRECTOR BIOGRAPHIES

JACQUES AUDIARD

Following in his father's footsteps, Jacques Audiard began his career in film as a screenwriter; indeed father and son have collaborated on a number of projects. Writing scripts for such film-makers as Josiane Blalasko, Denys Granier Feferre, and Claude Miller encouraged him to make films in his own right. Made at the age of 40 his first film, *Regarde les hommes tomber*, was met with enthusiastic critical acclaim and won the *César* for best film from a new director at Venice in 1994. A crime thriller about the activities of three men whose lives intersect, the film clearly demonstrated his skill as a creator of inventive and intelligent narratives and showed a marked ability to establish and sustain tone and tension. *Un Héros très discret* is his second film, again demonstrating his narrative flair and inventive plotting, suggestive of his former training as a screenwriter.

1994 *Regarde les hommes tomber*
1996 *Un Héros très discret*
1998 *Norme Française*

JOSIANE BALASKO

Josiane Balasko is one of the best-loved actress/film-makers in France today. Born in Paris in 1950, she achieved notoriety as a comedian in the *café-théâtres*, small highly accessible comedy playhouses which flourished in Paris in the 1970s. Having made her débuts in the *Café de la Gare*, Balasko transferred to its contemporary, *Le Splendid*, in 1976, where she worked alongside other rising stars of French comedy, including Thierry Lhermitte, Gérard Jugnot and Christian Clavier, and under the auspices of director Jean-Marie Poiré. She played her first film lead in Poiré's *Les Petits calins* (1978), but it was her role as the bourgeois director of a telephone helpline in the cult classic *Le Père Noël est une Ordure* (Poiré, 1980) which brought more recognition. Balasko developed an interest in operations behind the scenes and, in 1981, she wrote the scripts for Poiré's *Les Hommes préfèrent les grosses* and played the lead. She directed her first feature, *Sac de noeuds*, in 1985 and, after a period of ten years released her most acclaimed production to date, *Gazon maudit*. Her role as Gérard Depardieu's mistress in Bertrand Blier's melodrama *Trop belle pour toi* (1989) introduced her to international audiences. Elements of Blier's approach can be identified in Balasko's work including a focus on gender, use of comedy and manipulation of narrative structure. Their collaboration continues today – Balasko has recently starred as herself in Blier's latest release, *Les Acteurs* (2000). Balasko's work challenges misogyny, both within the media of the cinema and theatre and society in general. She is interested in questioning social conventions of 'femininity' and 'womanhood', particularly perceptions of female beauty. Her roles demonstrate the attractiveness of the larger woman through the seduction of established sexual icons such as Thierry Lhermitte, Richard Berry (she plays Berry's lover in her latest production, *Un Grand Cri d'amour* (1998)) and, of course, Victoria Abril in *Gazon maudit* (1995). It is this desire to subvert social and generic convention which constitutes the hallmark of Balasko's work and, along with her equally prolific and acclaimed female contemporary Coline Serreau, she has broadened the scope of the comic film, rendering it both accessible and attractive to other female directors.

1985 *Sac de noeuds*
1987 *Les Keufs*
1991 *Ma Vie est un enfer*
1995 *Gazon maudit*
1998 *Un Grand Cri d'amour*

ALAIN BERLINER

Born in Brussels on 21 February 1963, Alain Berliner studied in Brussels at the *INSAS* (the Belgian equivalent of *La Fémis* in France). After graduating with honours, he went on to work in various capacities on a number of public television projects for TF1: *Monsieur Victor* (1993), *La Guerre des privés* (1993), *Extrême Limit* (1992), *A l'ombre de la gloire* (1992), and *Les Galettes de Maimie* (1991). In cinema, he began as a scriptwriter before directing three shorts: *Rencontre* (1988), *Le Jour du chat* (1991), and *Rose* (1993). *Rose*, the story of a teacher in love with a rose who ends up finding happiness with a woman, was much admired by Chris Vander Stappen, who was to write the basis of the script for *Ma Vie en rose*, Berliner's first full-length film.

Agnès Brunet and Michel Pascal have identified Berliner as belonging to the young Belgian cinema, from which directors such as Jaco Van Dormael have emerged. It has been commented that Berliner has been visually inspired by the paintings of Magritte and Delvaux, and his work certanly contains pronounced surreal and oneiric elements. However, Brunet and Pascal also assimilate Berliner to a wider category of French-language film directors (including Robert Guédiguian, Manuel Poirier, Bruno Dumont and Laurence Ferreira-Barbosa) which, they assert, forms a 'new tendency on French cinema' with the emphasis on social commitment. The common factor uniting these directors, apart from their relative youth, are acute awareness of social exclusion, a popular appeal, and a mixture of affectionate humanism and pointed political critique. Berliner himself says that he likes to mix the probable and the improbable, the oneiric and the real, but that his main reason for directing films is to tell essentially human stories that provoke questions.

As well as making his own films, Berliner continues to be a reader and script analyst for the production house of D'Erwin Provoost in Brussels and he also teaches a class on scriptwriting at the CRRAV in Lille.

1988 *Rencontre* (short)
1991 *Le Jour du chat* (short)
1993 *Rose* (short)
1997 *Ma Vie en rose*
1998 *Le Mur*
2000 *Passion of Mind*

CLAUDE BERRI

Born Claude Langman in Paris in 1934, Berri has worked within a variety of genres, directing a form of populist cinema that is defined by its familiar, well-known stars and high production values. He won an Oscar for his short *Le Poulet* (1963) and drew in part from his own life experience with *Le Vieil homme et l'enfant* (1967), *Mazel Tov ou le mariage* (1968) and *Sex-shop* (1973). He followed his comically social commentaries, *Le Maître d'école* (1981) and *Tchao Pantin* (1983), with two important European heritage projects, *Jean de Florette* (1986) and *Manon des sources* (1986), becoming an internationally renowned director, earning both critical and commercial success. He has also taken on big-budget literary adaptations – *Uranus* (1990) and a version of *Germinal* (1990) – and produced several key French films such as *Les Amants du pont-neuf* (1991), *La Reine Margot* (1994), *La Séparation* and *Gazon maudit* (1995).

1963 *Le Poulet* (short)

1963 *Les Baisers*
1964 *La Chance et l'amour* (segment "La Chance du guerrier")
1967 *Le Vieil homme et l'enfant*
1969 *Mazel Tov ou le marriage*
1971 *Le Cinéma de papa*
1970 *Le Pistonné*
1973 *Sex-shop*
1975 *Le Mâle du siècle*
1976 *La Première fois*
1977 *Un moment d'égarement*
1979 *A nous deux*
1980 *Je vous aime*
1981 *Le Maître d'école*
1983 *Tchao Pantin*
1986 *Jean de Florette*
1986 *Manon des sources*
1990 *Uranus*
1993 *Germinal*
1997 *Lucie Aubrac*
1999 *La Débandade*

LUC BESSON

Born in 1959, Besson worked on various film sets in France and America before shooting his first full-length film, *Le Dernier Combat* (1982), a low-budget science fiction feature set in an apocalyptic urban landscape. Since the Gaumont-produced *Subway* (1985), Besson's name has become one of the most famous, and most bankable, in French cinema. *Subway* placed Besson in the emerging current of the '*cinéma du look*', the stylish urban thriller genre which marked French film production of the 1980s. *Le Grand Bleu* (1988) returned to his early love of the underwater world: it was a critical failure but a cult success, a situation which has been frequent in Besson's career and has led to a famously stormy relationship with the critical establishment. Besson returned once again to undersea filming in the little-known *Atlantis*, a semi-documentary made in 1991. *Nikita* (1990) may still be his best-known film. It was re-made in America as *The Assassin*, with Bridget Fonda, in 1992. In 1994, Besson shot *Léon* in New York and in the English language. However, his most transatlantic films are still marked by French film culture, and Besson himself emphasises that, although he dislikes 'sticking a flag' in films, he still considers his work primarily French.

He has worked with favourite actors in several films, for example Tchéky Karyo (Bob in *Nikita*) and Jean Reno (in all his films up to *Léon*, where of course he plays the protagonist). Besson's last two films, *Le Cinquième élément* (1997) and *Jeanne d'Arc* (1999), starring his now ex-wife Mila Jovovich, featured star-studded international casts. His presidency of the Cannes Film Festival in 2000 suggests that his importance to French cinema is at last obtaining official recognition.

1981 *L'Avant dernier* (short)
1983 *Le Dernier combat*
1985 *Subway*
1988 *Le Grand Bleu*
1990 *Nikita*
1991 *Atlantis*
1994 *Léon*
1997 *Le Cinquième Elément*
1999 *Jeanne d'Arc*

CATHERINE BREILLAT

Catherine Breillat was born in 1948. She published her first novel, *L'Homme facile*, at the age of seventeen. In addition to her career as a novelist, she worked as a scriptwriter in the 1970s and 1980s (notably writing the screenplay to David Hamilton's *Bilitis* (1975) and Maurice Pialat's *Police* (1985)). In 1976, she attempted unsuccessfully to adapt one of her own novels, *Une Vraie Jeune Fille*, for cinema (the film finally received a cinema release in France in July 2000). Her first successful feature film, *Tapage nocturne*, was released in 1979. This was followed by *36 fillette* (1988), *Sale comme un ange* (1991) and *Parfait amour!* (1996). Since *Romance* (1999), she has continued her exploration of female sexuality in *Fat Girl* (2000).

1988 *36 fillette*
1990 *Sale comme un ange*
1995 *A propos de Nice, la suite* (segment "Aux Niçois qui mal y pensent")
1996 *Parfait amour!*
1999 *Romance*
2000 *Une Vraie Jeune Fille*
2000 *Fat girl*

KARIM DRIDI

Born in Tunis to a French mother and Tunisian father, Karim Dridi spent his childhood moving between Tunisia and Paris (he is now based in France). After studying at university he worked as an 'industrial' film-maker, producing factual and promotional documentaries for private companies and organisations. Having directed a number of short films in the late 1980s and early 1990s, his first feature, *Pigalle* (1994), won awards at the 1994 Venice Film Festival. His second feature, *Bye-Bye* (1995), gained similar critical acclaim; winning the *Prix de la Jeunesse* in the *Certain Regard* section at Cannes in 1995 and attracting more than 120,000 spectators in France. Since the mid 1990s Dridi has worked closely with the independent production company ADR Productions, producing both fictional features and documentary films.

1985 *Mains de...* (short)
1987 *Dans le sac* (short)
1988 *La Danseuse de Saba* (short)
1989 *New Rêve* (short)
1990 *Jalousie* (short)
1992 *Zoë le boxeuse* (short)
1993 *Le Boxeur endormi* (short)
1994 *Pigalle*
1995 *Bye-Bye*
1996 *Citizen Ken Loach* (documentary)
1998 *Hors Jeu*

ROBERT GUEDIGUIAN

Guédiguian was born in 1953 in the port of L'Estaque, near Marseilles, of an Armenian mother and German father. He studied history, and was a member of the French Communist Party, which he left on making his first film in 1980. In the early 1980s his production cooperative, Agat, helped finance the films of a number of the current generation of young film-makers, several of whom participated with Guédiguian in the return to the political of 1997. This was also the year in which he came to national prominence at Cannes with his seventh film, *Marius et Jeannette*.

All of his films to date have been set in L'Estaque, and he has consistently used the same troupe of actors, whom he met when a student. His films are low-budget, and could be described as sentimentally social-realist regional films. Their themes revolve around a post-1968 nostalgia for revolutionary action, generational conflict, and resisting communities, paradigmatically the communities of L'Estaque. *Marius et Jeannette* was followed in 1998 by *A la Place du coeur*, an equally sentimental and moralising tract about racial and generational tolerance.

1980 *Dernier été*
1985 *Rouge midi*
1985 *Ki lo sa?*
1989 *Dieu vomit les tièdes*
1992 *L'Argent fait le bonheur*
1997 *Marius et Jeannette*
1998 *A la Place du coeur*
2000 *A l'attaque!*
2000 *La Ville est tranquille*

CEDRIC KLAPISCH

Cédric Klapisch attended film school at New York University and worked on short films in the United States from 1983 to 1985, first as a camera operator and subsequently as a director. After returning to France he directed a number of industrial films and documentary pieces for French television. From 1987 to 1989 he worked on several short films, including *Ce qui me meut* which was nominated for a *César* and was awarded prizes at the Cannes and Berlin film festivals. In 1990 Kapisch directed a television documentary on the Masai people of Kenya for Canal +. His first feature film was *Riens du tout*, released in 1992 and also nominated for a *César*. This film was swiftly followed by his second feature, *Le Péril Jeune*, in 1993. Both of these films were comedies. In 1996 he made *Chacun cherche son chat* and then, in 1997, the highly successful *Un Air de famille*. His most recent full-length film is the science fiction extravaganza *Peut-être* (1999), set in a Paris of the future. Klapisch has also continued to direct short films, notably *Poison Rouge* (1994), his contribution to the AIDS prevention campaign *3000 Scénarios contre un virus*.

1992 *Riens du tout*
1993 *Le Péril jeune*
1996 *Chacun cherche son chat*
1997 *Un Air de famille*
1999 *Peut-être*

JEAN-MARIE POIRÉ

Son of former Gaumont producer, the late Alain Poiré, Jean-Marie Poiré started his career as an assistant to Claude Autant-Lara and Gérard Oury. Born in 1945, scriptwriter and photographer Poiré also had a brief career as a rock singer before turning to directing films in 1977. His first feature, *Les Petits Calins*, 'a serious film', was a modest success. It is only with his third film, *Les Hommes préfèrent les grosses* – a *café-théâtre* style comedy, that Jean-Marie Poiré really came to public attention in 1981. Poiré's next film, *Le Père Noël est une ordure* (1982), adapted from the *Théâtre du Splendid* play of the same title also starred some of the *Splendid* actors – Balasco, Clavier, Jugnot and Lhermitte. A favourite with French schoolchildren and television viewers of all ages, Poiré's 1982 box-office hit was considered his best work until *Les Visiteurs*. Since 1982, Jean-Marie Poiré has worked with Christian Clavier and the French actor has both starred in and co-scripted Poiré's comedies. Poiré has been described as a spiritual heir of several trends, the Michel Audiard-Georges Lautner mould (Poiré wrote scripts for both film directors), the *Splendid* comic style, parody, and the burlesque tradition.

1978 *Les Petits Calins*
1980 *Retour en force*
1981 *Les Hommes préfèrent les grosses*
1982 *Le Père Noël est une ordure*
1983 *Papy fait de la résistance*
1986 *Twist again à Moscou*
1988 *Mes meilleurs copains*
1990 *L'Opération corned beef*
1992 *Les Visiteurs*
1995 *Les Anges gardiens*
1998 *Les Couloirs du temps: Les Visiteurs II*

SANDRINE VEYSSET

Born in Avignon in 1967, Sandrine Veysset studied literature and art at the University of Montpellier. She got a job building sets on Léos Carax's *Les Amants du Pont-Neuf*; giving up her studies to work on sets for several years. She then went to Paris and, through a friend she had met while working on

Amants, got a job driving Carax around Paris. He encouraged her to write about her rural childhood and with his encouragement she wrote the script of *Y aura-t-il de la neige à Noël?* She successfully applied for the *Avance sur recettes*, advance on box-office receipts, a French government subsidy for original – usually first – films, and made *Y aura-t-il de la neige à Noël?*, winning the César for best first film and the Louis Delluc prize in 1997. In 1998 her second film, *Victor ... pendant qu'il est trop tard*, was released to a mixed critical reception.

1996 *Y aura-t-il de la neige à Noël?*
1998 *Victor... pendant qu'il est trop tard*

BIBLIOGRAPHY

Allen-Mills, T. (1998) 'French cinema flickers towards the final reel', *The Sunday Times*, 13 December.

Audé, F. (1981) *Ciné-modèles, cinéma d'elles*. Lausanne: Editions L'Age d'Homme.

Austin, G. (1996) *Contemporary French Cinema: An Introduction*. Manchester: Manchester University Press.

Balasko, J. (1995) 'French Twist (*Gazon maudit*)', *France.com* URL: http://www.france.com/mag/cinema/gazonmaudit/

Barbancey, P. (1997) '*Ma Vie en rose*', in *L'Humanité*, 13 May.

Baudii, B. (1993) 'Christian Clavier: une pêche d'enfer', *Le Figaro*, 29 January.

—— (1997) 'Alain Berliner: vive la différence', *Le Figaro*, 29 May.

Berthemy, O. (1993) 'Godefroy, Jacquouille ... et Oedipe', *L'Evènement du jeudi*, 1–7 April.

Bhabha, H. K. (1994) *The Location of Culture*. London and New York: Routledge.

Bosséno, C. (1992) 'Immigrant cinema: national cinema – the case of *Beur* film', in R. Dyer and G. Vincendeau (eds) *Popular European Cinema*. London and New York: Routledge.

Bouquet, S. (1995) 'Les Enracinés', *Cahiers du cinéma*, 494, 36–8.

Breillat, C. and C. Denis (1999) 'Le Ravissement de Marie: Dialogue entre Catherine Breillat et Claire Denis', *Cahiers du cinéma*, 534, 42–7.

Bright, M. (1993) '*Les Visiteurs*', *Sight and Sound*, 4, 2, 61–2.

Brunet, A. and M. Pascal (1997) 'Cinéma français: le réveil', *Le Point*, 2 June.

Butler, J. (1990) *Gender Trouble: Feminism and the Subversion of Identity*. London: Routledge.

—— (1991) 'Imitation and Gender Insubordination', in J. Rivkin and M. Ryan (eds) *Literary Theory: An Anthology*. Malden: Blackwell, 722–30.

Cairns, L. (1999) '*Gazon maudit*: French National and Sexual Identities', *French Cultural Studies*, 9, 2, 26, 225–37.

Capvert, C. (1994) '*Les Visiteurs*: mais qu'est-ce que c'est que ce bin's?', *L'Humanité*, 25 January.

Caro, J. (1999) 'Romance', *Film Review* , November, 34.

Chevassu, F. (1996) '*Y aura-t-il de la neige à Noël?*', bifi. Fr. Services Saison 96 Notices 96 – 442 html.

Cohen, C. (1997) 'Le rêve du bonheur: *Marius et Jeannette* de Robert Guédiguian', *Cahiers du cinéma*, 518, 55–7.

Cook, P. (1996) *Fashioning the Nation*. London: BFI.

Corner, J. and S. Harvey (eds) (1991) *Enterprise and Heritage: Cross-Currents in National Culture*, London: Routledge.

Coveney, P. (1982) 'The Image of the Child' in Chris Jenks (ed.) *The Sociology of Childhood*. York: Batsford, 63–87.

Custen, G. (1992) *Bio-Pics: How Hollywood Constructed Public History*. Indiana: Rutgers University Press.

Danel, I. (1997) 'Entre drame et comédie', *Télérama*, 28 May.

Darke, C. (1987) 'Monsieur Memory', *Sight and Sound*, 7, 4, 24.

——— (1997) 'The Dark Realism of a Fairytale Debut', *Independent Eye*, 3 October.

——— (2000) *Light Readings: Film Criticism and Screen Arts*. London: Wallflower Press.

Dawson, G. (1994) *Soldier Heroes: British Adventure, Empire and the Imagining of Masculinities*. London and New York: Routledge.

De Baecque, A. and S. Toubiana (1997) 'Le goût de L'Estaque: Entretien avec Robert Guédiguian', *Cahiers du cinéma*, 518, 58–61.

De Bruyn, O. (1997) 'L'Internationale à l'aïoli', *L'Evénement*, 20 November.

De la Bretèque, F. (1991) 'Un cinéma de la deférence: une "certaine tendance" du cinéma français des années 80', *Cahiers du cinéma*, 451, 45–75.

——— (1992) 'Images of Provence: Ethnotypes and Stereotypes of the south in French cinema' in R. Dyer and G. Vincendeau (eds) *Popular European Cinema*. London and New York: Routledge, 58–71.

——— (1993) 'Atouts et Faiblesses du cinéma français', *CinémAction* 66.

De la Fuente, A. M. (1999) 'French Kissing in the USA', *Screen International*, 1225, 10.

De Lauretis, L. (1994) *The Practice of Love: Lesbian Sexuality and Perverse Desire*. Bloomington, Indiana University Press.

Deleuze, G. (1985) *Cinéma 2: L'Image-Temps*. Paris: Minuit.

Derobert, E. and S. Goudet (1997) 'Entretien avec Robert Guédiguian', *Positif*, 442, 42–8.

Dridi, K. (1995a) 'Propos de Karim Dridi', *Cahiers du cinéma*, 494, 39–41.

——— (1995b) Interview on 'Droit de Ciné', *Saga Cités*, France 3, October 14.

Dubet, F. and D. Laperyronnie (1992) *Les Quartiers d'Exil*. Paris: Seuil.

Duras, M. (1964) *Hiroshima mon amour*. Paris: Gallimard.

——— (1982) *La Maladie de la mort*. Paris: Minuit.

Durmelat, S. (1998) 'Petite histoire du mot beur: ou comment prendre la parole quand on vous le prête', *French Cultural Studies*, 9, 26, 191–207.

Dyer, R. (1977) 'Entertainment and Utopia', in S. During (ed.) *The Cultural Studies Reader*. London and New York: Routledge.

Fanon, F. (1986) *Black Skin, White Masks.* trans. C. Frarrington, London: Pluto.

Felperin, L. and L. R. Williams (1999) 'The Edge of the Razor', *Sight and Sound*, 9, 10, 12–14.

Fenby, J. (1998) *On the Brink: The Trouble with France.* London: Warner.

Ferenczi, A. (1998) 'Le Business Jacquouille', *Télérama*, 18 February, 2510, 20–5.

Ferro, M. (1988) *Cinema and History.* New York: Wayne State University Press.

Forbes, J. (1992) *The Cinema in France after the New Wave.* London: BFI.

Frodon, J-M. (1997a) 'Un artisan du septième art', in *Le Monde*, 20 November.

────── (1997b) 'Robert Guédiguian, réalisateur: "J'ai voulu prendre position contre la peur et la démission"', *Le Monde*, 20 November.

Frodon, J-M. and J-C. Loiseau (1987) *Jean de Florette: La Folle Aventure.* Paris: Herscher.

Fumaroli, M. (1991) *L'Etat culturel: Une religion moderne.* Paris: Editions de Fallois.

Garbaz, F. (1997) 'Le Renouveau social du cinéma français', *Positif*, 442, 74–5.

Gilles, E. (1995) 'Karim Dridi: amour, respect, dignité et responsibilité', *L'Humanité*, 14 September.

Goupil, R. (1997) 'Douze cinéastes témoignent de leur engagement citoyen', *Le Monde*, 19 March.

Gravari-Barbas, M. (1996) 'Le "sang" et le "sol"', *Géographie et cultures*, 20, 55–67.

Guédiguian, R. (1996) 'Un cinéma de quartier: Entretien avec Robert Guédiguian par Emmanuelle Eydt', *CinémAction*, 88, 152–6.

Guédiguian, R. and J-L. Milesi (1997) *Marius et Jeannette: Un conte de L'Estaque.* Paris: Arte Editions/Hachette.

Hargreaves, A. G. (1996) 'A deviant construction: the French media and the 'Banlieues', *New Community*, 22(4), 607–18.

────── (1997) 'Gatekeepers and Gateways: post-colonial minorities and French television', in A. Hargreaves and M. McKinney (eds) *Post Colonial Cultures in France.* London and New York: Routledge, 84–98.

Hayward, S. (1993) *French National Cinema.* London: Routledge.

────── (1998) *French Film Directors: Luc Besson.* Manchester and New York: Manchester University Press.

Herpe, N. (1998) 'Y aurait-il un jeune cinéma français?', *Positif*, 443, 53–5.

Higson, A. (1991) 'Representing the national past: nostalgia and pastiche in the heritage film', in L. Friedman (ed.) *British Cinema and Thatch-*

erism: Fires Were Started. London: University College of London, 109–29.

——— (ed.) (1996) *Dissolving Views: Key writings on British cinema*, London and New York: Cassell.

Holland, P. (1992) *What is a Child?* London: Virago.

Hollinger, K. (1998) 'Theorizing Mainstream Female Spectatorship: The Case of the Popular Lesbian Film', *Cinema Journal*, 37, 2, 3–15.

Honoré, C. (1998), 'La triste moralité du cinéma français', *Cahiers du cinéma*, 521, 4–5.

Hurd, G. (1984) (ed.) *National Fictions: World War Two in British Film and Television*. London: BFI.

Hutcheon, L. (1989) *The Politics of Postmodernism*. London: Routledge.

Jäckel, A. (1996) '*Les Visiteurs*: a popular form of cinema for Europe?', in W. Everett (ed.) *European Identity and Cinema*. Exeter: Intellect, 35–44.

Jeancolas, J-P. (1992) 'Un cinéma inexportable?', paper presented at the Popular European Conference, Warwick University, 14–17 September 1989.

——— (1997) 'Une bobine d'avance: du cinéma et de la politique en février 1997', *Positif*, 434, 56–8.

Johnson, B. (1998) *The Feminist Difference*. Cambridge, Massachusetts: Harvard University Press.

Johnson, C. (ed.) History/Production/Memory, Special Event at Edinburgh Film Festival: Edinburgh Festival '77 Magazine No. 2.

Jousse, T. (1999) 'Les Mystères de l'organisme', *Cahiers du cinéma*, 534, 40–1.

Kaes, A. (1989) *From Hitler to Heimat: The Return of History as Film*. Harvard: HUP.

Konstantarakos, M. (1999) 'Which Mapping of the City? *La Haine* and the *cinéma de banlieue*', in Phil Powrie (ed.) *French Cinema in the 1990s: Continuity and Difference*. Oxford: Oxford University Press, 160–71.

Lamassoure, P. (1998) 'Une "Romance" torride pour Breillat et Lepetit', *Film Français*, 2725, 5.

Lefort, G. (1997) 'La Fête de l'humanité: *Marius et Jeannette*, conte drole, émouvant et protestataire', *Libération*, 19 November.

Lejeune, P. (1987) *Le Cinéma des femmes*. Paris: Editions Atlas.

Libiot, X. (1998) '*Romance*', *Première*, 258, 107–8.

Loiseau, J-C. (1997) 'Le triomphe de la gènérosité', *Télérama*, 2500.

Lorcerie, F. and V. Geisser (1997) 'Maghrébins en France – Chronique', in *Annuaire de l'Afrique du Nord, XXXIV: 1995*. Paris: CNRS, 907–42.

Lyotard, J-F. (1987) *The Postmodern Condition: a Report on Knowledge*.

Manchester: Manchester University Press.

Malouk, A. and D. Lederman (1999) *1,2,3 ... Cités!*. Paris: Ramsay.

Martel, F. (1996) *Le rose et le noir: les homosexuels en France depuis 1968*, trans. Jane Marie Todd, Stanford: University of Stanford Press.

McHale, B. (1987) *Postmodernist Fiction*. New York: Methuen.

McLennan, G., D. Held and S. Hall (1984) *State and Society in Contemporary Britain: A Critical Introduction*. Cambridge: Polity Press.

Mérigeau, P. (1997) 'Tous en choeur', *Le Nouvel observateur*, 20 November.

Metz, C. (1982) *Psychoanalysis and Cinema: The Imaginary Signifier*. London: Macmillan.

Mulvey, L. (1975) 'Visual Pleasures and Narrative Cinema', *Screen*, 16, 3, 6–18.

Murphy, K. (1999) 'A Matter of Skin ... Catherine Breillat's metaphysics of film and flesh', *Film Comment*, 35, 5, 16–20.

Mury, C. (1996) '*Gazon maudit*', *Télérama*, 11 September, 115.

Nesselson, L. (1997) '*Ma Vie en rose*', *Variety*, 19–25 May, 57.

———— (1998) '*The Corridors of time: The Visitors II*', *Variety*, 23 February–1 March, 74.

Neve, B. (1998) 'The Reception of American Film in Britain and in France in the Late Twentieth Century: the case of *Jurassic Park*', paper presented (jointly with A. Jäckel) at 'Hollywood and its spectators', Commonwealth Fund Conference, UCL, London 12–14 February.

Nevers, C. (1993) 'Les Visiteurs font de la résistance', *Cahiers du cinéma*, 465, 83.

Nevers, C. and F. Strauss (1993) 'Entretien avec Jean-Marie Poiré et Christian Clavier', *Cahiers du cinéma*, 465, 84–9.

Olivier, C. (1980) *Les Enfants de Jocaste*. Paris: Denoël/Gonthier.

Ostria, V. and L. Roth (1996) '*Y aura-t-il de la neige à Noël?*: Entretien avec Sandrine Veysset', *Cahiers du cinéma*, 508, 56–8.

Palmer, M. (1996) 'GATT and culture: a view from France', in A. van Hemmel, H. Mommaas and C. Smithuijsen (eds) (1997) *GATT, European Cultural Policies and the Transatlantic Market*. Amsterdam: Boekman Foundation, 27–38.

Parkinson, D. (1999) '*Romance*', *Empire*, 125, 24.

Penley, C. (ed.) (1988) *Feminism and Film Theory*. London: BFI Publishing.

Perrin, E. (1995) '*Gazon maudit*', *Têtu* 1, 22.

Philbert, B. (1984) *L'Homosexualité à l'écran*. Paris: Henri Veyrier.

Ploquin, F. (1993) '*Les Visiteurs*', *Le Français dans le Monde*, 257, 11.

Powrie, P. (1997) *French Cinema in the 1980s: Nostalgia and the Crisis of Masculinity*, Oxford: Oxford University Press.

———— (1998) 'Heritage, History and the "New Realism"', *Modern &*

Contemporary France, 4, 479–92.

———— (ed.) (1999) *French Cinema in the 1990s: Continuity and Difference*. Oxford: OUP.

Prédal, R. (1996) *50 ans de cinéma français*. Paris: Nathan.

Rémy, V. (1995) 'Beur … je refuse ce mot!', *Télérama*, 2381, 51–2.

Remy, V. and A. Ferenczi (1999) '*Romance*', *Télérama*, 2570, 32–4.

Renouard, G. (1996) '*Gazon maudit*: une sacrée réussite', *Film Français*, 19 January, 13.

Richou, P. (1996) 'Blanche Neige, l'ogre et les sept nains', *Cahiers du cinéma*, 508, 56–8.

Rigoulet, L. (1997b) 'Cinq de ses membres racontent l'alchimie de la "famille" Guédiguian', *Libération*, 19 November.

———— (1997a) 'Les partis pris de Guédiguian', *Libération*, 9 May.

Rollet, B. (1999) 'Unruly Woman? Josiane Balasko, French Comedy and *Gazon maudit*', in P. Powrie (ed.) *French Cinema in the 1990s: Continuity and Difference*, Oxford and New York: OUP, 127–36.

Romney, J. (1997) 'She sent her star to work in the fields and turned the set into a labour camp', *The Guardian*, 7 November, 16–17.

Rose, J. (1984) *The Case of Peter Pan or the Impossibility of Children's Fiction*. London: Macmillan.

Rosello, M. (1998) *Declining the Stereotype: Ethnicity and Representation in French Cultures*. Hanover NH: University Press of New England.

Royer, P. (1995) 'Le Panier, un quartier vu sans hypocrisie', *La Croix*, 30 August.

———— (1997) 'Avec *Marius et Jeannette*, Guédiguian quitte son cinéma de quartier', *La Croix*, 19 November.

Séguret, Olivier (1997) 'Ludovic, sept ans et toutes ses robes', *Libération*, 22 May.

Sklar, R. (1999) 'A Woman's View of Shame and Desire: An Interview with Catherine Breillat', *Cinéaste*, 25, 1, 24–6.

Sorlin, P. (1991) *European Cinemas, European Societies: 1939–1990*. London: Routledge.

Tarr, C. (1997) 'French Cinema and Post-Colonial Minorities', in A. Hargreaves and M. McKinney (eds) *Post Colonial Cultures in France*. London and New York: Routledge, 59–83.

———— (1999) 'Ethnicity and Identity in the *cinéma de banlieue*', in P. Powrie (ed.) *French Cinema in the 1990s: Continuity and Difference*. Oxford: OUP, 172–84.

Temple, M. (1997) '*Ma Vie en rose*', *Sight and Sound*, 7, 11, 48.

Toubiana, S. (1986) 'L'Opéra Pagnol', *Cahiers du cinéma*, 387, 49–51.

———— (1997) '*Marius et Jeannette* de Robert Guédiguian', *Cahiers du cinéma*, 514, 25.

Tremois, C-M. (1995) '*Gazon maudit*', *Télérama*, 13 February, 28.

—— (1997) *Les Enfants de la liberté: Le jeune cinéma français des années 90*. Paris: Seuil.

Trotter, D. A. (1993) 'L'Esprit Gaulois: Humour and National Mythology', in K. Cameron (ed.) *Humour and History*. Oxford: Intellect, 70–83.

Ulrichs, K. H. (1868*) Memnon: Die Geschlechtsnatur des mannliebenden Urnings*. Schleiz: Hubscher-Heyn.

Vassé. C. (1996) '*Parfait Amour!*: Anatomie d'une histoire de sexe', *Positif*, 429, 29–30.

—— (1999) '*Romance*: Nouvelle Eve de glaciation', *Positif*, 458, 43–4.

Vavasseur, P. (1993) 'Les ressorts d'un succès', *Le Parisien*, 20 Aug.

Vincendeau, G. (1993) 'Gérard Depardieu: The Axiom of Contemporary French Cinema', *Screen*, 34, 4, 343–61.

—— (1996a) 'Twist and Farce', *Sight and Sound*, 6, 2, 24–6.

—— (1996b) '*Gazon maudit*', *Sight and Sound*, 6, 3, 41–2.

—— (1999) '*Romance*', *Sight and Sound*, 9, 11, 51–2.

Warren, S. (1996) '*French Twist* Takes a New Turn on Love Triangles', in *Outlines*, March, 1–2 (http://suba.com~outlines/march96/ french.html).

Wharton, S. (1997) 'Financial (Self-) Identification: the Pink Economy in France', in S. Perry and M. Cross (eds) *Voices of France: Social, Political and Cultural Identity*. London and Washington: Pinter, 172–84.

Zimmer, J. (1988) 'Exploitation: 8 ans de box-office', *La Revue du cinéma*, 442, 64.

Zizek, S. (1997) *The Plague of Fantasies*. London: Verso.

INDEX